CATALOGUE

OF THE

VERMONT STATE LIBRARY,

SEPTEMBER 1, 1872.

MONTPELIER:
J. & J. M. POLAND, PRINTERS.
1872.

CONTENTS.

VERMONT STATE LIBRARY.

The real growth and life of the VERMONT STATE LIBRARY dates from 1858. As to what was done in the way of obtaining or preserving books before the first State House was occupied in Montpelier, in 1808, even tradition is silent; and during most of the next generation we cannot learn that anything was accomplished or attempted.

The first dawn of legislation we can discover is the following joint resolution of the Governor and Council and the General Assembly in 1825:

IN COUNCIL, Nov. 17, 1825.

Resolved, the general assembly concurring herein, That it shall be the duty of the governor and council, annually, to appoint some suitable person, whose duty it shall be to take charge of, and keep in good order, all the books and publick documents, deposited in the state-house, in Montpelier; and that a suitable room in the state-house be placed under the control of such person, for a place of deposit for such books and documents: and such person, in the discharge of his duty, shall be governed by such rules and regulations as the governour and council shall, from time to time, prescribe.

[*Concurred Nov.* 17, 1825.]

From this time there has been, at least in form, a Library and a Librarian.

The Librarian was first required to be appointed by the Governor and Council; then the appointment was given to the Governor; and in 1848 the annual election of a Librarian was given to the Senate and House of Representatives. And from 1825 to 1856 legislation was ample in quantity, but quite small, inexpensive and unprogressive in result.

In 1856 the following joint resolution was passed by the Legislature :

JOINT RESOLUTION RELATING TO THE LIBRARY.

Resolved by the Senate and House of Representatives, That the governor be instructed to appoint one efficient person to act conjointly with the librarian, to collect all books and property belonging to the state library, classify the same, prepare a catalogue, and report to the next legislature their action in full, together with such recommendations of repairs, purchases and regulations, for the future government of the library, as to them seem expedient.

IN SENATE, Nov. 15, 1856.

Read and adopted.

C. H. CHAPMAN, *Secretary.*

IN HOUSE OF REPRESENTATIVES, November 15, 1856.

Read and adopted in concurrence.

B. F. FIFIELD, *Assistant Clerk.*

Under this resolution, Joseph H. Barrett was appointed Commissioner.

At the October session, 1857, the Librarian, Mr. Webster, and Mr. Commissioner Barrett made their several reports, which are printed in the Senate Journal of that session, pp. 264 and 284. Mr. Webster reports an immensly large list of missing volumes and broken sets of books. Mr. Barrett reports the condition of things in the Library, and says, " From such evidence as can readily be procured, it does not appear that any State in the Union, all circumstances considered, is worse off in regard to its Library than Vermont."

The Legislature at that session passed the Act of 1857, which is substantially embodied in Chap. VII. General Statutes. This law placed the management and control of the Library in the hands of Trustees and a Librarian elected by them. The Trustees organized their Board Nov. 16, 1858.

PRESENT :

His Excellency, HILAND HALL.
Chief Justice, ISAAC F. REDFIELD.
Secretary of State, BENJAMIN W. DEAN.
Resident Trustees, { FERRAND F. MERRILL, E. P. WALTON, CHARLES REED. }

At this meeting, Charles Reed was elected Librarian and Secretary, and has occupied that position to this date.

Under the present administration, the Library has trebled in size, and while it may still justify the remark that Jared Sparks made while in it, "IT IS VERY SMALL FOR A STATE," it has certainly ceased to be the disgrace that Commissioner Barrett thought it. Later Legislatures have seen the growth of the Library with evident pleasure, and have not failed to supply funds when asked.

A catalogue of the Library was printed in 1850, and also in 1858, after the fire which destroyed the State House.

At the fire, (January 6, 1857,) most of the books were thrown from the second story windows into the snow, and thence carefully gathered up and piled into the parlor and out-buildings of Hon. Daniel Baldwin. The loss of books of the Library by this fire is supposed to have been small ; and, as it was a bitterly cold night, they were not damaged by wet.

While the State House was building, the Masonic Hall was used for the Library, and it was well accommodated there during the session of 1857.

This Library is not yet complete in a single department. Even in Vermont Documents, the Library is destitute of some of the original Session Laws and Journals. It is strongest in American Law Reports, of which it requires only a score of volumes to be complete.

Our State Library and Historical Society should have all the materials from which to write our State history in all its branches. Nothing should be omitted in this direction to the full extent of our means.

The clerical work of making this Catalogue has been performed entirely by HIRAM A. HUSE, Esq., Assistant Librarian. It is printed under the provisions of Chapter 7, General Statutes.

The laws of the State in force in relation to the Library, and also the rules of the Library, will be found on pages ix–xiv.

LIBRARY LAWS IN FORCE.

OF THE STATE LIBRARY.

SECTION 1. The State Library shall consist of such books, maps, charts, and other documents, as are, or shall be, received or acquired by the State or any public officer for the use of the State government, and shall be under the direction of nine trustees, three of whom shall be styled *ex officio* trustees, three state trustees, and three resident trustees; and the following persons are hereby constituted said trustees, with powers and duties as hereinafter mentioned, viz.:

The Governor, The Chief Justice of the Supreme Court, The Secretary of State,	*Ex officio.*
*Erastus Fairbanks, of St. Johnsbury, *Norman Williams, of Woodstock, *George F. Houghton, of St. Albans,	*State.*
E. P. Walton, of Montpelier, Charles Reed of Montpelier, Joseph Poland, of Montpelier,	*Resident.*

SECT. 2. Said trusrees shall have the following powers, viz.:

To fill all vacancies in the offices of state and resident trustees.

To appoint and remove a secretary, who shall also act as librarian, and, when necessary, to appoint an assistant librarian.

To prescribe rules and by-laws for the government of the library.

To expend the money appropriated for the library; to sell or exchange imperfect or duplicate books belonging to the library.

To arrange and carry on domestic and foreign exchanges of books for the benefit of the library, and for this purpose one hundred copies of all publications by the authority of the state, shall be deposited in the library.

SECT. 3. It shall be the duty of said trustees to report annually to the legislature, all accessions to the library, and as to exchanges made, and generally all transactions concerning the

* Since deceased.

library; to make, as often as they may deem expedient, a full and perfect catalogue of all the books, maps, medals, &c., in the library, which catalogue shall be printed; to prescribe the duties of the secretary and librarian, and of the assistant librarian, and see that they observe them, and, generally, to superintend the interests and management of the library; and to make distribution of the judicial reports, acts, journals, and other documents, as provided by law, in all cases where such distribution shall not be devolved by law upon some other person or officer.

SECT. 4. No salary or compensation shall be allowed to said trustees for their services.

SECT. 5. For the appointment of secretary and librarian, and assistant librarian, and for the adoption of rules and by-laws, and for the election to fill vacancies in the board of trustees, six members shall constitute a quorum. For the transaction of ordinary business, any three members present shall constitute a quorum.

SECT. 6. The annual compensation of the secretary and librarian shall be one hundred and twenty-five dollars, and the assistant librarian shall be paid one dollar and fifty cents per day for his services during such portions of the sessions of the general assembly as the trustees shall deem such services necessary for the public interest.

SECT. 7. The debenture of such assistant librarian shall be allowed and certified by the governor and librarian, and when so allowed and certified, the auditor of accounts shall draw an order upon the state treasurer for the same.

SECT. 8. If any person shall violate any of the rules which have been, or may hereafter be, prescribed by the trustees of the state library, for the regulation thereof, such person shall be liable to pay the state, for the benefit of said library, the several amounts and penalties, by any of such rules required and prescribed.

SECT. 9. All the aforesaid sums and penalties may be sued for and recovered in an action on the case, brought in the name of the state.

SECT. 10. There shall be, and hereby is, appropriated an annual sum of money, not to exceed two hundred dollars, to be expended under the direction of the trustees of the state library, in the purchase of books, maps, documents, and historical works, for the use and improvement of the state library.

SECT. 11. The said trustees shall cause an accurate account of such expenditures to be kept, and such account shall be audited by the auditor of accounts, who shall draw orders on the treasury therefor.

SECT. 12. Said trustees shall, at all times, be subject to the order and control of the general assembly.

An Act to Appropriate Money for the State Library.

It is hereby enacted by the General Assembly of the State of Vermont:

Sec. 1. An additional annual sum of three hundred dollars is hereby appropriated, to be expended under the direction of the trustees of the State Library, in the manner now provided by chapter seven of the General Statutes, entitled "Of the State Library."

Sec. 2. This act shall take effect from its passage.

Approved, November 19, 1866.

An Act Relating to the Salary of the State Librarian, and Pay of Assistants Thereof.

It is hereby enacted by the General Assembly of the State of Vermont:

Sec. 1. The salary of the State Librarian shall be three hundred and fifty dollars annually, and be paid quarterly. The provisions of this act shall extend to the salary of the present year, commencing October 1, 1870.

Sec. 2. The State Librarian is hereby authorized to employ two assistants during each session of the legislature, whose pay shall not exceed three dollars per day each.

Sec. 3. This act shall take effect from its passage.

Approved, November 23, 1870.

Joint Resolution Concerning the State Library and Other Matters—[1870].

Resolved by the Senate and House of Representatives:

That the Governor is hereby authorized to appoint three Commissioners to devise a plan for the better accommodation for the State Library, the State Cabinet, and the collections of the Vermont Historical Society, and to prepare designs and estimates for the same, and to report to the legislature at its next session.

C. H. JOYCE,
Speaker of the House of Representatives.

CHARLES H. HEATH,
President pro tem. of the Senate.

An Act in Relation to the Vermont Historical Society.

It is hereby enacted by the General Assembly of the State of Vermont:

Sec. 1. Whenever the Vermont Historical Society shall be dissolved, the books, collections, and all the property thereof shall become the exclusive property of the State of Vermont; and said society shall have no right or power to sell or dispose of any part of its books or collections, except by way of exchange; and all such sales or disposal shall be void.

Sec. 2. The Secretary of State, the Auditor of Accounts and the State Librarian shall be *ex officio* members of the Historical Society aforesaid, and of the board of curators thereof.

Sec. 3. The sum of two hundred and fifty dollars is hereby appropriated to aid the said Historical Society in the preservation of its valuable collections, and to put the same in suitable condition for examination and use.

Sec. 4. The aforesaid sum of money shall be paid to the curators of said society on the order of the Governor, and said curators shall settle with the Auditor of Accounts for the proper expenditure of said sum of money.

Sec. 5. This act shall not take effect until the said society shall by a vote thereof at a meeting regularly called and holden accept of and adopt this act.

Approved November 9, 1869.

RULES OF THE LIBRARY.

1.

The Library shall be kept open each day, at suitable hours, of every session of the Legislature and Constitutional Convention, when the Librarian or his Assistants shall be present. And no person shall be allowed access to the Library at any time except in the presence of the Librarian or Assistants.

2.

Books may be taken from the Library by the Governor and Lieutenant Governor ; the Secretary of Civil and Military Affairs; members of the Senate and House and their Clerks ; members of of the Constitutional Convention and its Clerks ; Heads of Departments ; Judges of the Supreme Court ; Trustees of the Library ; Secretary and members of the Board of Education.

3.

The right to take and keep books by the members and clerks of a Legislature, or Constitutional Convention, is limited to the time said Legislature or Convention may be in session, and no other person shall keep a book from the Library more than twenty days.

4.

The Librarian shall keeps records in which he shall enter all books taken from the Library ; and every person taking a book shall be responsible for its return agreeably to the rules of the Library, until the Librarian shall cancel the charge. And no book shall be taken from the Library until the same has been so charged.

5.

Every book placed on the shelves of the Library shall be stamped on the outside and inside, when practicable, with the words, "Vermont State Library," in such a manner as to be indelibly inscribed.

6.

The Librarian, in suitable books, shall keep a record of all the transactions of the Library in the purchase and exchange of books, and also of all the expenses of the Library, for the examination of the Trustees and the Committee on the Library.

7.

The Librarian, in the discharge of his duties, shall in all matters be subject to the control of the Trustees of the Library, and shall keep a full record of all their proceedings.

8.

The Library and Library Rooms shall be under the control and charge of the Librarian, and he shall carefully preserve the books and all other property belonging to the Library; and if any loss or damage to the same shall happen from his want of care, or any violation of the rules of the Library, by him permitted, he shall be personally responsible for the same.

9.

If on notice to any person that the time for which any book or books have been drawn from the Library by such person, has expired, such person shall neglect to return such book or books to the Library for more than three days after such notice, such person shall be liable to pay to the State double the value of such book or books, which value shall be estimated at the cost of replacing the same.

10.

If any person shall take from the Library any book or other article belonging to the same, without being properly authorized so to do, such person shall be liable to pay to the State double the value of such book or other article, and shall also pay a penalty of ten dollars.

11.

If any person shall have in his possession any book or other article belonging to the Library, and shall neglect to return the same to the Library on demand, such person shall be liable to pay to the State double the value of such book or other article, and also a penalty of ten dollars.

12.

If any book shall be damaged while the same shall be drawn from the Library by any person, such person shall be liable to pay to the State the amount of such damage.

OFFICERS OF THE LIBRARY,

SEPTEMBER 1, 1872.

STATUTE LAW.

STATUTE LAW.

ALABAMA.

Digest of the Laws of Alabama; containing the statutes and resolutions in force at the end of the general assembly, in January, 1823. By Harry Toulmin. Cahawba, 1823.

Digest of the Laws of Alabama; containing all the statutes of a public and general nature in force at the close of the session of the general assembly, in February, 1843. By C. C. Clay. Tuscaloosa, 1843.

Code of Alabama; prepared by J. J. Ormond, A. P. Bagby, and G. Goldthwaite, 1852. Montgomery, 1852.

Penal Code of Alabama; prepared by G. W. Stone and J. W. Shepherd, and adopted in 1865–6. Montgomery, 1866.

Revised Code of Alabama; prepared by A. J. Walker, February, 1867. Montgomery, 1867.

Acts passed at the first session of the first General Assembly of the Alabama Territory, 1818. 12°. St. Stephens, 1818.

Acts of the General Assembly of the State of Alabama, 1822 [its 4th session] to 1829–30; 1832–3 [extra and annual sessions]; 1834–5; 1835–6; 1837 [called session, June]; 1837; 1838–9; 1840–1; 1841 [called session, April]; 1841–2; 1842–3; 1843–4; 1845–6; 1849–50 [second biennial session under amended constitution of 1846]; 1851–2; 1855–6; 1857–8; 1859–60; 1865–6 [first annual session under constitution of 1865]; 1866–7; 1868 [first annual session under constitution of November, 1867]; 1870–1. 22v. in 16. Cahawba, Tuscaloosa, and Montgomery, 1823–71.

ARIZONA.

Compiled Laws of the Territory of Arizona; including the Howell code and the session laws from 1864 to 1871. By Coles Bashford. Albany, 1871.

Acts, Resolutions and Memorials adopted by the Legislative Assembly of the Territory of Arizona, 1864 to 1868, [being the first to the fifth session]. 5v. Prescott and Tucson, 1865–9.

ARKANSAS.

Revised Statutes of Arkansas; adopted at the October session of the general assembly, 1837. By W. McK. Ball and S. C. Roane. With notes and index, by Albert Pike. Boston, 1838.

Digest of the Statutes of Arkansas; embracing all the laws of a general and permanent character in force at the close of 1846; with notes of the decisions of the supreme court upon the statutes. By E. H. English. Examined and approved by Samuel H. Hempstead. Little Rock, 1848.

Digest of the Statutes of Arkansas; embracing laws in force at close of session of 1856; with notes of decisions, &c. By Josiah Gould. Examined and approved by George C. Watkins. Little Rock, 1858.

Acts of the General Assembly of Arkansas, 1840 to 1860–1 [third to thirteenth biennial sessions]; 1864–5 [first legislature under constitution of 1864]; 1866–7; 1868–9 [adjourned session of first legislature under constitution of 1868]; 1871. 15v. Arkadelphia and Little Rock, 1841–71.

CALIFORNIA.

Compiled Laws of California; containing all the acts of the legislature of a public and general nature now in force, passed at the sessions of 1850–53. By S. Garfielde and F. A. Snyder. Benicia, 1853.

Statutes of California, passed in 1851 [being the second annual session]; 1852; 1854 to 1863; 1863–4 [being the fifteenth session under the constitution of 1849, or the first biennial session under the constitution as amended in 1862] to 1869–70. 16v. San Jose, San Francisco and Sacramento, 1851–70.

The same, 1852 and 1858. [In Spanish.] San Francisco and Sacramento, 1852–8.

Supplement to the Statutes of 1869–70. (Pamphlet.) Sacramento, 1870.

CANADA.

Revised Acts and Ordinances of Lower Canada; published under the superintendence of the commissioners for revising said acts and ordinances. Montreal, 1845.

Consolidated Statutes for Lower Canada; proclaimed and published under the authority of the act 23 Vict., cap. 56, A.D. 1860. Quebec, 1861.

Revised Statutes of Upper Canada to the time of the Union [1841]. Vol. 1, Public Acts. 4°. Toronto, [1843 ?]

Consolidated Statutes for Upper Canada; proclaimed and published under authority of the act 22 Vict., cap. 30, A.D. 1859. Toronto, 1859.

CANADA :

Consolidated Statutes of Canada ; proclaimed and published under the authority of the act 22 Vict., cap. 29, A.D. 1859. Toronto, 1859.

Statutes of the Province of Canada, 1852–3 ; 1856 to 1858 ; 1860 to 1866. 14v. Toronto, Quebec and Ottawa, 1853–66.

Statutes of [the Dominion of] Canada, passed 1867 to 1871. 5v. Ottawa, 1867–71.

Note.—See ONTARIO and QUEBEC.

CHEROKEE NATION.

Laws passed during the years 1839–1867 ; compiled by authority of the national council. St. Louis, 1868.

CHICKASAWS.

Constitution, Laws and Treaties of the Chickasaws. By authority. Tishemingo City, 1860.

CHOCTAW NATION.

Acts and Resolutions of the General Council of the Choctaw Nation, from 1852 to 1857. Fort Smith, (Ark.,) 1858.

COLORADO.

Revised Statutes of Colorado, as passed at the seventh session of the legislative assembly, convened December, 1867. Central City, 1868.

Session Laws of 1861 [being first annual session] ; 1862 ; 1870 [being the eighth session, or the first biennial session under revised statutes of 1868]. 3v. Denver, 1861–70.

CONNECTICUT.

Acts and Laws of His Majesty's English Colony of Connecticut in New England in America. New-London: printed by Timothy Green, Printer to the Governor and Company of the above said Colony, 1750. Folio. [This also contains the charter of Charles II., and bound with it are the acts and laws passed by the general court at its sessions from 1750 to 1758.]

Acts and Laws of the State of Connecticut, in America. Hartford, 1796.

Public Statute Laws of Connecticut, as revised and enacted by the general assembly, in May, 1821. Hartford, 1821.

The same, with the acts of the three subsequent sessions incorporated. Hartford, 1824.

CONNECTICUT:

Public Statute Laws of the State of Connecticut; passed subsequent to the revision in 1821. [This is a compilation of the session laws of 1822, 1823 and 1824]. Hartford, 1824.

The same; passed since the session in 1824. [This is a compilation of the session laws of 1825 and 1826, and is paged as a continuation of the Revision of 1824]. Hartford, 1826.

Public Statute Laws of Connecticut; compiled in obedience to a resolve of the general assembly, passed May, 1835. Hartford, 1835.

Public Statute Laws of Connecticut; compiled in obedience to a resolve of the general assembly, passed May, 1838. Hartford, 1839.

Revised Statutes of Connecticut. Hartford, 1849.

Statutes of the State of Connecticut; compiled and published by authority of the general assembly. New Haven, 1854.

General Statutes of the State of Connecticut; published by authority of the general assembly. New Haven, 1866.

Resolves and Private Laws of the State of Connecticut, 1789 to 1865. 5v. in 4. Hartford and New Haven, 1837–71.

Acts and Resolves made and passed by the general assembly of Connecticut, from October, 1798, to May, 1808. (May sessions, 1799 to 1805, and October session, 1804, wanting.) [12 pamphlets, paged in continuation of session laws prior to October, 1798, and designed with them to form 1 v.] Hartford, 1798–1808.

The same, October, 1808, to 1821. (The laws of the following years are wanting: 1809, *except special February session;* 1810, *except October session;* 1811, *except May session;* 1812; 1821.) [19 pamphlets, paged (except the special session of February, 1809,) as portions of a volume entitled "Public Statute Laws of the State of Conn. Book II."] Hartford, 1808-21.

The same, 1822 to 1835. (The laws passed in 1824; 1825; 1827; 1828; 1832; 1834 wanting.) [8 pamphlets, paged as belonging to 1 vol.] Hartford, 1822–35.

Public Acts, passed by the general assembly of the State of Connecticut, 1836 to 1871. (Acts of 1856 wanting.) 37v. in 34. Hartford and New Haven, 1836–71.

Private Acts and Resolutions, passed by the general assembly of the State of Connecticut, 1837 to 1871. [35 vols., of which all, except the 10 vols. for 1838, 1839, 1841, 1842–3, 1844, 1845, 1849, 1853, 1854, and 1856, are bound with the public laws for the corresponding years.] 10v. Hartford and New Haven, 1837–71.

DAKOTA.

Laws, Memorials and Resolutions of the Territory of Dakota, passed by the legislative assembly, 1862 to 1867–8, [being first to seventh sessions.] 7v. Yankton, 1862–8.

DELAWARE.

Laws of the State of Delaware, from 1700 to 1797. 2v. New Castle, 1797.

The same, from 1798 to 1805; and from 1806 to 1813, [being numbered vols. 3 and 4, as a continuation of the above New Castle edition.] 2v. Wilmington, 1816.

Laws of the State of Delaware, to 1829, inclusive. Revised edition. Wilmington, 1829.

Revised Statutes of the State of Delaware, to 1852, inclusive. Dover, 1852.

Laws of the State of Delaware, passed at the [annual] sessions of the general assembly, from 1813 to 1832 (those for 1819, 1820, 1823 and 1828 wanting); and at the [biennial] sessions from 1833 to 1861 (those of a special session in 1836 ? and the regular sessions of 1845 and 1851 wanting); November, 1861 [a special session]; 1866 [an adjourned session]; 1867; 1869; 1871. 34v. in 16. Wilmington, Milford and Dover, 1813–71.

FLORIDA.

Manual or Digest of the Statute Law of the State of Florida, of a general and public character, in force on the 6th day of January, 1847. By Leslie A. Thompson. Boston, 1847.

Code of Procedure, 1870. Tallahassee, 1870.

Acts of the Legislative Council of the Territory of Florida; passed in 1824 [being the third session]; 1825; 1833; 1835; 1836; 1839; 1842; 1843; 1844; 1845. 11v. in 8. Tallahassee, 1825–45.

Acts and Resolutions of the General Assembly of the State of Florida, passed in 1845 [being first session]; 1845 [an adjourned session]; 1846; 1848; 1849; 1850; 1852; 1858; 1859; 1868 [first session under constitution of 1868]; 1869; 1869 [extra session]; 1870; 1870 [extra session]; 1871. 15v. in 11. Tallahassee, 1845–71.

GEORGIA.

Compilation of the Laws of the State of Georgia, from November, 1800, to December, 1810. By Augustin S. Clayton. 4°. Augusta, 1812.

Digest of the Laws of the State of Georgia, passed previous to December, 1820. By O. H. Prince. Milledgeville, 1822.

The same. 2d ed. Laws passed previous to December, 1837. Athens, 1837.

Compilation of the Laws of the State of Georgia, passed by the general assembly, since the year 1819 to the year 1829. By Wm. C. Dawson. 4°. Milledgeville, 1831.

GEORGIA:

Codification of the Statute Laws of Georgia, including the English statutes of force. With a collection of state papers of English, American, and State origin. By W. A. Hotchkiss. New York, 1845.

Analysis of the Statutes of Georgia, in general use, with the forms and precedents necessary to their practical operation. By Howell Cobb. New York, 1846.

Digest of the Statute Laws of the State of Georgia, in force prior to 1851. By Thos. R. R. Cobb. Athens, 1851.

Compilation of the General and Public Statutes of the State of Georgia, with the forms and precedents necessary to their practical use. By Howell Cobb. New York, 1859.

Code of the State of Georgia. By R. H. Clark, Thos. R. R. Cobb, and D. Irwin. Atlanta, 1861.

The same. Revised and corrected by David Irwin. Atlanta, 1867.

Acts of the General Assembly of the State of Georgia, 1823; 1824; 1827 to 1869, (1836 *wanting*). [The sessions from 1843 to 1857 were biennial.] 36v. in 31. Milledgeville, Columbus, Savannah, Macon and Atlanta, 1824–69.

GREAT BRITAIN AND IRELAND.

Index to the Statutes, public and private, passed from the union with Ireland to the termination of the eighteenth parliament of the United Kingdom. 1801 to 1865. 2v. [London, 1867.]

IDAHO.

Laws passed by the Legislative Assembly of the Territory of Idaho, from the 1st to the 4th session: 1863–4 to 1866–7. 4v. Lewiston, 1864–67.

ILLINOIS.

Revised Code of Laws of Illinois; containing those of a general and permanent nature, passed in 1828, and those enacted previous thereto. Shawneetown (printed at Cincinnati), 1829.

Revised Laws of Illinois; containing all laws of a general and public nature, passed in 1832–3; with all laws required to be republished. Vandalia, 1833.

Revised Statutes of Illinois; adopted in 1844–5. Revised, with notes, &c., by M. Brayman. Springfield, 1845.

Statutes of Illinois; embracing all the general laws of the State in force December 1, 1857; with marginal notes. By Samuel H. Treat, W. B. Scates, and R. S. Blackwell. 2v. Chicago, 1858.

ILLINOIS:

Laws [public and private] of the State of Illinois; passed by the general assembly at its [biennial] sessions, 1820–1; 1822–3; 1824–5; 1830–1; 1834–5; 1838–9 to 1869; 1871–2 [public]; also, at special sessions, June, 1837; 1839–40; October, 1849; June, 1852; February, 1854; April, 1861; June, 1867. Bound in 37 vols. Vandalia and Springfield, 1821–72.

INDIANA.

Revised Laws of Indiana; adopted and enacted by the general assembly at their 8th session. Corydon, 1824.

Revised Laws of Indiana; comprising all such acts of a general nature as are in force; adopted and enacted by the general assembly at their 15th session. Indianapolis, 1831.

Revised Statutes of Indiana; adopted and enacted by the general assembly at their 22d session. Indianapolis, 1838.

Revised Statutes of Indiana. Indianapolis, 1843.

Revised Statutes of Indiana, passed at the 36th session of the general assembly. 2v. Indianapolis, 1852.

Session Laws, passed in 1817–18 [second session] to 1820–1; 1822–3; 1825–6 to 1829–30; 1832–3 to 1835–6; 1838–9 to 1850–1; 1853 [being 37th session of the legislature or the first biennial session under amended constitution of 1851] to 1869, (including special sessions of 1858, 1861 and 1865.) [It would seem from title pages of succeeding sessions that the special session of 1865 is classed as the 44th regular session.] 39v. in 33. Corydon and Indianapolis, 1818–69.

Laws of a Local Nature, passed at the 2d, 19th, 20th, 28th, 29th and 33d sessions of the general assembly. 6v. in 5. Corydon and Indianapolis, 1818–49.

IOWA.

Code of Iowa, passed at the session of the general assembly of 1850–51. Iowa City, 1851.

Revision of 1860; containing all statutes of a general nature of the State of Iowa which are now in force, as the result of the legislation of the 8th general assembly. Des Moines, 1860.

Educational Laws. Des Moines, 1860.

School Laws, with forms, etc. Des Moines, 1868.

Acts, Resolutions and Memorials of the General Assembly; passed at their regular [biennial] sessions, from the first session, 1846–7 to 1872 (1854 *wanting*); also those passed at the special sessions of 1848, 1856 and 1862. 16v. Iowa City and Des Moines, 1847–72.

JAMAICA.

Acts of Assembly, passed in the Island of Jamaica; from 1681 to 1737 inclusive. Printed by John Baskett, Printer to the King's Most Excellent Majesty. Folio. London, 1738.

KANSAS.

Statutes of the Territory of Kansas, passed at the 1st session of the legislative assembly, 1855; and the act of congress organizing said territory, and other acts of congress having immediate relation thereto. Shawnee M. L. School, 1855.

General Laws of the State of Kansas, in force at the close of the session of the legislature, ending March 6th, 1862. Published by authority. Topeka, 1862.

General Statutes of Kansas. Revised by J. M. Price, S. A. Riggs and J. McCahon: adopted in 1868. Lawrence, 1868.

Laws of the Territory of Kansas, passed at the sessions of 1857–8; 1859; 1860. 3v. Lecompton, 1858–60.

Laws of the State of Kansas, passed by the general assembly at the sessions of 1861 [being the 1st annual session]; 1863; 1865; 1869 to 1872. 7v. Lawrence and Topeka, 1861–72.

KENTUCKY.

Digest of the Statute Laws of Kentucky, of a public and permanent nature, from the commencement of the government to 1834; with references to judicial decisions. By C. S. Morehead and Mason Brown. 2v. Frankfort, 1834.

Revised Statutes of Kentucky. By C. A. Wickliffe, S. Turner and S. S. Nicholas; approved and adopted by the general assembly, 1851 and 1852. Frankfort, 1852.

Code of Practice in Civil and Criminal Cases for the State of Kentucky. Prepared by M. C. Johnson, James Harlan and J. W. Stevenson, commissioners. Frankfort, 1854.

Revised Statutes of Kentucky; approved and adopted in 1851 and 1852, with amendments made to session of 1859–60, and an appendix. By Richard H. Stanton. 2v. Cincinnati, 1860.

Digest of the General Laws of Kentucky, enacted between December 4, 1859, and June 4, 1865; embracing laws passed since Stanton's edition; with appendix, containing laws of 1865–6. By Harvey Myers. Cincinnati, 1866.

Acts of the General Assembly, passed in 1815–16 [being the annual session of the 24th legislative assembly]; 1816–17; 1820; 1822 to 1845–6; 1847–8; 1848–9; 1849–50; 1853–4 [being the second biennial session under constitution of 1850]; 1855–6; 1859–60; called session, 1861; May session, 1861; 1861–2–3; 1863–4; adjourned session, 1865. 42v. Frankfort, 1816–65.

LOUISIANA.

Laws of Las Siete Partidas, which are still in force in the State of Louisiana. Translated from the Spanish, by L. Moreau Lislet and Henry Carleton. 2v. New Orleans, 1820.

LOUISIANA:

General Digest of the Acts of the Legislature of Louisiana, from the year 1804 to 1827, inclusive. By L. Moreau Lislet. 2v. New Orleans, 1828.

Civil Code of the State of Louisiana; with annotations. By Wheelock S. Upton and Needler R. Jennings. New Orleans, 1838.

Consolidation and Revision of the Statutes of the State, of a general nature. Prepared by Levi Peirce, Miles Taylor and W. W. King, February 5th, 1852. New Orleans, 1852.

Revised Statutes of Louisiana; compiled by U. B. Phillips, under direction of the legislature. New Orleans, 1856.

Civil Code of the State of Louisiana, with Statutory Amendments from 1825 to 1866. By James O. Fuqua. New Orleans, 1867.

Code of Practice in Civil Cases, with Statutory Amendments from 1825 to 1866. By James O. Fuqua. New Orleans, 1867.

Revised Civil Code. New Orleans, 1870.

Code of Practice. New Orleans, 1870.

Revised Statute Laws, from the organization of the Territory to 1869. New Orleans, 1870.

Acts of the General Assembly of the State of Louisiana, 1816–17 [being the third legislature]; 1819; 1823 to 1825; 1827; 1828; 1830 to 1841 (including Nov. session, 1831, and Dec. sessions of 1837 and 1841); 1845 to 1848; December session, 1848; 1850; 1852 to 1854; 1856 to 1860; 1864–5 [being the first sessions under constitution of 1864]; 1866; 1867; 1868 [being the first session under constitution of 1868]; 1869; 1870. (In English and French.)—40v. Baton Rouge and New Orleans, 1817–70.

MAINE.

Revised Statutes, passed October 22, 1840; with the other public laws of 1840 and 1841. Augusta, 1841.

Revised Statutes, passed April 17, 1857. Bangor, 1857.

Revised Statutes, passed January 25, 1871. Portland, [1871.]

Laws relating to Public Schools. 12°. Augusta, 1867.

Public Acts of the Legislature of the State of Maine, 1823 [third legislature] to 1830. 8v. in 2. Portland, 1823–30.

Acts and Resolves, passed by the Legislature, 1831 to 1871 (1851 *wanting*). 40v. Portland and Augusta, 1831–71.

MARYLAND.

Laws; from the end of the year 1799, to February, 1819. With a full index. Revised and prepared, under the authority of the legislature, by William Kilty, Thomas Harris, and John N. Watkins. V. 3 to 7. Annapolis. (n. d.)

Index to the Laws and Resolutions of Maryland, 1832 to 1837. Annapolis, 1838.

MARYLAND:

Statutory Testamentary Law of Maryland; with the decisions of the courts thereof explanatory of the same. By Clement Dorsey. Baltimore, 1838.

General Public Statutory Law and Public Local Law, from the year 1692 to 1839, inclusive, with annotations thereto, and a copious index. By Clement Dorsey. 3v. Baltimore, 1840.

Maryland Code. Public General Laws compiled by Otho Scott and Hiram McCullough, commissioners; adopted by the legislature, January session, 1860; the acts of that session being therewith incorporated. With an index by H. C. Mackall. 2v. Baltimore, 1860.

Collection of the British Statutes in force in Maryland. By Julian J. Alexander. Baltimore, 1870.

Laws passed by the General Assembly in 1811–12; 1814–15 to 1816–17; 1819–20; 1822–3 to 1841–2; 1843–4; 1844–5; 1849–50; 1852 [being first biennial session under constitution of 1851] to 1864, including special sessions of 1853, April and December, 1861; 1865 [first biennial session under constitution of 1864]; extra session, 1866; 1867; 1868 [first biennial session under constitution of 1867]; 1870. 41v. in 38. Annapolis, 1812–70.

MASSACHUSETTS.

NOTE.—See Plymouth Colony Records, Vol. 11, and Records of the Governor and Company of Massachusetts Bay, for old Colonial Laws.

Laws of the Commonwealth of Massachusetts, passed from 1780 to end of 1800. 2v. Boston, 1801.

Public and General Laws of the Commonwealth, passed from February 28, 1807, to February 16, 1816. [Being vol. 4 of a series of which the preceding are vols. 1 and 2.] Boston, 1816.

General Laws, from adoption of Constitution to February, 1822. Revised by A. Stearns, L. Shaw and T. Metcalf. 2v. Boston, 1823.

Revised Statutes of Massachusetts, passed November 4, 1835. Printed and published under the supervision and direction of T. Metcalf and H. Mann. Boston, 1836.

The same. General Statutes; revised by commissioners appointed under a resolve of February 16, 1855, amended by the legislature and passed 1859. Edited [by Joel Parker, W. A. Richardson and A. A. Richmond.] Boston, 1860.

Acts and Resolves, public and private, of the Province of Massachusetts Bay. Vol. 1. 1692–1714. Boston, 1869.

Private and Special Statutes. Vols. 9, 10 and 11 [1849 to 1865]. 3v. Boston, 1860–9.

Laws passed by the General Court, at their sessions, 1815 to 1834. 20v. in 7. Boston, 1815–34.

Acts and Resolves passed by the General Court, 1835 to 1871. (*Acts* of 1838 *wanting.*) 37v. Boston, 1835–71.

MICHIGAN.

Laws of the Territory of Michigan [enacted by the Governor and Judges, 1818–21]; with marginal notes, ordinance and acts of Congress relating to the Territory. Detroit, 1820, [1821.]

The same; comprising acts of a public nature revised by commissioners appointed by the first legislative Council, and passed by the second Council; acts and resolutions of the first and second Councils; and acts, now in force, adopted by the Governor and Judges. Detroit, 1827.

Revised Statutes, passed at the adjourned session of 1837, and the regular session of 1838. Published under the supervision of E. B. Harrington and E. Roberts. Detroit, 1838.

Revised Statutes, passed and approved, May 18, 1846. Published under the superintendence of Sanford M. Green. Detroit, 1846.

Compiled Laws. Arranged by Thomas M. Cooley. 2v. Lansing, 1857.

School Laws, with notes, etc. Lansing, 1869.

Acts passed by the Legislative Council of the Territory, 1824; 1825; 1828; 1829. 4v. in 1. Detroit, 1824–9.

Acts of the the Legislature of the State of Michigan. Adjourned session, 1837; 1838 to 1850; 1851 [first biennial session under constitution of 1850]; 1853; 1857 to 1871 (including extra sessions of 1858, 1862, 1864 and 1870). 32v. Detroit and Lansing, 1838–71.

MINNESOTA.

Revised Statutes, passed at the second session of the legislative assembly, 1851. Published under the supervision of M. S. Wilkinson. Saint Paul, 1851.

Public Statutes. 1849 to 1858. Compiled by Moses Sherburne and W. Hollinshead. Saint Paul, 1859.

General Statutes. Revised [by S. J. R. McMillan, E. C. Palmer, Thomas Wilson and Gordon E. Cole], and passed 1866. Saint Paul, 1867.

Acts, Joint Resolutions, and Memorials, passed at the first legislative assembly of the Territory, 1849. Saint Paul, 1850.

Session Laws of the Territory, 1852; 1857; extra session, 1857. 3v. Saint Paul, 1852–7.

Special Laws of the State of Minnesota, 1857–8; 1861 to 1864, [those from '61 to '64 bound with General Laws for corresponding years.] Saint Paul, 1858–64.

General Laws of the State of Minnesota, 1857–8 to 1871. 13v. Saint Paul, 1858–71.

MISSISSIPPI.

Revised Code; comprising all such acts of a public nature as were in force at the end of 1823. Natchez, 1824.

Laws of the State; embracing all acts of a public nature, from 1824 to 1838. Jackson, 1838.

Statutes of the State of Mississippi. Compiled by V. E. Howard and A. Hutchinson. New Orleans, 1840.

Code of Mississippi; an analytical compilation of the public and general statutes of the Territory and State, with references to the local and private acts, from 1798 to 1848. By A. Hutchinson. Jackson, 1848.

Revised Code; published by authority of the Legislature. Jackson, 1857.

The same; adopted 1871. Jackson, 1871.

Laws of the State of Mississippi; passed by the legislature in 1827 [10th annual session]; 1828 [11th do.]; January, 1830, to January, 1833 [13th to 16th do.]; November, 1833 [1st biennial session under constitution of 1832]; 1838 [3d do.]; 1839 [an adjourned session]; 1840; 1841 [an adjourned session]; 1842; 1848; 1850; 1856; 1856–7 [an adjourned session]; 1865 [a biennial session held at the time provided by the constitutional amendment of 1854–6, being the first session under the amended constitution of 1865]; 1866–7 [a called session]; 1870 [first annual session under constitution of 1868–9]. 19v. in 14. Jackson, 1827–70.

MISSOURI.

Laws of the State. Revised and digested by authority of the general assembly. Vol. 2. St. Louis, 1825.

Laws of a public and general nature of the District of Louisiana, of the Territory of Louisiana, of the Territory of Missouri, and of the State of Missouri. Vol. 1 [to 1824]. Jefferson City, 1842.

Revised Statutes. Digested by the 8th general assembly, 1834–35. St. Louis, 1835.

Revised Statutes. Digested by the 13th general assembly, 1844–45. Printed under the superintendence of W. C. Jones. St. Louis, 1845.

Revised Statutes. Digested by the 18th general assembly, 1854–55; Charles H. Hardin, commissioner. 2v. City of Jefferson, 1856.

General Statutes. Revised [by C. C. Simmons and W. Currier; edited by] A. F. Denny. Passed March 20, 1866. City of Jefferson, 1866.

Local Laws and Private Acts, passed by the General Assembly, 1844–5; 1855 [an adjourned session]. 2v. City of Jefferson, 1845–55.

MISSOURI:

Acts of the General Assembly, passed at the regular biennial sessions 1826–7 to 1864–5 (those of 1834–5 and 1844–5 *wanting*); 1867 [first biennial session under constitution of 1865] to 1871; also at the extra sessions of June, 1821 [being second session of the first general assembly]; January, 1826; October, 1857; 1859–60; May, 1861; 1863–4; 1868; 1871–2. 29v. in 23. City of Jefferson, 1821–72.

NEBRASKA.

Revised Statutes of the Territory of Nebraska, in force July 1, 1866. By E. Estabrook. Omaha, 1866.

Laws, Joint Resolutions and Memorials, passed by the Legislative Assembly of the Territory, (4th to 12th sessions,) 1857–8 to 1867. [Those of 11th session, 1866, with Revised Statutes.] 8v. Omaha, 1858–67.

The same, passed by the Legislative Assembly of the State, 1867. [With Territorial laws of the same year.]

NEVADA.

Laws of the Territory, passed by the Legislative Assembly (1st to 3d sessions), 1861; 1862; 1864. 3v. Virginia City, 1862–4.

Laws of the State, passed by the Legislature, 1864–5 to 1871. [1st to 5th sessions, that of 1867 being the first biennial.] 5v. Carson City, 1865–71.

NEW HAMPSHIRE.

Laws of the State; together with the Constitution of New Hampshire; and the Constitution of the United States. Portsmouth, 1792.

The same. Portsmouth, 1797.

The same. Exeter, 1815.

The same. Hopkinton, 1830.

Revised Statutes of New Hampshire, passed December, 1842. Concord, 1843.

Compiled Statutes of the State. Concord, 1853.

General Statutes of the State. Manchester, 1867.

Laws of the State, passed by the Legislature, 1812 to 1870. Bound in 46 vols. Concord, 1812–70.

NEW JERSEY.

Laws. Revised by William Paterson. Newark, 1800.

Laws. Revised and published under the authority of the legislature. Trenton, 1821.

NEW JERSEY:

Statutes of the State. Revised and published under the authority of the legislature. Trenton, 1847.

Digest of the Laws of New Jersey. By Lucius Q. C. Elmer. 2d ed., containing all the laws of general application, now in force, from 1709 to 1855, by John T. Nixon. Philadelphia, 1855.

The same. 3d ed., [to 1861]. Bridgeton and Trenton, 1861.

Acts of the Legislature, 1820 to 1822 [public]; 1824 to 1871, (those of 1852 and 1862 *wanting*). 50v. in 37. Trenton, 1820–71.

NEW MEXICO.

Laws of the Territory, passed by the Legislative Assembly, 1851–2 (first session); 1852–3; 1853–4; 1856–7; 1857–8. 5v. in 4. Santa Fe, 1852–8.

Revised Statutes and Laws of the Territory, in force February 2, 1865. St. Louis, 1865.

NEW YORK.

Laws and Ordinances of New Netherland, 1638–1674. Compiled and translated from the original Dutch records, by E. B. O'Callaghan. Albany, 1868.

Acts of Assembly, passed in the Province of New York, from 1691 to 1718. Folio. London, 1719.

Laws of New York, from 1691 to 1773. 2v. in 1. Folio. New York, 1774.

Laws of the State; revised and passed at the 36th session of the legislature. By W. P. Van Ness and John Woodworth. 1783–1813. Vols. 1 and 2. Albany, 1813.

Revised Statutes of the State of New York, passed during the years 1827 and 1828. 3v. Albany, 1829.

The same. 2d ed. 3v. Albany, 1836.

The same; to close of session of 1858. Prepared by A. J. Parker, Geo. Wolford and Edward Wade. 5th ed. 3v. [Vol. 2 *missing.*] Albany, 1859.

General Index to the Laws of the State. [1777 to 1858, and 1858 to 1865; first vol. prepared by T. S. Gillett, second by H. H. Havens.] 2v. Albany, 1859–66.

Laws of the State, passed by the Legislature, (34th to 94th sessions), 1811 to 1871, (42d session, 1819, *wanting*). In 64 vols. Albany, 1811–71.

NORTH CAROLINA.

Revised Statutes, passed at the session of 1836–37, including an act concerning the revised statutes. Published by Fred. Nash, James Iredell, and W. H. Battle. 2v. Raleigh, 1837.

NORTH CAROLINA:

Revised Code, enacted at the session of 1854. Published by B. F. Moore, Asa Biggs, and W. B. Rodman. Boston, 1855.

Laws passed by the General Assembly, 1822 to 1824; 1826–7 to 1828–9; 1831–2 to 1835–6; 1836–7 [being the first biennial session under constitutional amendment of 1835]; 1842–3 to 1858–9; 1865 [a session held under an ordinance of the convention of 1865,] and special session 1866, with certain acts from 1859 to 1864 reprinted; 1866–7; 1868–9 [first annual session under constitution of 1868]; 1869–70; 1870–1. In 18 vols. Raleigh, 1823–71.

OHIO.

Statutes of a general nature, in force December 7, 1840. Collated, with references to the decisions of the courts and to prior laws. By J. R. Swan. Columbus, 1841.

Public Statutes at Large, from the close of Chase's Statutes, February, 1833, to the present time. With references to the judicial decisions construing those statutes; and supplement, containing all laws prior to February, 1833, now in force. Edited by Maskell E. Curwen. 4v. Cincinnati, 1853–61.

Statutes of a general nature, in force January 1st, 1854; with references to prior repealed laws. By J. R. Swan. Cincinnati, 1854.

Revised Statutes of a general nature, in force August 1, 1860. Collated by Joseph R. Swan. With notes of the decisions of the supreme court, by Leander J. Critchfield. 2v. Cincinnati, 1860.

Supplement to the Revised Statutes, 1860 to 1868. Collated by J. R. Swan. With notes by Milton Sayler. Cincinnati, 1868.

Militia Law of Ohio; passed March 28, 1857. Columbus, 1857.

Ohio School Laws. Prepared by the State school commissioner, for use and government of school officers. 2d ed. Columbus, 1858.

The same. 3d ed. Columbus, 1862.

The same. 4th ed. Columbus, 1865.

Index to Ohio Laws, general and local, and to the resolutions of the general assembly, from 1845–6 to 1857, inclusive. With index to the documents in the journals of the House and Senate, from 1802 to 1836. By William T. Coggeshall. Columbus, 1858.

Laws passed by the General Assembly of the State: *general*—vol. 15, 1816–17; vol. 22, 1823–4, with revised and reprinted laws; vol. 23, 1824–5; vol. 29, 1830–1, with revised and reprinted laws; vol. 33, 1834–5; vol. 34, 1835–6: *general and local*—vol. 32, 1833; vols. 35 to 68, 1836–7 to 1871. 40v. Columbus, 1817–71.

ONTARIO.

Statutes of the Province, passed 1867–8 [first session of the first parliament]; 1870–1. 2v. Toronto, 1868–71.

OREGON.

General and Special Laws, [enacted by the Council and House of Representatives, by the House of Representatives, and by the Legislative Assembly, from 1838 to 1849. *Title page wanting.* Salem, 1853 ?]

Statutes of Oregon ; enacted and continued in force by the legislative assembly [territorial] at the 5th and 6th sessions. Oregon, 1855.

Code of Civil Procedure and other General Statutes, enacted at session commencing September, 1862. Oregon, 1863.

Organic and other General Laws: 1845–1864. Compiled by M. P. Deady. Portland, 1866.

Laws of the Legislative Assembly of the Territory, 7th to 9th sessions, 1855–6 to 1857–8. 3v. in 1. Salem, 1856–8.

Acts and Resolutions of the Legislative Assembly of the State, 1859, extra session ; 1866 ; 1870. 3v. Salem, 1859–70.

PENNSYLVANIA.

Laws of the Commonwealth of Pennsylvania, from October 14, 1700, to April 6, 1802. Republished, under the authority of the legislature, by M. Carey and J. Bioren. 6v. Philadelphia, 1803.

The same. 1802 to 1808. Republished, under the authority of the legislature, by John Bioren. Vols. 7 and 8. Philadelphia, 1806–8.

Laws, from the 14th October, 1700, to 1829. Republished under authority of the legislature ; with notes and references. 10v. (Vol. 9 *wanting.*) Philadelphia, 1810–44.

Digest of the Laws of Pennsylvania from 1700 to May 21, 1861. Originally compiled by J. Purdon. Revised by F. C. Brightly. Philadelphia, 1862.

Common School Laws. Prepared by the Superintendent. Harrisburg, 1848.

The same. Harrisburg, 1857.

The same ; revised by T. H. Burrowes. Harrisburg, 1862.

The same ; revised by J. P. Wickersham. 16°. Harrisburg, 1870.

Election Laws ; digested and arranged with notes and judicial decisions, to 1868. Harrisburg, 1868.

Laws of the Commonwealth of Pennsylvania, 1801–2 to 1805–6. [These three vols. of session laws seem to be numbered as a continuation of A. J. Dallas's 4 vol. folio edition of laws.] Vols. 5, 6, 8. Lancaster and Octoraro, 1802–6.

Acts of the General Assembly, 1817–18 ; 1818–19 ; 1820–1 to 1846 ; 1848 to 1853 ; 1855 to 1861 ; 1863 to 1871. 50v. in 41. Harrisburg, 1818–71.

QUEBEC.

Statutes of the Province, passed 1867–8 [first session of the first parliament]; 1869. 2v. Quebec, 1868–9.

RHODE ISLAND.

Public Laws, as revised and finally enacted at the session in January, 1798. Providence, 1798.

The same, as revised in January, 1822. Providence, 1822.

Supplements to the Revision of 1822, [containing public laws from January, 1822, to July, 1842.] (May, 1829, to January, 1831, and May, 1839, to January, 1840, *wanting.*) 5v.

Public Laws, as revised and enacted in January, 1844. Providence, 1844.

Supplements to the Revision of 1844. [1844 to 1857.] 6v.

Revised Statutes of the State of Rhode Island and Providence Plantations. Providence, 1857.

Public Laws, passed from January, 1858, to January, 1867. Providence, 1867.

The same, from May, 1867, to January, 1869. (Pamphlet.) Providence, 1869.

Acts relating to the Public Schools. Providence, 1857.

The same. Providence, 1867.

Index to the printed Acts and Resolves of, and of the Petitions and Reports to, the General Assembly, 1758 to 1850. By John Russell Bartlett. Providence, 1856.

The same, 1850 to 1862. Providence, 1863.

Acts and Resolves passed by the General Assembly, [and Reports,] 1850–1 to 1869–70. 20v. Providence, 1850–70.

SOUTH CAROLINA.

Alphabetical Digest of the Public Statute Law of South Carolina. By Joseph Brevard. 3v. Charleston, 1814.

Statutes at Large. Edited under authority of the legislature, by Thomas Cooper, and David J. McCord. 10v. Columbia, 1836–41.

Acts of the General Assembly, 1817; 1819; 1823; 1829; 1836; 1839; 1840; 1842 to 1845; 1847 to 1853; 1855 to 1870–1. [With these are bound the *Resolutions and Reports* for 1817; 1819; 1823; 1829 and 1842; the *Journals* for 1835; and the *Resolutions, Reports* and *Journals* for 1836; 1839; 1840; 1843; 1847 to 1853; and 1855 to 1859.] In 25 vols. Columbia, 1818–71.

TENNESSEE.

Statute Laws of the State, of a public and general nature. By John Haywood and Robert L. Cobbs. 2v. Knoxville, 1831.

Compilation of the Statutes of Tennessee, of a general and permanent nature, from the commencement of the government to the present time. By R. L. Caruthers and O. P. Nicholson. Nashville, 1836.

Code of Tennessee; enacted by the general assembly of 1857–8. Prepared and edited by Return J. Meigs and William F. Cooper. Nashville, 1858.

Acts passed by the General Assembly [at its regular biennial sessions], 1819 to 1825; 1833, [public]; 1839–40; 1843–4; 1847–8 to 1853–4; 1857–8; 1859–60; 1865–6 to 1871: also [at extra sessions of] 1820; 1822; 1824; 1826; 1832, [public]; January, 1861; April, 1865; 1866; 1866–7; 1868. 28v. in 24. Nashville and Knoxville, 1819–71.

TEXAS.

Laws and Decrees of the State of Coahuila and Texas, in Spanish and English. Also, the Colonization Law of the State of Tamaulipas, and Naturalization Law of the General Congress, 1824 to 1835. Houston, 1839.

Digest of the Laws. To which are prefixed the constitutions of the United States, of the Provisional Government of the Republic, and of the State of Texas. By Oliver C. Hartley. Philadelphia, 1850.

Penal Code [and] Code of Criminal Procedure of the State of Texas, adopted by the 6th legislature. 2v. in 1. Galveston, 1857.

Digest of the General Statute Laws of the State; also, the Repealed Laws of the Republic and State of Texas, by which rights have accrued; also, the Colonization Laws of Mexico, Coahuila, and Texas, in force before the declaration of independence by Texas. By W. S. Oldham and George W. White. Austin, 1859.

Digest of the Laws, containing Laws in force and Repealed Laws on which rights rest. By Geo. W. Paschal. Galveston, 1866.

General and Special Laws, passed by the Legislature, 1846 to 1859–60 [biennial sessions]; 1859 to 1864 [general]; 1866; 1870. Austin, 1846–70.

UNITED STATES.

Laws of the United States of America, [1789 to March 3, 1797. Folwell's edition.] 3v. Philadelphia, 1796.

Laws, arranged and published under the authority of an act of Congress, 1789, to March 3, 1845. 10v. Washington City, 1815–45. [Vols. 1 to 5 edited by John Bioren, W. John Duane, and R. C. Weightman; v. 6 and 7 by William A. Davis and P. Force; and v. 8, 9, and 10 compiled by the Clerk of the House of Representatives.] (Vols. 2, 5, 6 and 10 *wanting.*)

UNITED STATES:

Laws, Resolutions of Congress under the Confederation, Treaties, Proclamations, and other documents having operation and respect to the Public Lands. Washington, 1817.

The same. Washington, 1828.

Statutes at Large, from the organization of the government, in 1789, to March 3, 1871. Edited, by authority of Congress, by R. Peters, G. Minot and G. P. Sanger. 16v. Boston, 1845–71.

Synoptical Index to the Laws and Treaties of the United States, from March 4, 1789, to March 3, 1851. Prepared under the direction of the Secretary of the Senate. Boston, 1852.

Analytical Digest of the Laws of the United States, from the adoption of the constitution to end of 34th Congress; 1789–1857. By Frederick Charles Brightly. Philadelphia, 1858.

The same. Vol. 2. 1857–1869. Philadelphia, 1869.

Statutes of the United States relating to revenue, commerce, navigation and the currency. Compiled by Lewis Heyl. Boston, 1868.

Session Laws, 1800–1 to 1870–1 (1801–2; 1806–7; 1825–6 and 1834–5 *wanting.*) In 47v. Washington, 1801–71.

UTAH.

Acts, Resolutions and Memorials, passed at the several annual sessions of the Legislative Assembly of the Territory; with Declaration of Independence, Constitution of the State of Deseret, Deseret Laws and Organic Act of Utah. Great Salt Lake City, 1855.

Acts, Resolutions and Memorials, passed in 1851; 1853; 1859–60. Great Salt Lake City, 1852–60.

VERMONT.

NOTE.—For a list of sessions of the Vermont Legislature, see Legislative Directory for 1870–71, pp. 134, 135 and 136. This list is correct, except that an adjourned session held at Rutland in February and March, 1797, is omitted. The laws of the first three sessions (March, June and October, 1778) are not known to be extant in print or manuscript. They were never recorded in the office of the Secretary of State. William Slade (Vermont State papers, p. 287,) says they were published in pamphlet form toward the close of the year 1778. Henry Stevens of Barnet, first President of the Vt. Historical Society, claimed that the Laws of 1778 were never printed, but that town clerks and particular officers had manuscript copies furnished them. Certainly a committee was appointed to get them printed; see Journal of the General Assembly for October 24, 1778, on p. 285 of Vermont State Papers.

GENERAL STATUTES.

Acts and Laws passed by the General Assembly of the representatives of the freemen of the State of Vermont at their session at Bennington, February 11th, A.D. 1779. [Slade calls this the "general code of 1779"; (see Vt. State Papers, p. 287.) The title page is wanting.] 4°. [Hartford, (Conn.) 1779?]

Statutes of the State of Vermont, passed by the Legislature in February and March, 1787. 4°. Windsor, 1787. (3 copies.)

VERMONT:

Laws of the State, revised and passed in the year 1797; with laws regulating proprietors' meetings, &c. Rutland, 1798. (4 copies.)

Laws of the State, digested and compiled [by Thomas Tolman]. 2v. in 1. Randolph, 1808. (4 copies.)

The same. To the close of the session of the legislature in 1816. Vol. 3. Rutland, 1817. (4 copies.)

Compilation of the Laws, coming down to and including the year 1824. By William Slade. Windsor, 1825. (4 copies.)

Laws of Vermont, from 1824 down to and including the year 1834. By Daniel P. Thompson. Montpelier, 1835. (4 copies.)

Revised Statutes of the State, passed November 19, 1839; to which are added several public acts now in force. Burlington, 1840. (4 copies.)

Compiled Statutes of the State, being such of the revised statutes, and of the public acts, and the laws passed since, as are now in force. By Charles L. Williams. Burlington, 1851. (4 copies.)

General Statutes of the State; passed at the annual session of the general assembly, commencing October 9, 1862; together with certain of the public acts of the year 1862. Cambridge, (Mass.,) 1863. (4 copies.)

The same. 2d edition. With appendix [by Wm. G. Shaw] comprising public laws enacted since; [1862 to 1869.] Cambridge, (Mass.,) 1870. (4 copies.)

MISCELLANEOUS.

Act for regulating and governing the Militia of the State of Vermont, passed 1793. Windsor, 1793.

The same; passed March 10, 1797. [Bound with above. This law, though printed in the *Revision* of 1797, was never printed with the regular session laws for the February session, 1797. Title page wanting; the heading of the act in this edition is "Militia Law."]

Act establishing Fees, passed October, 1798. [This act is also found in regular session laws of 1798.] Vergennes, 1798.

Act for regulating and governing the Militia of Vermont, with report of Board of Officers to organize the Militia of this State. Montpelier, 1837.

Statutes relating to the Grand List, in force January 1, 1855. Montpelier, 1855.

SESSION LAWS.

NOTE.—As to session laws of 1778, see note preceding General Statutes, *ante*. The "General Code" of 1779 and the Statutes passed February and March, 1787, comprise the result of the legislation of the February sessions of 1779 and 1787, and are themselves all the "session laws" originally published of the same.

Acts and Laws made and passed by the General Assembly of the representatives of the freemen of the State of Vermont, at their session at Windsor, June 2d, A.D. 1779. [Bound with "General Code" of 1779, and paged in continuation thereof.] 4°.

VERMONT:

The same; session at Manchester, October, 1779. [Bound with "General Code" of 1779.] 4°. Hartford, (Conn.) 1780.

The same; session at Bennington, October, 1780. [Imperfect. Bound with "General Code" of 1779.] 4°.

The same; session at Windsor, February, 1781. [Bound with "General Code" of 1779.] 4°.

The same; session at Windsor, April, 1781. [Imperfect. Bound with "General Code" of 1779.] 4°.

NOTE.—The session laws of permanent interest of the nineteen sessions from February, 1779, to October, 1786, are reprinted in Slade's Vermont State Papers, p. 287 to p. 510; which see. For laws regulating proprietors' meetings, granting land taxes, and privileges for locks, toll bridges and turnpike roads, passed from 1779 to 1787, see Appendix to Revision of 1797.

Acts and Laws passed by the Legislature of the State of Vermont, at their session at Newbury, October, 1787. [Bound with Statutes of 1787.] 4°.

The same; session at Manchester, October, 1788. [Bound with Statutes of 1787.] 4°.

The same; session at Westminster, October, 1789. [Bound with Statutes of 1787.] 4°.

The same; session at Castleton, October, 1790. [Bound with Statutes of 1787.] 4°.

The same; adjourned session at Bennington, January, 1791. Bennington, 1791.

The same; session at Windsor, October, 1791. [Imperfect.] Windsor, 1791.

Statutes of the State of Vermont, revised and established by authority, in the year 1787, including those passed since that period, until the session of the assembly of said State, holden at Bennington, in January, 1791. [Added to these are the session laws of the regular October sessions of 1791, 1792 and 1793. The book, therefore, contains a reprint of the session laws from 1787 to 1793. It has been known as "Haswell's Revision."] Bennington, 1791.

Acts and Laws passed by the General Assembly, 1792 to 1795. [This book contains the session laws from 1792 to 1795; a reprint of those of 1792, 1793, and 1795, bound with the original edition of those of 1794. Bennington.]

Acts and Laws passed by the General Assembly, 1793 to 1801. 10v. Windsor, Bennington, and Rutland, 1793–1801. [3 copies of 1800; 2 copies each of 1794; 1795; February session, 1797; 1798; 1799 and 1801.]

Acts and Laws passed by the General Assembly, 1802 to 1870. 70v. Bennington, Windsor, Randolph, Danville, Rutland, Middlebury, Poultney, Woodstock, Burlington, Bradford, and Montpelier, 1802–70. [4 copies.]

VIRGINIA.

Abridgment of all the Public Acts of Assembly of Virginia, in force and use, January 1, 1758. Glasgow, 1759.

Collection of such Acts of the General Assembly as are now in force, 1802. Vol. 1. Richmond, 1803.

The same. Vol. 2. January, 1807. Richmond, 1808.

Statutes at Large; being a collection of all the laws, from 1619. By William Waller Hening. 13v. Richmond, New York, etc., 1819–23.

Statutes at Large, from October session, 1792, to December session, 1807. New series, being a continuation of Hening, by Samuel Shepherd. 3v. Richmond, 1835–36.

Revised Code; a collection of all acts of the general assembly, of a public nature, now in force. 2v. Richmond, 1819.

Code of Virginia. With the declaration of rights and constitution of Virginia. Richmond, 1849.

The same. 2d edition. Including legislation to the year 1860. Richmond, 1860.

Acts passed by the General Assembly of the Commonwealth; 1810–11 to 1812–13; 1815–16; 1822–3 to 1841–2; 1844–5; 1847–8 to 1871–2. 47v. in 35. Richmond and Alexandria, 1811–71.

NOTE.—The session laws from 1847-8 to 1870-1 are as follows:—1847-8 to 1850-1 [last four annual sessions under old constitution]; 1852 [first biennial session under constitution of 1851]; 1852-3 [a special session, at which the time of the biennial meeting of the legislature was changed to December of odd years]; 1853-4 to 1865-6 [regular biennial sessions]; 1869-70 [first annual session under constitution of 1869] to 1871-2; also, special sessions of 1861; 1862; 1863; 1865; 1866-7, and sessions of the Pierpont loyal legislature in 1863-4 and 1864-5.

WASHINGTON.

Statutes of the Territory of Washington, being the code passed by the legislative assembly at their first session, February 28, 1854, with Declaration of Independence, &c. Olympia, 1855.

Laws passed by the Legislative Assembly at its [annual] sessions, 1854–5 to 1860–1. 7v. in 5. Olympia, 1855–61.

WEST VIRGINIA.

Ordinances and Acts of the restored government of Virginia, prior to the formation of the State of West Virginia; with the constitution and laws of the State of West Virginia, to March 2, 1866. Reprinted by order of the legislature. Wheeling, 1866.

Code of West Virginia. Comprising legislation to the year 1870, with appendix, containing legislation of that year. Wheeling, 1868. [1871 ?]

West Virginia:

Acts of the Legislature of West Virginia, July, 1861 [extra session]; June, 1868 [extraordinary session]; and at annual sessions, 1866 to 1871. 8v. Wheeling, 1861–71.

WISCONSIN.

Statutes of the Territory, passed at a session commencing in November, 1838, and an adjourned session commencing in January, 1839. Albany, 1839.

Revised Statutes, passed at the second session of the Legislature, commencing January 10, 1849. Southport, 1849.

The same; approved May 17, 1858. Chicago, 1858.

Laws relating to Common Schools. Madison, 1859.

Laws passed by the Legislature of the Territory, 1842; 1843; 1848. 3v. Madison, 1842–48.

General Laws, passed by the Legislature of the State, 1849 to 1860; 1862 to 1871: private and local laws, 1854 to 1860; 1862; 1864 to 1871. 38v. Madison, 1849–71.

JOURNALS

AND

DOCUMENTS.

JOURNALS AND DOCUMENTS.

ALABAMA.

Senate and House Journals, 1857–8 ; 1859–60. 4v.

State Documents, 1869–70.

Second Biennial Report on the Geology of Alabama. By M. Tuomey. Montgomery, 1858.

ARIZONA.

Journals of the Legislature, 1864 to 1867. 4v.

Constitution and Schedule of Provisional Government and Proceedings of Convention. 12°. Tucson, 1860.

ARKANSAS.

Senate and House Journals, 1858–9 ; 1864–5 to 1871. 11v.

Message and Documents, 1856–7 ; 1858–9. 2v.

Reports of Auditor, Superintendent of Public Instruction, &c. 1868.

Journal of Convention of Delegates, 1864, [with House Journal, 1864–5].

Debates and Proceedings of the Convention, 1868. Official. J. G. Price, Secretary, Little Rock, 1868.

Constitution of the State, adopted in 1868, with marginal notes and documentary history. By J. M. Pomeroy. Little Rock. 1870.

First and Second Reports of a Geological Reconnoisance, [1857–1860.] By David Dale Owen. 2v. Little Rock, 1858, and Philadelphia, 1860.

CALIFORNIA.

House and Senate Journals and Appendices, 1st to 18th sessions, 1850 to 1869–70. (Appendix to 12th session *wanting.*) 56v.

Transactions of State Agricultural Society, 1858 ; 1859. [The same also in appendices to State Journal, 10th and 11th sessions].

CALIFORNIA :

Second Report of Superintendent of Public Instruction. San Francisco, 1853.

First, Third and Fourth Biennial Reports of Superintendent of Public Instruction for 1864–65 and 1868 to 1872. [The same also in Appendices to Journals].

Law Regulating Common Schools, with notes, etc. San Francisco, 1853.

Report of Commissioner in Lunacy, Dec, 2, 1871.

Catalogue of State Library, 1857 ; 1860 ; 1866 : 1871. 5v.

Debates in the Convention on the Formation of the Constitution, 1849. By J. Ross Browne. Washington, 1850.

The same. (In Spanish).

CANADA.

Journals of the Legislative Council and Assembly of the PROVINCE; with appendix, or sessional papers.

CONTENTS.

Assembly. V. 8. 1849. Appendix. V. 8. Pts. 1–3.	4v. Folio. Montreal, 1849.
Council. V. 9. 1850. Assembly. V. 9. 1850. Appendix. V. 9. Pts. 1–2.	4v. Folio. Montreal, 1850.
Assembly. V. 10. 1851. Appendix. V. 10. Pts. 1–4.	5v. Folio. Montreal, 1851.
Council. V. 11. 1852-3. Assembly. V. 11. Pts. 1-2. 1852-3. Appendix. V. 11. Pts. 1–9. (Part 2 of Appendix *wanting*.)	11v. Quebec, 1852-3.
Council. V. 14. 1856. Assembly. V. 14. 1856. Appendix. V. 14. Pts. 1–6.	8v. Toronto, 1856.
Council. V. 15. 1857. Assembly. V. 15. 1857. Appendix. V. 15. Pts. 1–10.	12v. and 2v. folio. (appended maps and plans.
Council. V. 16. 1858. Assembly. V. 16. Pts. 1-2. 1858. Appendix. V. 16. Pts. 1–9.	12v. Toronto, 1858.
Council. V. 17. 1859. Assembly. V. 17. 1859. Appendix. V. 17. Pts. 1–5.	6v. and 1v. folio. Toronto, 1859.
Council. V. 18. 1860. Assembly. V. 18. 1860. Sessional Papers. V. 18, Pts. 1–4.	6v. Quebec, 1860.
Council. V. 19. 1861. Assembly. V. 19. 1861. Sessional Papers. V. 19. Pts. 1–4.	6v. Quebec, 1861.
Council. V. 20. 1862. Assembly. V. 20. 1862. Sessional Papers. V. 20. Pts. 1–5.	7v. Quebec, 1862,
Council. V. 21. 1863. (1st session.) Assembly. V. 21. 1863. Sessional Papers. V. 21. Pts. 1–6.	8v. Quebec, 1863.
Council. V. 22. 1863. (2d session.) Assembly. V. 22. Sessional Papers. V. 22.	3v. Quebec, 1863.
Council. V. 23. 1864. Assembly. V. 23. Sessional Papers. V. 23. Pts. 1–4.	6v. Quebec, 1864.
Council. V. 24. 1865. (1st session.) Assembly. V. 24. Sessional Papers. V. 24. Pts. 1–3, Parliamentary Debates on Confederation of British North American Provinces.	6v. Quebec, 1865.

CANADA :

Council. V. 25. 1865. (2d session.)
Assembly. V. 25.
Sessional Papers. V. 25. Pts. 1—2. } 4v. Ottawa, 1865.

Council. V. 26. 1866.
Assembly. V. 26. 1866.
Sessional Papers. V. 26. Pts. 1—4. } 6v. Ottawa, 1866.

Journals of the Senate and House of Commons of the DOMINION of Canada ; with Sessional Papers.

CONTENTS.

Senate. V. 1. 1867-8.
Commons. V. 1.
Sessional Papers. V. 1. Nos. 1—9. } 11v. Ottawa, 1868.

Senate. V. 2. 1869.
Commons. V. 2.
Sessional Papers. V. 2. Nos. 1—6. } 8v. Ottawa, 1869.

Senate. V. 3, 1870.
Commons. V. 3.
Sessional Papers. V. 3. Nos. 1—6. } 8v. Ottawa, 1870.

Senate. V. 4. 1871.
Commons, V. 4.
Sessional Papers. V. 4. Nos. 1—6. } 8v. Ottawa. 1871.

General Index to the Journals of the Legislative Assembly of Canada in the 1st, 2d and 3d Parliaments, 1841-51. By Alfred Todd. Folio. Montreal, 1855.

Government Map of Canada, from Red River to Gulf of St. Lawrence. Compiled by Thomas Devine. 1859. [In sheets].

Maps, Reports and Estimates relative to Improvements of Navigation of the River St. Lawrence, and proposed Canal connecting the River St. Lawrence with Lake Champlain. Folio. 1856.

Map of the North West part of Canada, Indian Territory, and Hudson's Bay .By Thomas Devine. [Folded in 4° case.] Toronto, 1857.

Tables of Trade and Navigation, 1850 ; 1852 to 1858. [The same also found in sessional papers and appendices ; for tables of succeeding years see sessional papers.] 8v.

Census of Canada, 1851-2 ; 1860-61. 4v.

Canada at the Universal Exhibition of 1855. [The same also in No· 5 of Appendix, vol. 14].

Report of Normal, Model and Common Schools in Upper Canada, 1851 ; 1855 ; 1857 ; 1858. [See also Appendices.] 4v.

Report of Superintendent of Education for Lower Canada, 1855; 1857 ; 1858. [See also Appendices]. 3v.

Catalogue of the Library of Parliament, Canada. General Library. Toronto, 1857.

The same. Works relating to America. Pamphlets and manuscripts. Index to authors and subjects. Toronto, 1858.

Geological Survey, Reports of Progress, 1847-8 ; 1849-50 ; 1853-4-5-6 ; 1858 ; from its commencement [1843] to 1863 ; atlas, 1863; 1863 to 1866 ; 1866 to 1869 ; 1870-71. [See also sessional papers.] 8v.

The same. Figures and Descriptions of Organic Remains. Decade III. Montreal, 1858.

Seigniorial Tenure. 4v. Quebec, 1852-53. (Vol. 3 *wanting.*)

COLORADO.

House and Council Journals, 1861 ; 1862 ; 1870. 3v.

CONNECTICUT.

Senate and House Journals, 1840 ; 1842 ; 1844 to 1846 ; 1849 to 1871. Senate Journal, 1848. House Journals, 1838 ; 1847. 60v.

General Assembly Reports, &c., 1853; 1855; 1856; 1858; 1860. 5v.

Legislative Documents of Connecticut, 1861 to 1871. 11v.

Catalogue of Connecticut Volunteer Organizations to July 1, 1864. Hartford, 1864.

The same, 1861–5. Hartford, 1869.

Report of Bank Commissioners, 1859. [For other years see Legislative Documents.]

Seventh Reform School Report, 1859. [See Documents for other years.]

Report of Joint Committee on Petition of Hartford and New Haven R. R. Company, 1839.

Report of Directors of State Prison, 1839 ; 1859. [For other years see Documents].

Third and Fourth Annual Reports of Secretary of State Board of Agriculture, 1868 ; 1869.

NOTE.—For Transactions of Conn. State Agricultural Society see *General Library*.

Statistics of Certain Branches of Industry, 1845. Prepared by D. P. Tyler. Hartford, 1846.

Report of Committee of School Fund, 1839.

Report of Trustees of State Normal School, 1859. [For other years see Legislative Documents.]

Reports [on] Common Schools, 1842 ; 1859. [See Assembly Reports and Legislative Documents for other years.]

[Reports of Directors of American Asylum for Deaf and Dumb are found in Legislative Documents. See also *General Library* under AMERICAN ASYLUM.]

Report on Geological Survey. By C. U. Shepard. New Haven, 1837.

Report on Geology. By J. G. Percival. New Haven, 1842.

Public Records of the Colony. [See *General Library* under HOADLEY and TRUMBULL.] 5v.

New Haven Colonial Records. [See *General Library* under HOADLEY.] 2v.

DAKOTA.

House and Council Journals, 1862 ; 1863-4 to 1867-8. 12v.

DELAWARE.

Memoir of the Geological Survey of the State. By James C. Booth. Dover, 1841.

FLORIDA.

Senate and House Journals and Appendices, 1848 ; 1850 ; 1856 ; 1858 ; 1859. Senate Journal and Appendix, 1852. 10v.

FRANCE.

Administration des Douanes. Tableau General des Mouvements du Cabotage, pendant l'annee 1848. Folio.

Agriculture Francaise. Departement des Cotes-du-Nord. Paris, 1844.

Rapport sur les questions coloniales a la suite d'un voyage aux Antilles et aux Guyanes, 1838-39. Par J. Lechevalier. 2v. Folio.

GEORGIA.

Senate and House Journals 1821 to 1869. (Senate Journals for 1828 and 1838, and House Journals for 1827, 1830, 1833 and 1838 *wanting.*) 84v.

Governor's Message, May, 1825, wlth documents. [On Creek and Cherokee affairs.] Milledgeville, 1825.

Catalogue of State Library, 1869. By John L. Conley.

Journals of the State [Constitutional] Convention, 1839 ; 1850 ; 1861 ; 1865 ; 1867-8. 5v.

Analysis of Constitution, 1868. By John L. Conley.

GREAT BRITAIN.

Journals of the House of Lords. V. 1-31. 1509 to 1767. 31v. Folio.

General Index to [vols. 1-19 of] the Journals of the House of Lords, 1509 to 1714. V. 1-2. 2v. Folio.

Calendar of the Journals of the House of Lords from 1509 to 1826. 2v. Folio.

Journals of the House of Commons. V. 9-36 and V. 100-118 ; 1667 to 1778 and 1845 to 1863. 47v. in 48. Folio.

GREAT BRITAIN:

General Index to [vols. 1–75 of] the Journals of the House of Commons, 1547 to 1820. V. 1–6. [Edited by Cunningham, Flexman, Forster, Moore, Dunn and Burney.] 6v. Folio.

The same; [to vols. 46–55] 1790 to 1800. Folio. London, 1803.

House of Commons Reports: Reports from Committees, reprinted by order of the House; 1715–1773. V. 1–4. 4v. Folio.

Rotuli Parliamentorum, 1278–1503. 6v. Folio.

The same: Index to. Folio. London, 1832.

Parliamentary Register, 1774 to 1780. 17v.

The same, 1780 to 1783. 11v.

Report on the Geology of Trinidad. By G. P. Wall and J. G. Sawkins. London, 1860.

Report from the Select Committee on the Hudson's Bay Company; with Proceedings of Committee and Minutes of Evidence. Folio. [1857].

[Sessional Papers: arranged under the four heads of] Bills Public, Reports of Committees, Reports of Commissioners, and Accounts and Papers:

—1857–8. Vols. 1–62. (V. 25 and V. 38, Part 1 *wanting.*) 60v. in 69. Folio.
—1859. 1st session. Vols. 1–27. 27v. in 29. Folio.
—1859. 2d Session. Vols. 1–35. 35v. in 39. Folio.
—1860. Vols. 1–73. 73v. in 74. Folio.
—1861. Vols. 1–69. 69v. in 74. Folio.
—1862. Vols. 1–66. 66v. in 67. Folio.
—1863. Vols. 1–76. (V.38; 51; 61 *wanting.*) 73v. in 75. Folio.

Chronicles and Memorials of Great Britain and Ireland during the Middle Ages. [See *General Library* under CHRONICLES.] 23v,

HAWAII.

Transactions of Royal Hawaiian Agricultural Society, at its 4th session, 1854. Vol. 2. Part 1. Honolulu, 1854.

IDAHO.

House and Council Journals, 1863–4; 1866–7; 1870–71. 5v.

ILLINOIS.

Senate and House Journals, 1834–5 to 1869. (Senate Journal 1834–5 and 1852 *wanting.*) 49v.

Reports made to the General Assembly, 1838–9 to 1871. 25v.

Adjutant General's Report, Jan. 1863. [This is also found in vol. 1 of Reports to the General Assembly, 1863.] Springfield, 1863.

ILLINOIS :

Adjutant General's Report, 1861–6. 8v. Springfield, 1867.

First and Second Reports of Trustees of Industrial University. [See also the same in Reports to General Assembly.] 2v.

First Report of Commissioners of Public Charities ; presented Dec. 20, 1870. [See also Reports, 1871].

First Report of Railroad and Warehouse Commission, 1871. [See also Reports].

Transactions of State Agricultural Society. Vols. 1–8, 1853 to 1870. 8v. Springfield, 1855–71.

Fourth, Sixth, Seventh and Eighth Biennial Reports of Superintendent of Public Instruction, 1861–2 ; 1865 to 1870. [See also Reports to General Assembly.] 4v.

Journals of Constitutional Convention, 1847 ; 1862 ; 1869–70. 3v.

Debates and Proceedings of the Constitutional Convention, 1869–70. 2v. 4°. Springfield, 1870.

Geological Survey of Illinois. A. H. Worthen, Director. 4v. 4°. [Springfield,] 1866–70.

INDIANA.

Senate and House Journals, 1857 ; 1863 ; 1865. 6v.

Documents of the General Assembly, 1849–50 ; 1857 ; 1861 ; 1863 ; [Part 1 and Vol. 2 of Part 2] ; 1865, [Vol. 1 of Part 1, and Part 2.] 7v.

Annual Reports, for 1871. Indianapolis, 1872.

Reports of the Officers of State to the Governor, for 1860 and 1861 ; 1863. 2v.

Report of [W. H. H. Terrell] the Adjutant General, 1861–5. 8v. Indianapolis, 1869–7.

Fifth Report of the State Board of Agriculture, containing transactions for 1856. Indianapolis, 1858.

Thirteenth Report of Superintendent of Public Instruction, 1863 and 1864. [See also Documents.] Indianapolis, 1865.

Catalogue of State Library, 1859 ; 1872. 2v.

Second Report of Geological Survey, made 1870. By E. T. Cox. Indianapolis, 1871.

IOWA.

Senate and House Journals, 1848 to 1870. (Senate Journal 1848–9 *wanting.*) 30v.

Legislative Documents, 1856–7 ; 1860 to 1872. 12v.

Adjutant General's Reports, 1861 to 1867, viz : Dec. 31, 1861 ; Jan. 1, 1863 ; Jan. 11, 1864 ; Jan. 1, 1865 ; Jan. 1, 1866 ; Jan. 1, 1867, 2v. 7v. Des Moines, 1862–67.

IOWA :

Census Returns, 1856 ; 1859 ; 1863 ; 1867. 4v.

Biennial Report of the Superintendent of Public Instruction, made Dec. 2, 1850.

Report of the Secretary of Board of Education, made Dec. 5, 1859. [See also Legislative Documents.]

Journal of the Constitutional Convention, 1857. Muscatine, 1857.

Debates of the Constitutional Convention, 1857. Vol. 1. Davenport, 1857.

Report of the Geological Survey of the State, 1855-6-7. By James Hall and J. D. Whitney. Vol. 1. Parts 1 and 2. 2v. 4°. [Albany.] 1858.

First and Second Annual Report of Progress by the State Geologist. Des Moines, 1868.

Report of the Geological Survey, 1866-7-8-9. By Charles A. White. 2v. 4°. Des Moines, 1870.

KANSAS.

House and Council Journals, 1855 ; 1857 ; 1859 ; 1860 ; 1860, special session. Senate Journal, 1862. Senate and House Journals, 1863 ; 1864 ; 1865 ; 1867 ; 1868 ; 1870. 23v.

Public Documents of the State Officers for the year 1870 ; 1871. 2v.

Proceedings in the Cases of the Impeachment of Charles Robinson, Governor, J. W. Robinson, Secretary of State, and G. S. Hillyer, Auditor. Lawrence, 1862.

KENTUCKY.

Senate and House Journals, 1849-50 ; 1853-4 ; 1865 ; 1865-6. 8v.

Reports to the Legislature, (or Legislative Documents,) 1843-4; 1844-5 ; 1845-6 ; 1848-9 ; for 1852, [to the Governor] ; 1853-4 ; 1863-4 ; for 1864 ; 1865-6. 10v.

Auditor's Reports, 1846 ; 1860 ; 1862 ; 1865. 4v.

Insurance Commissioner's Report of business of the year 1870.

First and Second Reports of the State Agricultural Society, 1856 to 1859. 2v. Frankfort, 1857-60.

Reports of Superintendent of Public Instruction for 1859 ; 1860; 1862 to 1864. [See Legislative Documents for other years.] 5v.

First and Fourth Reports of the Geological Survey, 1854-55 and 1858-59. David Dale Owen, Principal Geologist. 2v. 4°. Frankfort, 1856-61.

LOUISIANA.

Executive Journal of the Senate, 1850, 1853. House Journal, 1853. Senate and House Journals, 1860 ; 1864 to 1867 ; 1870. 17v.

Documents of the Legislature, 1853, [bound with House Journal for that year] ; 1860 ; 1864 ; 1866 to 1870. 6v.

Debates of the House of Representatives, 1870.

Journals of Constitutional Convention, 1844–5 ; 1861 ; 1864 ; 1867–8. 4v.

Debates in Constitutional Convention, 1844–5 ; 1864. 2v.

Constitution as adopted in Convention, 1852.

MAINE.

Senate and House Journals, 1869 to 1871. 6v.

Documents printed by order of the Legislature, 1845 to 1849 ; 1851–2 to 1867. Legislative Documents and Public Documents, 1868 to 1871. 35v.

Adjutant General's Reports, 1861 to 1866. 5v.

Report of Committee on North Eastern Boundary, 1841.

First Report of Commissioners of Fisheries, 1867. [See also Public Documents].

First Report of Bank and Insurance Examiner, 1868. [See also Public Documents].

Third Report of Insurance, made Jan. 1, 1871. [See also Public Documents].

Report of Commissioner on "Paper Credits," 1870.

Maine Legislative Manual, 1868 ; 1869. [See also Public Documents].

Rules and Orders of the Legislature, 1864. 16°. Augusta, 1864.

Provisional Report upon Water Power of Maine. By Walter Wells. [See also Public Documents, 1868].

Agriculture, Reports of the Secretary of the State Board ; 1860 to 1870. [See also Documents.] 11v.

Common Schools, Reports of State Superintendent, 1859 to 1862; 1864 ; 1865 ; 1867 ; 1870. [See also Public Documents.] 8v.

Catalogue of State Library, 1850.

Second Report on the Geology of the State. By Charles T. Jackson. Augusta, 1838.

Documentary History. See *General Library* under MAINE HISTORICAL SOCIETY.

MARYLAND.

Senate and House Journals and Documents, 1841-2 ; 1849-50 ; 1852 to 1870. (Documents for 1841-2 and 1849-50 *wanting*.) 39v.

Reports on Standards of Weight and Measure for the State ; and on Construction of the Yard-Measures. By J. H. Alexander. 1845.

First Report of State Agricultural Chemist, 1860. [See also Documents].

Proceedings of the Conventions of the Province, 1774-5-6. Baltimore, 1836.

Debates of the Constitutional Convention, 1864. 3v.

Constitution [of 1867] with marginal notes, etc. By Edward Otis Hinkley. Baltimore, 1867.

MASSACHUSETTS.

Journals of each Provincial Congress of Massachusetts, in 1774 and 1775, and of the Committee of Safety, &c. Boston, 1838.

House Journal, 1857.

Public Documents, 1844 to 1870. (Those printed 1848 to 1851 and 1855 *wanting*.) 64v.

NOTE.—These Documents are Reports. Before 1863 the date attached to them, in binding, was that of the year of the session at which they were made. In 1863 this was changed, and the date now attached is that of the year whose business is reported.]

Plans to accompany [Senate Document 76] Report of Commissioners for Enlargement of State House.

Documents submitted to the General Court by the Secretary of the Commonwealth, 1848 ; 1849 ; 1850 ; 1851. [Containing abstracts of agricultural, banking, insurance, pauper and prison returns of the years 1847 to 1850 ; also the 6th and 7th registration reports.] 4v.

Reports of Railroad Corporations, 1849.

Report on Insanity and Idiocy, under resolve of 1854. [See also Documents].

Report of Commissioners on Sanitary Survey of the State, presented April 27, 1850.

Pleuro Pneumonia. Hearing before the Committee on. Extra session, 1860.

Abstract exhibiting condition of Banks, October, 1838.

Abstract of the Census of Massachusetts, 1855. Prepared under direction of F. DeWitt. Boston, 1857.

Industry of Massachusetts. Statistical tables exhibiting condition and products of. For the year ending April 1, 1837. By John P. Bigelow, Boston, 1838.

The same. Statistics for year ending April 1, 1845. By J. G. Palfrey. Boston, 1846.

MASSACHUSETTS:

The same. Statistical Information relating to, for year ending June 1, 1855. By F. DeWitt. Boston, 1856.

The same. For year ending May 1, 1865. By Oliver Warner. Boston, 1866.

Laws of the Commonwealth for Government of the State Prison, with Rules and Regulations of Board of Inspectors. Boston, 1839.

Manual for the General Court, 1864; 1866, By S. N. Gifford and Wm. S. Robinson. 2v. 16°. Boston, 1864–66.

Abstract from Returns of Agricultural Societies, 1846. Boston, 1847.

Transactions of the Agricultural Societies of Massachusetts, 1847; 1848; 1851; 1852. 4v. Boston, 1848–53.

Agriculture of Massachusetts, containing Report of Secretary of Board of Agriculture and Abstract of Returns from the Societies. By Charles L. Flint. 1853 to 1862. 10v. (*Abstract of Returns* 1854 *wanting.*) 10v. Boston, 1854–63,

NOTE.—The *Reports* are also found in Public Documents.

Transactions of Massachusetts Society for the Promotion of Agriculture, 1856. Boston, 1857.

Board of Education. First to Thirty-Third Annual Reports. [See also Public Documents.] 33v in 20. Boston, 1838–70.

Catalogue of Library of General Court, 4°. 1846.

Catalogue of State Library, 1858,

Journal of the Constitutional Convention, 1853.

Debates in the Constitutional Convention, 1853. 4v. 4°.

NOTE.—See *General Library* under CURTIS, G. T.

Report on the Geology, Mineralogy, Botany and Zoology of Massachusetts. By Edward Hitchcock. Amherst, 1863.

Final Report on Geology of Massachusetts. 4°. Amherst, 1841.

Report on the Sandstone of the Connecticut Valley, especially its Fossil Footmarks. By Edward Hitchcock. 4°. Boston, 1858.

Tables of Bearings, Distances, Latitudes, Longitudes, &c., ascertained by the Astronomical and Trigonometrical Survey. 4°. Boston, 1846.

EARLY HISTORY.

Judicial Acts of the Colony of New Plymouth, 1636—1692. 4°. Boston, 1857. (Plymouth Colony Records, v. 7).

Laws of the Colony of New Plymouth, 1623—1682. 4°. Boston, 1861. (Plymouth Colony Records, v. 11).

Records of the Colony of New Plymouth, in New England. Edited by N. B. Shurtleff and D. Pulsifer. 11v. in 9. 4°. Boston, 1855–61.

Records of the Governor and Company of Massachusetts Bay, in New England, 1628—1686. [Edited by N. B. Shurtleff.] 5v. in 6. 4°. Boston, 1853–54.

MASSACHUSETTS :

ELECTION SERMONS.

By Ebenezer Emmons, May 25, 1757.

By Abraham Williams, May 26, 1762.

By Edward Barnard, May 28, 1766.

By Jason Haven, May 31, 1769.

By Samuel Stillman, May 26, 1779.

By Samuel Cooper. [At commencement of the Constitution, and inauguration of the new government.] Oct. 24, 1780.

By Moses Hemmenway, May 26, 1784.

By Daniel Foster, May 26, 1790.

By Samuel Parker, May 29, 1793.

By Jonathan French, May 25, 1796.

By Nathaniel Emmons, May 30, 1798.

MICHIGAN.

Senate and House Journals, 1850 to 1871. 44v.

Senate and House Documents, 1850 to 1867. 19v.

Joint Documents of the State of Michigan for the years 1849; 1851; 1853; 1855 to 1870. 21v.

Adjutant General's Reports, 1862 to 1866. [For Report of 1861 see Joint Documents for that year.] 5v.

Census and Statistics of Michigan, 1854; 1860. 2v.

Statistics of Michigan, compiled from Census of 1860.

Transactions of the State Agricultural Society, v. 1 to 11, 1849 to 1850. (V. 3, 1851, *wanting*.) 10v.

State Board of Agriculture, Third to Sixth and Eighth Annual Reports of the Secretary, 1864 to 1867; 1869. 5v.

System of Public Instruction and Primary School Law. By Francis W. Shearman. Lansing, 1852.

School Funds and School Laws, with notes, &c. By John M. Gregory. Lansing, 1859.

Reports of the Superintendent of Public Instruction, 1838; 1853; 1855 to 1860; 1862 to 1870. 17v. in 15. [See also Joint Documents].

Catalogue of State Library, 1859.

The same. Prepared by J. E. Tenney, Nov. 1868.

The same. Prepared by Harriet A. Tenney, Lansing, 1870.

Appeal by the Convention of Michigan to the people of the United States, with other documents, in relation to the Boundary Question between Michigan and Ohio. Detroit, 1835.

Journal of Constitutional Convention, 1850; 1867. 2v.

MICHIGAN:

Debates and Proceedings of the Constitutional Convention, 1867. 2v. 4°.

First Biennial Report of Progress of Geological Survey. [By A. Winchell.] Lansing, 1861.

MINNESOTA.

House and Council Journals, 1849 to 1857. (House Journal for 1855 *wanting.*) 15v. in 14.

Senate and House Journals, 1857; 1861 to 1871. 24v.

Executive Documents, 1860 to 1870. (1864 *wanting.*) 11v.

First and second Annual Reports of the Commissioner of Statistics. 2v. Hartford and St. Paul, 1860–62.

Journal of the Constitutional Convention, 1857. [Democratic Branch].

Debates and Proceedings of the Constitutional Convention, 1857. Reported by Francis H. Smith. St. Paul, 1857.

Debates and Proceedings of the Constitutional Convention, 1857. F. F. Andrews, Reporter, St. Paul, 1858.

NOTE.—The Territorial Convention of 1857 divided into two separate "Conventions"; one Democratic and the other Republican. Mr. Smith reported the proceedings of the former, and Mr. Andrews those of the latter.

MISSISSIPPI.

Senate and House Journals, 1840; 1841; 1850; 1850, [called session]; 1858; 1870. 12v. in 11.

Journal of Proceedings and Debates in the Constitutional Convention, 1865.

Constitution of the State as amended, 1865.

Report on Agriculture and Geology, 1854. By B. L. C. Wailes.

MISSOURI.

Senate and House Journals, 1836–7; 1838–9; 1842–3 to 1869. 44v.

Appendices to Journals. To House Journal, 1863–4. To Senate and House Journals, 1865–6; 1867; 1869. [Appendices of other sessions are bound with Senate and House Journals.] 9v.

Adjutant General's Reports, 1863 to 1865, [See also the same in Appendices to Journals.] 3v.

Report of Committee to investigate the Conduct and Management of the Militia. [See also the same in Appendix to House Journal, 1863–4].

First, Third and Fourth Annual Reports of the State Board of Agriculture, made 1865; 1867; 1868. [See also Appendices to Journals.] 3v. Jefferson City, 1866–69.

MISSOURI :

Report of Superintendent of Common Schools to 21st General Assembly. [See also Appendices.] Jefferson City, 1861.

First and Second Annual Reports of the Geological Survey. By G. C. Swallow. Jefferson City, 1855.

NEBRASKA.

House and Council Journals, 1855 to 1865. (Council Journal of 7th session, 1860–61, *wanting.*) 19v.

Senate and House Journals of the State Legislature, 1st, 2d and 3d sessions, 1866–7. 2v.

Third Annual Report of the State Board of Agriculture, for 1870, Des Moines, 1871.

NEVADA.

Council and House Journals, 1861. 2v. in 1.

Senate and Assembly Journals, 1864–5 to 1871. 10v.

Appendix to Senate Journal, 1864–5. [Appendices of other sessions are bound with Journals].

Catalogue of State Library, 1865. (Pamphlet).

Official Report of Debates and Proceedings in the Constitutional Convention, 1864. San Francisco, 1866.

NEW BRUNSWICK.

Ninth Annual Report of Board of Agriculture of the Province, 1868. Fredericton, 1868.

NEW HAMPSHIRE.

Senate and House Journals, 1810 to 1870. (Senate Jonrnals, 1816 ; 1822 ; November session, 1824 ; 1830 : and House Journals, 1810 to 1815 ; 1818 ; June session, 1820 ; 1822 ; 1824, *wanting.*) In 66v.

Bank Commissioners' Reports, 1844 ; 1846 to 1850 ; 1852 ; 1854 to 1857. [See also the same in Appendices to Journals.]

Governors' Messages, 1819 ; 1820 ; 1823 ; 1824 ; 1836 ; 1838 to 1840 ; 1842 to 1855. [See also the same in Journals].

Insurance Commissioners' Reports, 1853 to 1858. [See also Appendices].

International Exchanges. Address of Alexandre Vattemare, June 28, 1849.

Railroad Commissioners' Reports, 1849 to 1855 ; 1857 ; 1858. [See also Appendices].

NEW HAMPSHIRE:

Reports of Warden of State Prison, 1841; 1842; 1845; 1849 to 1851; 1853; 1855; 1857; 1867. [See also Appendices].

Reports on House of Reformation, 1852; 1856; 1858; 1867; with printed bill introduced, 1853. [See also Appendices].

Reports of Board of Visitors, Asylum for Insane, 1860. [See also Appendices].

Transactions of State Agricultural Society, 1850 to 1860. In 9v. Concord, Manchester and Dover, 1853–61.

Reports [of State Board and Superintendent] upon Common Schools, 1848; 1850; 1851; 1854 to 1868. [See also Appendices.] 18v.

Catalogue of State Library, 1857.

First Annual Report on Geology, 1841. By Charles T. Jackson.

Final Report on the Geology and Mineralogy of the State. By Charles T. Jackson. 4°. Concord, 1844.

Provincial Papers. Documents and Records relating to the Province. Edited by Nathaniel Bouton. V. 1-3. 1623—1722. 3v. Concord, 1867–69.

NEW JERSEY.

Council Journals and Minutes of the General Assembly, 1841–2 to 1843–4. 6v.

Senate Journals and Minutes of the General Assembly, 1845 to 1859; 1866 to 1871. 41v.

Legislative Documents, 1860 to 1871. 12v.

New Jersey in the Rebellion. By John Y. Foster. Newark, 1868. [See *General Library*].

Official Register of the Officers and Men of New Jersey in the Revolutionary War. Compiled by W. S. Stryker, Adjutant General. Trenton, 1872.

Register of the Commissioned Officers and Privates of the New Jersey Volunteers in the Service of the U. S. Jersey City, 1863.

Report on Condition of State Prison, January, 1858. [For other Reports, see Documents].

Report of Trustees of Lunatic Assylum, for 1860. [See also Documents, 1861].

Report of Agricultural Society, for 1860. [See also Documents, 1861.]

Journal of Proceedings of Convention to form a Constitution, 1844.

Description of the Geology of the State, being a final report by Henry D. Rogers. Philadelphia, 1840.

Geology of New Jersey. By George H. Cook. 4°. Newark, 1868.

Geological Survey. Maps. 4°. 1868.

NEW MEXICO.

Council Journal, 1853, and House Journals, June and December Sessions, 1851. (In Spanish and English.) 6v. in 5.

NEW YORK.

Journal of the Legislative Council of the Colony; 9th day of April, 1691, to April 3, 1775. 2v. 4°. Albany, 1861.

Journal of Votes and Proceedings of the General Assembly of the Colony, 1691 to 1765. 2v. Folio. New York, 1764–66.

Assembly Journal, 4th Session, 1st meeting, 1780. [Reprint.] 4°. Albany, 1859.

Senate and Assembly Journals, 1848 to 1870. (Senate Journal, 1853, *wanting.*) 54v.

Senate and Assembly Documents, 1848 to 1870. (Vol. 3, Senate Documents, 1849, and all Documents of 1854 *wanting.*) 272v.

NOTE.—The above 272 volumes are as follows:

	Senate Documents.	*House Documents.*
1848	3 vols.	7 vols.
1849	2 vols.	7 vols.
1850	3 vols.	9 vols.
1851	3 vols.	6 vols.
1852	3 vols.	7 vols.
1853	3 vols.	6 vols.
1855	3 vols.	7 vols.
1856	3 vols.	7 vols.
1857	4 vols.	5 vols.
1858	3 vols.	6 vols.
1859	2 vols.	5 vols.
1860	1 vol.	6 vols.
1861	2 vols.	8 vols.
1862	6 vols.	10 vols.
1863	5 vols.	9 vols.
1864	4 vols.	12 vols.
1865	3 vols.	10 vols.
1866	2 vols.	10 vols.
1867	3 vols.	18 vols.
1868	7 vols.	15 vols. in 16.
1869	8 vols.	12 vols.
1870	4 vols.	13 vols.

Senate Documents, 77 v. and House Documents, 195 v. Total, 272 v.

Analysis and Classification of Rules of Proceeding in the Legislature. By Sherman Crosswell. 16°. Albany, 1858.

Manual for Use of Legislature, 1868; 1869; 1870. 3v. 16°.

General Index to the Documents of the State of New York, [1777 to 1857]. Prepared by T. S. Gillett. Albany, 1860.

Cases of Breaches of Privileges of the House, 1777 to 1871. By C. W. Armstrong.

Cases of Contested Elections in Assembly, 1777 to 1871. Prepared by C. W. Armstrong.

NEW YORK:

Canals, Report of Commissioners on; made 1817.

Canal Fund, Report of Commissioners; made 1842.

Canals, Report of State Engineer and Surveyor on; made January, 1853. [See also Documents].

Census of the State, 1855. By F. B. Hough. Folio. Albany, 1857.

The same, 1865. By F. B. Hough. Folio. Albany, 1867.

Census, Instructions for taking, 1865.

Draft of a Penal Code. Albany, 1864.

Homœopathic Medical Society. Transactions. V. 4 and 6, 1866 and 1868. [See also Documents].

Insurance Department. Reports of Superintendent, 1861; 1862; 1864. 4v.

International Exchanges. Report of Joint Library Committee, 1847.

Military Forces, General Regulations for. 12°. Albany, 1858.

Prison Association. 3d, 5th, 21st [Part 1], 23d to 26th Reports of Executive Committee, for 1847; 1849; 1865; 1867 to 1870. [See also Documents.] 7v.

Prisons and Reformatories of United States and Canadas. Report on, made by E. C. Wines and T. W. Dwight; made 1867. [See also Documents].

Prison, State. 2d and 3d Reports of Inspectors, 1850; 1851. [See also Documents].

Prisons, State. Report of Commissioners to investigate Pecuniary Affairs of, 1855. [See also Documents].

Report of Secretary of State on Criminal Statistics, made 1848. [See also Documents].

Railroad Accidents, Report of Committee to examine Causes of, 1853. [See also Documents].

Railroads, Report of State Engineer and Surveyor on, made 1848. [See also Documents].

Regents of the University. Instructions to Academies, 1845.

The same. 3d, 4th, 13th, 14th, 16th, 17th, 19th, 20th and 22d Reports on Condition of State Cabinet of Natural History, 1850; 1851; 1860; 1861; 1863; 1864; 1866; 1867; 1869. [See also Documents.] 9v.

The same. Annual Reports, 1843 to 1849; 1854: 1855; 1858; 1861 to 1870. [See also Documents.] 20v.

Roads and Bridges, Report of Committee on, against a bridge over the Hudson, at Albany. 1844.

State Library. Reports of Trustees, 1848; 1851 to 1853; 1856; 1858; 1859; 1861 to 1867; 1869 to 1871. [See also Documents.] 17v.

NEW YORK:

Transactions of the State Agricultural Society; with Proceedings of the County Agricultural Societies. V. 1 to 28, 1841 to 1868. [See also Documents.] 29v. Albany, 1842–69.

Transactions of the American Institute of the City of New York. Annual Reports for 1845 to 1852; 1854 to 1860; 1863 to 1869–70. [See also Documents.] 22v. Albany, 1846–70.

Superintendent of Public Instruction, Annual Reports of, 1863; 1864; 1871. [See also Documents.] 3v.

Catalogue of State Library, 1850.

Catalogue of Maps and Surveys in offices of Secretary of State, State Engineer and Surveyor, and in the State Library, 1851.

Catalogue of State Library, 1855–1856. 3v. 4°.

Catalogue of Bibliography, &c.; State Library, 1858. 4°.

Catalogue of State Library; General Library, First Supplement, 1861. 4°.

Catalogue of State Library; Law Library, First Supplement. 1865. 4°.

Journal of Convention, 1867–8.

Documents of the Convention, 1867–8. 5v.

Proceedings and Debates of the Constitutional Convention, 1867–8. 5v.

Convention Manual. [Part 2, Statistics].

[Annotated] Constitution, 1846. By F. B. Hough. 4°. Albany, 1867.

Revision Documents of the Constitutional Convention, 1867–8. 4°.

Geological Survey. Report, made 1840.

Documentary History. Arranged under the Direction of the Hon. Christopher Morgan, Secretary of State, by E. B. O'Callaghan. 4v. 4°. Albany, 1850–51.

The same. 4v. Albany, 1849–51.

Documents relative to the Colonial History of the State; procured in Holland, England and France, by J. R. Brodhead. Edited by E. B. O'Callaghan. 10v. 4°. Albany, 1853–58.

The same. General Index. Prepared by E. B. O'Callaghan. 4°. Albany, 1861.

Report of J. Romeyn Brodhead relative to Colonial History; with Calendar to Holland Documents. 1845.

Natural History of New York. 21v in 22. 4°. Viz:

Part 1. zoology; or, the New York Fauna. By James E. DeKay. 5v. 4°. Albany, 1842–43.

2. Flora. By John Torrey. 2v. 4°. Albany, 1843.

3. Mineralogy. By Lewis C. Beck. 4°. Albany, 1842.

4. Geology. By William W. Mather, Ebenezer Emmons, Lardner Vanuxem, and James Hall. 4v. 4°. Albany, 1842–43.

5. Agriculture. By Ebenezer Emmons. 5v. Albany. 1846–54.

6. Palæontology. By James Hall. 4v. in 5. 4°. Albany, 1847–67.

NORTH CAROLINA.

Report of Superintendent of Public Instruction, 1869.

Proceedings of the General Assembly on the subject of International Exchanges. Raleigh, 1849.

Proceedings and Debates of the Convention called to amend the Constitution, 1835. Raleigh, 1836.

Geological Report of the Midland Counties. By Ebenezer Emmons. Raleigh, 1856.

OHIO,

Senate and House Journals, 1854 to 1870. 32v.

Executive Documents, 1843–4 ; 1853 ; 1854 ; 1856 to 1870. 34v.

Appendix to Senate Journal, 1857.

Report of Treasury Investigating Committee, 1859.

Annual Railway Reports, 1868 to 1870. 4v.

NOTE.—These Reports, except Vol. 1 for 1870, are also found in Executive Documents.

Proceedings of the State Board of Equalization, to 1853. Columbus, 1854.

The same ; 1859–60. Columbus, 1860.

Insurance Department. Third Annual Report. Part 1, Fire and Marine Insurance. 1870.

The Same. Fourth Annual Report. Part 2, Life Insurance, 1871.

Military Forces, General Regulations for, with laws pertinent thereto. Compiled by Henry B. Carrington. 2d ed. 1861.

State Library, 13th Annual Report of Commissioners, for 1858, with a historical sketch. [See also Executive Documents.]

Statistical Report of the Secretary of State, 1858 ; 1868. [See also Executive Documents.] 2v.

Annual Reports of the Board of Agriculture of the State, 5th to 24th, for the years 1850 to 1869. 20v. Columbus, 1851–70.

Fifth Annual Report of Commissioner of Common Schools, for year ending Aug. 31, 1858. [See also Executive Documents].

Report of Debates and Proceedings of the Convention for the Revision of the Constitution, 1850–1. 2v. 4°. Columbus, 1851.

Geological Survey. Reports of Progress for 1869 ; 1870. [With maps accompanying 1870.] 2v. Columbus, 1871.

OREGON.

House and Council Journals, 1854–5 to 1857–8. (Council Journal, 1854–5 *wanting.*) 7v.

Senate and House Journals, 1858–9 ; 1862 ; 1870. 6v. in 4.

Message and Documents, 1870.

PENNSYLVANIA.

Senate and House Journals, 1860 ; 1863 to 1871. 20v.

Executive Documents, 1862 to 1870. 13v.

Legislative Documents, 1860 ; 1863 to 1871. 13v.

Manual for the Government of the Senate and House of Representatives. By Jacob Ziegler. 1863. 16°.

Rules and Decisions of the General Assembly, Legislative Directory, 1869 ; 1870 ; 1871. By John A. Smull. 3v. 16°.

Adjutant General's Reports, 1862 to 1866. [See Documents also for corresponding years.] 5v.

Auditor General's Reports on Railroads, &c., 1863 ; 1865 to 1870. [See also Documents for corresponding years.] 7v.

Reports of Inspectors of Mines, 1870. [See Documents also].

Report of Board of Public Charities, 1870 ; 1871. [See Documents also.] 2v.

Report of Select Committee relative to Soldiers' National Cemetery, [at Gettysburg.] [See Documents also.] Harrisburg, 1864.

Revised Report of the same. [See Documents also.] Harrisburg, 1865.

The same ; with Addresses by Everett, Lincoln and Howard. Harrisburg, 1867.

Report of Inspectors of State Penitentiary, Eastern District, 1856 ; 1858 ; 1859. [For Reports of other years see Documents.] 3 (pamphlet) v.

Report of State Librarian, 1865. [For other years see Documents].

Pennsylvania School Architecture, a manual of directions and plans. Thomas H. Burrowes, Editor. 4°. Harrisburg, 1855.

Reports of Superintendent of Common Schools, 1860 ; 1862 to 1866 ; 1868 to 1870. [See also Documents.] 9v,

Catalogue of State Library. By Wallace De Witt. 1859.

Proceedings and Debates of the Convention to propose Amendments to the Constitution, 1837. 6v. Harrisburg, 1838.

Geology of Pennsylvania. A government survey. By Henry Darwin Rogers, State Geologist. 2v. 4°. Philadelphia, 1858.

Minutes of the Provincial Council, from the organization to the termination of the proprietary government, in 1776 ; and of the Supreme Executive Council from that date to termination of the Revolution. (March 10th, 1683, to December 20th, 1790.) 16v. Philadelphia and Harrisburg, 1852–53.

Pennsylvania Archives. Selected and arranged from original documents, by Samuel Hazard ; from 1664 to 1790. 12v. Philadelphia, 1852–56.

RHODE ISLAND.

Public Documents, or Reports ordered to be published, May, 1850 to January, 1870. [Bound with Acts and Resolves for the corresponding sessions].

Census of the Inhabitants of the Colony, taken in 1774. Arranged by J. R. Bartlett, Secretary of State. Providence, 1858.

Census, Report upon, 1865. By Edwin M. Snow. Providence, 1867.

Report upon Poor and Insane. By Thomas R. Hazard. 1851.

Second to Fifth, and Seventh Registration Reports, 1853–4 to 1857 ; 1859. [See also Public Documents.] 5v.

Acts relating to Public Schools, with remarks and forms, 1851.

Public School Reports, for 1851 ; 1853 to 1855 ; 1858 ; 1859 ; 1863 to 1870. [See also Public Documents.] 14v.

Records of the Colony of Rhode Island and Providence Plantations in New England. Printed by order of the Legislature. Ed. by J. R. Bartlett. 1636 to 1792. 10v. Providence, 1856–65.

SOUTH CAROLINA.

Senate and House Journals, 1835 ; 1836 ; 1839 to 1845 ; 1847 to 1853 ; 1855 to 1859 ; 1870–1. [Those for 1841 ; 1842 ; 1844 ; 1845 and 1870–1 are bound in separate volumes : those for the remaining years are bound with the Acts of the corresponding sessions.] 6v.

Reports and Resolutions, 1817 ; 1819 ; 1823 ; 1829 ; 1836 ; 1839 ; 1840 ; 1842 to 1845 ; 1847 to 1853 ; 1855 to 1859 ; 1870–1. [Those for 1870–1 are bound in a separate volume ; the remainder bound with Acts or Journals of corresponding years].

TENNESSEE.

Senate and House Journals, 1859–60 ; 1861, extra session ; 1865 to 1861. (House Journal 1865–6 *wanting.*) 20v.

Public Documents or Appendices to Journals, 1859–60 ; 1865 ; 1865–6 ; 1866–7 ; 1867–8 ; 1868–9 ; 1869–70 ; 1871. [Those for 1859–60 ; 1865–6 ; 1867–8 ; 1868–9 and 1869–70 in separate volumes : the remainder bound with Journals of corresponding sessions.] 6v.

First Report of Superintendent of Public Instruction, Oct. 7, 1860.

Catalogue of the General and Law Library of the State, 1871.

Journal of Proceedings of Convention of Delegates to amend, revise, or form and make a new Constitution, 1870.

Geological Reconnoisance, being First Biennial Report by James M. Safford. Nashville, 1856.

Geology of Tennessee. By James M. Safford. Nashville. 1869.

TEXAS.

Senate and House Journals, 1855 to 1859-60; 1866. 1870. 10v.

Journal of State Convention, 1866.

UTAH.

House and Council Journals, 1853-4.

UNITED STATES.

JOURNALS.

Journal of Congress; containing the proceedings from Sept. 5, 1774 to Nov. 3, 1788. Published by authority. 2d edition. 13v. Philadelphia, 1800-1801.

Secret Journals of the Acts and Proceedings of Congress, from the first meeting thereof to the dissolution of the Confederation by the adoption of the Constitution of the United States. 4v. Boston, 1821.

Journal of the Senate of the U. S, [1789 to 1815, or to close of 13th Congress.] Reprinted. 5v. Washington, 1820-21.

Journal of the Executive Proceedings of the Senate of the United States, 1798 to 1828. 3v. Washington, 1828.

Journal of the House of Representatives of the U. S. [1789 to 1815, or to the close of the 13th Congress,] Reprinted by order of the H. of R. 9v. Washington, 1826.

Journals of the Senate of the United States:

3d Cong., 1st sess., 1793-94.
2d sess., 1794-95.
6th Cong., 1st sess. 1799-1800
13th Cong., 2d sess., 1813-14.
3d sess., 1814-15.
14th Cong., 1st sess., 1815-16.
2d sess., 1816-17.
15th Cong., 1st sess., 1817-18.
2d sess., 1818-19.
16th Cong., 1st sess., 1819-20.
2d sess., 1820-21.
17th Cong., 1st sess., 1821-22.
2d sess., 1822-23.
18th Cong., 1st sess., 1823-24.
2d sess., 1824-25.
19th Cong., 1st sess., 1825-26.
2d sess., 1826-27.
20th Cong., 1st sess., 1827-28.
2d sess., 1828-29.
21st Cong. 1st sess., 1829-30.
2d sess., 1830-31.

22d Cong., 1st sess., 1831-32.
2d sess., 1832-33.
23d Cong., 1st sess., 1833-34.
2d sess., 1834-35.
24th Cong., 1st sess., 1835-36.
2d sess., 1836-37.
25th Cong., 1st sess., 1837
2d sess., 1837-38.
3d sess., 1838-39.
26th Cong., 1st sess., 1839-40.
2d sess., 1840-41.
27th Cong., 1st sess., 1841
2d sess., 1841-42.
3d sess., 1842-43.
28th Cong., 1st sess., 1843-44.
2d sess., 1844-45.
29th Cong., 1st sess., 1845-46.
2d sess., 1846-47.
30th Cong,, 1st sess., 1847-48.
2d sess., 1848-49 }
special, 1849 } in 1.

31st Cong., 1st sess., 1849-50. 2d sess., 1850-51.

UNITED STATES:

32d Cong., 1st sess., 1851–52.
2d sess., 1852–53.
33d Cong., 1st sess., 1853–54.
2d sess., 1854–55.
34th Cong. 1st sess., 1855–56 } in 1.
2d sess., 1856 }
3d sess., 1856–57.
35th Cong., 1st sess., 1857–68.
2d sess., 1858–59.
36th Cong., 1st sess., 1859–60.
2d sess., 1860–61.
37th Cong., 1st sess., 1861
37th Cong., 2d sess., 1861–62.
3d sess., 1862–63 } in 1.
special, 1863 }
38th Cong., 1st sess., 1863–64.
2d sess., 1864–65.
39th Cong., 1st sess., 1865–66.
2d sess., 1866–67.
40th Cong., 1st sess., 1867
2d sess., 1867–68.
3d sess., 1868–69.
41st Cong., 1st sess., 1869
2d sess. 1869–70.

63v. Small folio (2 vols. of 3d Cong.) and 8° (6th Cong. and *post*). Philadelphia (3 vols. of 3d and 6th Cong.) and Washington (13th Cong. and *post.*) 1797–1870.

Journals of the House of Representatives of the United States,
2d Congress, 1st session, 1791–92;
3d Congress, 1st session, 1793–94;
13th Congress, 2d session. 1813–14;
and for the succeeding sessions to the 1st session of the 42d Congress, 1871. [See sessions specified in list of Senate Journals above. The special sessions of 1849 and 1863 were of the Senate only, The 1st and 2d sessions of 34th Congress together form 1 vol.; and the 1st session of 36th Congress is in 2 vols.] 66v. (1 vol., 2d Congress, small folio; the rest octavo.) Philadelphia (1 vol., 2d Congress) and Washington, 1792—1871.

DOCUMENTS OF THE SESSIONS.

Documents published by the Congress of the United States, viz:

13th Congress, 2d session, 1813–14,	Senate Documents.	1 vol.
	House Documents.	2 vols. fo.
	House Documents.	2 vols.
3d session, 1814–15,	Senate Documents.	1 vol.
	House Documents.	1 vol. fo.
	House Documents.	1 vol.
14th Congress, 1st session, 1815–16,	Senate Documents.	1 vol. fo.
	House Documents.	2 vols.
	House Documents.	2 vols. fo.
2d session, 1816–17,	Senate Documents.	1 vol.
	House Documents.	2 vols.
	House Documents.	3 vols. fo.
15th Congress, 1st session, 1817–18,	House Documents.	8 vols.
2d session, 1818–19,	Senate Documents.	2 vols.
	House Documents.	8 vols.
16th Congress, 1st session, 1819–20,	Senate Documents	4 vols.
	House Documents.	8 vols.
	Reports of Comm.	1 vol.
2d session, 1820–21,	Senate Documents.	5 vols. (Vol. 5 *wanting.*)
	House Documents.	9 vols.
	Reports of Comm.	1 vol

UNITED STATES :

17th Congress, 1st session, 1821–22, Senate Documents. 3 vols.
(Vols. 1 and 2 *wanting.*)
House Documents. 9 vols.
(Vols. 3, 6, 7, 8, 9 *wanting.*)
Reports of Comm. 2 vols.
(Vol. 1 *wanting.*)
2d session, 1822–23, Senate Documents, 2 vols.
(Vol. 1 *wanting.*)
House Documents. 10 vols.
(Vol. 9 *wanting.*)
18th Congress, 1st session, 1823–24, House Documents. Vols. 2 & 7
2d session, 1824–35, House Documents. Vols.1,5 & 7
19th Congress, 1st session, 1825–26, House Documents. 10 vols.
Reports of Comm. 2 vols.
2d session, 1826–27, Senate Documents. 3 vols.
(Vols. 1 and 3 *wanting.*)
House Documents. 10 vols. in 11.
Reports of Comm. 3 vols.
20th Congress, 1st session, 1827–28, Senate Documents. 5 vols.
House Documents. 7 vols.
Reports of Comm. 4 vols.
2d session, 1828–29, Senate Documents. 2 vols.
House Documents. 6 vols.
Reports of Comm. 1 vol.
21st Congress, 1st session, 1829–30, Senate Documents. 2 vols.
House Documents. 4 vols.
Reports of Comm. 3 vols.
2d session, 1830–31, Senate Documents. 2 vols.
House Documents. 4 vols.
Reports of Comm. 1 vol.
22d Congress, 1st session, 1831–32, Senate Documents. 3 vols.
(Vol. 3 *wanting.*)
House Documents. 8 vols.
Reports of Comm. 5 vols.
(Vol. 1 *wanting.*)
2d session, 1832–33, Senate Documents. 2 vols.
(Vol. 2 *wanting.*)
House Documents. 3 vols.
Reports of Comm. 1 vol.
23d Congress, 1st session, 1833–34, Senate Documents. 14 vols.
House Documents. 6 vols.
Reports of Comm. 5 vols.
2d session, 1834–35, Senate Documents. 4 vols.
House Documents. 5 vols.
Reports of Comm. 2 vols.
24th Congress, 1st session, 1835–36, Senate Documents. 6 vols.
(Vol. 1 *wanting.*)
House Documents. 7 vols.
Reports of Comm. 3 vols.
2d session, 1836–37, Senate Documents. 3 vols.
House Documents. 4 vols.
Reports of Comm. 3 vols.
25th Congress, 1st session, 1837, Senate Documents. 1 vol.

UNITED STATES:

25th Congress, 1st session, 1837, House Documents. 2 vols.
(Vol 2, atlas, *wanting.*)
Reports of Comm.
[Bound with House Docs.]
2d session, 1837-38, Senate Documents. 6 vols.
(Vol. 1 *wanting.*)
House Documents. 12 vols.
Reports of Comm. 4 vols.
(Vol. 4 *wanting.*)
3d session, 1838-39, Senate Documents. 5 vols.
House Documents. 6 vols.
(Vol. 3 *wanting.*)
Reports of Comm. 2 vols.
Index to Documents, 22d to 25th Cong., inc. 1 vol.

26th Congress, 1st session, 1839-40, Senate Documents. 8 vols.
House Documents. 7 vols.
Reports of Comm. 4 vols.
2d session, 1840-41, Senate Documents. 5v. in 6.
[Vol. 5 in 2 parts.]
House Documents. 6 vols.
Reports of Comm. 1 vol.

27th Congress, 1st session, 1841, Senate Documents. 1 vol.
House Documents. 1 vol.
Reports of Comm.
[Bound with House Docs.]
2d session, 1841-42, Senate Documents. 5 vols.
House Documents. 6 vols.
Reports of Comm. 5 vols.
3d session, 1842-43, Senate Documents. 4 vols.
House Documents. 8 vols.
Reports of Comm. 4 vols.

28th Congress, 1st session, 1843-44, Senate Documents. 7 vols.
(vol 6 *wanting.*)
House Documents. 6 vols.
Reports of Comm. 3 vols.
2d session, 1844-45, Senate Documents. 13v. in 14
[Vol. 10 in 2 parts and 1 vol. of plates.]
House Documents. 5v .in 6.
[Vol. 4 in 2 parts.]
Reports of Comm. 1 vol.

29th Congress, 1st session, 1845-46, Senate Documents. 9 vols.
House Documents. 8 vols.
Reports of Comm. 4 vols.
2d session, 1846-47, Senate Documents. 3 vols.
House Documents. 4 vols.
Reports of Comm. 1 vol.

30th Congress, 1st session, 1847-48, Senate Documents. 8 vols.
Repts. Comm., S. 1 vol.
Miscell. Docs. S. 1 vol.
House Documents. 9 vols.
Repts. Comm. H. 4 vols.
Miscell. Docs., H. 1 vol.

UNITED STATES:

30th Congress, 2d session, 1848–49,	Senate Documents. 4 vols.
	Repts. of Comm., S. 1 vol.
	Miscell. Docs., S. 2 vol.
	Senate special sess. 1 vol.
	House Documents. 7 vols.
	Repts. Comm., H. 2 vols.
	Miscell. Docs. H. 1 vol.
31st Congress, 1st session, 1849–50,	Senate Documents. 14 vols.
	Repts. of Comm., S. 1 vol.
	Miscell. Docs., H. 2 vols.
	House Documents. 11 v. in 14. [Vol. 3 in 3 parts, and vol. 6 in 2 parts.]
	Repts. Comm., H. 3 vols.
	Miscell. Docs. H. 2 vols.
2d session, 1850–51,	Senate Documents. 5 vols.
	Repts. of Comm., S. 1 vol.
	Miscell. Docs. S. 1 vol.
	House Documents. 8v. in 10. [Vols. 6 and 7 in 2 pts. each.]
	Repts. Comm., H. 1 vol.
	Miscell. Docs. H. 1 vol.
32d Congress, 1st session, 1851–52,	Senate Documents. 16v. in 17 and 1 vol. maps. [Vol. 5 in 2 parts.] (Vol. maps *wanting*)
	Repts. of Comm., S. 2 vols.
	Miscell. Docs., S. 1 vol.
	S. special sess. Docs. 3 vols.
	House Documents, 15v. in 19 and 1 vol. maps. [Vol. 2 in 3 parts and vols. 4 and 10 in 2 parts each.] (Vol. maps *wanting*.)
	Repts. Comm., H. 1 vol.
	Miscell. Docs, H. 1 vol.
2d session, 1852–53,	Senate Documents. 11v. in 12. [Vol 6 in 2 pts. Vol. 11 4°.]
	Repts. Comm., S. 1 vol.
	Miscell. Docs. S. 1 vol.
	S. special sess. Docs. 1 vol.
	House Documents. 11v in 13. [Vols. 1 and 9 in 2 pts. each. Vol 8, Coast Survey, 4°, and same as vol. 11 Senate Docs.]
	Repts. Comm., H. 1 vol.
	Miscell. Docs., H. 1 v.
	House List of Private Claims, 1st to 31st Cong. 3 vols. 4°. (Vols. 2 and 3 *wanting*.)
33d Congress, 1st session, 1853–54,	Senate Documents. 13v. in 14 and 1 vol. maps. [Vol. 12 in 2 parts. Vol. 13, 4°.]
	Repts. Comm.. S. 3 vols.
	Miscell. Docs., S. 1 vol.

UNITED STATES:

33d Congress, 1st session, 1853–54, House Documents. 19v in 30 and 1 vol. maps. [Vols. 4 (Coast Survey and same as vol. 13 Senate Docs.) and vol. 15 (Naval Astronomical Expedition) 4°. Vol. 1 in 3 parts. Vol. 7 in 2 parts. Vol. 15 in 6 parts. Vol. 18 in 4 pts] (Parts 1, 4, 5 of vol. 15, and Part 3 of vol. 18 *wanting*.)
Repts. Comm., H. 3 vols.
Miscell. Docs. H. 1 vol.

2d session, 1854–55, Senate Documents, 13v in 25. [Vols. 12 (Coast Survey), 13 (Pacific R. R. Survey) and 14 (Perry's Japan Expedition) 4°. Vol. 13 in 11 parts. Vol. 14 in 3 parts.] (Vol. 12; Part 1 of vol. 13; and Parts 1 and 3 of vol. 14 *wanting*.)
Repts. Comm., S. 1 vol.
Miscell. Docs., S. 3 vols.
House Documents. 14v in 28. [Vols. 6 (Coast Survey), 11 (Pacific R. R. Sur.) and 12 (Japan Ex.) 4°. Vols. 1 and 7 in 3 parts each. Vol. 11 in 11 pts., and vol. 12 in 2 pts.] (Vol. 6 and Part 1 of vol. 11 *wanting*.)
Repts. Comm., H. 1 vol.
Miscell. Docs., H. 1 vol.

34th Congress, 1st & 2d sess., 1855–56. Senate Documents. 20v in 25. [Vols. 17 (Coast Surv.), 18 and 19 (Commercial Relations with Foreign Nations) and 20 (U. S. and Mexican Boundary) 4°. Vol. 19 in 4 parts and vol. 20 in 3 parts.]
Miscell. Docs., S. 1 vol.
House Documents. 16v. in 26. [Vols. 3 (Coast Survey), 10 (Commercial Rela. with F. Nations) and 14 (U. S. and Mex. Boundary) 4°. Vols. 1 & 10 in 4 parts each. Vols. 6 & 14 in 3 parts each.]
Repts. Comm., H. 3 vols.
Miscell. Docs. H., 2 vols.
Repts. of Court of Claims. 2v.

3d session, 1856–57, Senate Documents. 16 vols. [Vols. 14 (Com. Rela.), 15 (Coast Surv.) and 16 (4th Meteorological Rept.) 4°.]

UNITED STATES:

3d session, 1856–57, Repts. of Comm., S. (and of special session). 1 vol.
Miscell. Docs., S., (and of special session). 1 vol.
Senate Docs., special sesssion 1857. (McClellan's Crimean Report). 1 vol. 4°.
House Documents. 12v. in 17. [Vols. 4 (Co. Surv.) and 7 (Com. Rela.) 4°. Vol. 1 in 3 parts. Vol. 8 in 4 parts.] (Part 3 of vol. 1 *wanting*.)
Repts. Comm., H. 3 vols.
Miscell. Docs., H. 1 vol.
Rept. of Court of Claims. 1v.

35th Congress, 1st session, 1857–58, Senate Documents. 16 vols. [Vols. 15 (C. S.) and 16 (C. R.) 4°.]
Senate Reports. 2 vols.
Senate Miscell. 4 vols.
House Documents. 14v. in 20. [Vols. 5 and 6 (C. S. and C. R.) 4°. Vols. 2 and 8 in 4 parts each].
House Reports. 6 vols.
House Miscell. 3 vols.
Repts. of Court of Claims. 3v.

2d session, 1858–59, Senate Documents. 18v. in 19. [Vols. 16 (C. S.), 17 (C. R.) and 18 (Pacific R. R. Rept. by Stevens) 4°. Vol. 6 in 2 parts].
Senate Reports. 1 vol.
Senate Miscell. 1 vol.
House Documents. 13v. in 20. [Vols. 6 (C. S.) and 8 (C. R.) 4°. Vol. 2 in 5 parts and Vol. 10 in 4 parts].
House Reports. 3 vols.
House Miscell. 2 vols.
Repts. of Court of Claims. 1v.

36th Congress, 1st session, 1859–60, Senate Documents. 15 vols. [Vols. 13 (Sickness and Mortality in U. S. Army), 14 (Delafield's Rept. on Art of War in Europe) and 15 (Mordecai's Rept. on Military Commission to Crimea, &c.) 4°].
Senate Reports. 2 vols.
Senate Miscell. 1 vol.

UNITED STATES:

36th Congress, 1st session, 1859–60,	House Documents. 15v in 17. [Vols. 2 (C. R.), 7 (C. Sur.), 10 (Meteorological Observations), 11 (Stevens' Northern Pacific R. R. Rept.) and 14 (Ives' Rept. on Colorado River of the West) 4°. Vols 10 and 11 in 2 parts each].
	House Reports. 5 vols.
	House Miscell. 7 vols.
	Repts. of Court of Claims. 5v.
2d session, 1860–61,	Senate Documents. 9v. in 11. [Vols. 9 (C. R.) 4°. Vols. 3 and 7 in 2 parts each].
	Senate Reports. 1 vol.
	Senate Miscell. 1 vol.
	House Documents. 10 vols. [Vol. 7 (C. S.) 4°.]
	House Reports. 3 vols. in 4. [Vol. 3 in 2 parts.]
	House Miscell. 1 vol.
	Repts. of Court of Claims. 3v.
37th Congress, 1st session, 1861,	Senate Documents, &c. 1 vol.
	House Documents, &c. 1 vol.
	House Miscell., &c. 1 vol.
2d session, 1861–62,	Senate Documents. 6 vols.
	Senate Reports. 1 vol.
	Senate Miscell. 1 vol.
	Maps accompanying Mess. 1v.
	House Documents. 12v. in 14. [Vols. 4 and 6, 4°. Vol. 5 in 3 parts].
	House Reports. 4 vols.
	House Miscell. 1 vol.
	Repts. of Court of Claims. 2v.
3d session, 1862–63,	Senate Documents. 1 vol.
	Senate Reports. 4 vols. [Vols. 2, 3, 4 being Rept. on Conduct of the War].
	Senate Miscell., (and Docs. of special session, 1863). 1 vol.
	House Documents. 12v. in 13. [Vol. 9, 4°. Vol. 10 in 2 pts.]
	House Miscell. 2 vols.
	Repts. of Comm. and Repts. of Court of Claims. 1 vol.
	Commerce & Navigation. 1v.
38th Congress, 1st session, 1863–64,	Senate Documents. 1 vol.
	Senate Reports. 1 vol.
	Senate Miscell. 1 vol.
	House Documents. 16 vols. [Vol. 8, 4°].
	Maps accompanying Mess. 1v.
	Repts. of Comm. 2 vols.

UNITED STATES :

38th Congress 1st session, 1863–64,	House Miscell. 4 vols. (Vol. 4 being Smithsonian Report.)
	Commerce & Navigation. 1v.
2d session, 1864–65,	Senate Documents. 1 vol.
	Senate Miscell. 1 vol.
	Senate Reports. 4 vols. [Vols. 2, 3, 4 being Rept. on Conduct of the War].
	House Documents. 15v. in 16. [Vol. 9, 4°. Vol. 10 in 2 pts.]
	Reports of Comm. 1 vol.
	House Miscell. 3 vols. [Vol. 2 being Smithsonian Report].
39th Congress, 1st session, 1865-66,	Senate Documents. 2 vols.
	Senate Reports. 1 vol.
	House Documents. 16v. in 24. [Vol. 13, 4°. Vol. 1 in 4 pts. Vol. 9 in 3 parts. Vols. 3, 4 and 11 in 2 parts each.]
	Reports of Comm. 3 vols.
	House Miscell. 3 vols.
	Supplemental Rept. on Conduct of War. 2 vols.
	Commerce and Navigation, 1865. 1 vol.
2d session, 1866-67,	Senate Documents. 2 vols.
	Senate Reports. 1 vol.
	Senate Miscell. 1 vol.
	House Documents. 16v. in 20. [Vol. 14, 4°. Vols. 1 and 16 in 3 parts each].
	Repts. of Comm. 4 vols.
	House Miscell. 1 vol.
	Commerce & Navigation. 1v.
40th Congress, 1st session, 1867,	Senate Documents (and special session). 1 vol.
	Senate Reports (and special session). 1 vol.
	House Documents. 1 vol.
	Reports of Comm. 1 vol.
	House Miscell. 2 vols.
2d session, 1867-68,	Senate Documents. 2 vols.
	Senate Miscell. 1 vol.
	Senate Reports. 1 vol.
	Reports of the Commissioners to the Paris Universal Exposition. 6 vols.
	House Documents. 20v in 25. [Vols. 1 and 2 in 2 parts each, and vol. 10 in 4 parts. Vol. 18, 4°.]
	Reports of Comm. 2 vols.

UNITED STATES:

40th Congress, 2d session, 1867–68, House Miscell. 2 vols.
Commerce & Navigation. 1v.
Rept. of Dept. of Agricul. 1v.
3d session, 1868–69, Senate Documents. 1 vol.
Senate Miscell. 1 vol.
Senate Reports. 1 vol.
House Documents. 14v. in 19. [Vols. 1 and 3 in 2 pts. each. Vol. 10 in 4 parts.] (Vol. 11, 4°, *wanting*).
Repts. of Comm. 4 vols.
House Miscell. 1 vol.
Commerce and Nav. 1 vol.
Rept. of Dept. of Ag. 1 vol.
Index to Reports of Comm., 1839 to 1869.
Index to Executive Documents, 1839 to 1869.

41st Congress, 1st session, 1869, Senate Documents. 6 vols.
Senate Repts. & Mis. Docs. 1v.
House Documents. 1 vol.
Repts. of Comm. 1 vol.
House Miscell. 1 vol.
2d session, 1869, Senate Documents. 3 vols.
Senate Reports. 1 vol.
House Documents. 13v. in 17. [Vol. 2 in 2 parts.] (Vol. 8, 4°, and vol. 9, in 4 parts, *wanting*).
Repts. of Comm. 3 vols.
Com. and Nav. 1 vol.
Rept. of Dept. of Ag. 1 vol.

NOTE.—For classified Table of Contents of Documents of the sessions, see Index to the Catalogue of Books in the upper hall of the Public Library of the City of Boston, 1861, page 842.

ANNALS, DEBATES AND GLOBE.

Annals of Congress. Debates and Proceedings in the Congress of the United States, from March 3d, 1798, to May 27, 1824. 42v. Washington, 1834–56.

Register of Debates in Congress, from 1824 to 1833. 9v. in 15. Washington, 1825–33. [For continuation of Debates see Congressional Globe].

Congressional Globe and Appendix, from Dec. 7, 1833 to May 27, 1871; 1st session, 23d Congress to 1st session, 42d Congress. (vol. 25, or Appendix for 1st session, 32d Congress, 1851–2, *wanting*.) 94v. 4°. Washington, 1834–71.

AMERICAN ARCHIVES.

American Archives; consisting of a collection of authentic records, State papers, debates, and letters, and other notices of public affairs. The whole forming a documentary history of the origin and progress of the North American Colonies; of the

UNITED STATES :

causes and accomplishment of the American Revolution ; and of the Constitution of Government for the United States, to the final ratification thereof. Published by M. St. Clair Clarke and Peter Force. 4th series ; from the King's message March 7, 1774 to July 4, 1776. 6v. Folio. Washington, 1837–46.

The same. 5th series ; from July 4, 1776 to Declaration of Treaty of Peace 1783. V. 1–3. Folio. Washington, 1848–53.

AMERICAN STATE PAPERS.

American State Papers. Documents, legislative and executive, of the Congress of the United States, from 1789 to 1859, selected and edited under the authority of Congress. First series. 22v. Folio. Washington, 1832–34. (vol. 2, Military Affairs, *wanting*).

CONTENTS.

Claims, 1 v., 1789-1823.
Commerce & Navigation, v. 1-2., 1789-1823.
Finance, v. 1-3. 1789-1822.
Foreign Relations, v. 1-4, 1789-1815.
Indian Affairs, v. 1-2., 1789-1827.
Military Affairs, v. 1-2., 1789-1825. (vol. 2, *wanting*.)
Miscellaneous, v. 1-2., 1789-1823.
Naval Affairs, v. 1, 1789-1825.
Post Office, 1 v., 1789-1823.
Public Lands, v. 1-5., 1789-1834.

The same. Second Series. Selected and Edited by the Secretary of the Senate and Clerk of the House of Representatives. 17v. Folio. Washington, 1858–61.

CONTENTS.

Finance, v. 4-5. 1822 to May 16, 1828.
Foreign Relations, v. 5-6. 1818 to May 24, 1828
Military Affairs, v. 3-7, 1823 to March 1, 1838.
Naval Affairs, v. 2-4, 1824 to June 15, 1836.
Public Lands, v. 4-8, 1823 to Feb. 28, 1837.

NOTE.—Each series contains vols. numbered as 4 and 5 of Public Lands ; thus making 10 vols. of Pnblic Lands.

State Papers and Public Documents of the United States, from the accession of George Washington to the Presidency ; exhibiting a complete view of our foreign relations since that time. 10v. Boston, 1817. (vols. 4, 5 and 10 *wanting*).

Diplomatic Correspondence of the American Revolution, edited by Jared Sparks. 12v. Boston, 1829–30.

AGRICULTURE.

Reports of the Commissioner, 1862 to 1864 ; 1866 to 1868 ; 1870. 7v. [See also Documents. Also see under PATENTS, *post.*]

ARMY AND NAVY DOCUMENTS.

[Blue Book. Biennial] Register of officers and agents, civil, military and naval, in the service of the United States on the 30th day of Sept., 1821 ; 1823 ; 1829 to 1851. 14v. 12°. Washington, 1822–51.

The same, 1857 to 1871. 8v. Washington, 1857–72.

Official Army Register for 1867 ; January, 1869 ; January, 1870, 3v. 12°. Washington, 1867–70.

Navy Register for 1852 ; 1853. 2v. 12°. Washington, 1852–53.

The same for 1864 ; 1865. 2v.

Rules and Regulations for field exercise and manœuvres of Infantry. Concord, 1817.

UNITED STATES:

Regulations for the Army of the United States, 1861. 12°. New York, 1861.

Revised Regulations, 1861, with a full index. By authority of the War Department. Philadelphia, 1861.

Regulations for the Uniform and Dress of the Army. 1851. Folio. [1852].

The same, for the Navy and Marine Corps. [Bound with above.] Folio. 1852.

Cavalry Tactics. By P. St. G. Cooke. 2v. 16°. Philadelphia, 1862.

Instruction for Field Artillery. 12°. Philadelphia, 1863.

Ordnance Department, Regulations for the government of. 12°. Washington, 1852.

Ordnance Manual. 3d ed. 12°. Philadelphia, 1862.

Small Arms, Reports of Experiments with. 1856.

Navy of the United States, 1775 to 1853. By G. F. Emmons. 4°. Washington, 1853.

Statistical Report of Sickness and Mortality in the Army, 1839 to 1855. By R. H. Coolidge. [The same in Documents, 34th Congress.] 4°. Washington, 1856.

Circulars No. 6 and 7, War Department, Surgeon General's Office; on materials for Medical and Surgical History of the Rebellion, and on Amputations at the Hip Joint. 2v. 4°. Washington, 1865–67.

Military Commission to Europe in 1855 and 1856, Report of Major Alfred Mordecai. [See also Documents, 1st Session, 36th Congress.] 4°. Washington, 1860.

Report on the Art of War in Europe in 1854, 1855 and 1856. By Richard Delafield, [See also Documents, 1st Session, 36th Congress.] 4°. Washington, 1860.

Report of Captain George B. McClellan; War in Europe in 1855 and 1856. [See also Documents, Special Session, 34th Congress.] 4°. Washington, 1857.

Report of Committee to examine U. S. Military Academy at West Point. [See also Documents, 2d session, 36th Congress.] 1860.

Statement of Expenditures for Naval and Military Establishments, from Jan. 1, 1797 to Dec. 31, 1801. 4°. Washington, 1803.

ASTRONOMICAL AND METEOROLOGICAL OBSERVATIONS.

Army Meteorological Register, 1843 to 1854. Prepared under direction of Thomas Lawson. 4°. Washington, 1855.

Astronomical Observations, made at the U. S. Naval Observatory, 1851 and 1852. 4°. Washington, 1867.

Astronomical and Meteorological Observations, made at the U. S. Naval Observatory, 1864 to 1869. 6v. 4°. Washington, 1866–72.

UNITED STATES :

Zones of Stars observed at the National Observatory, Washington. By M. F. Maury. Vol. 1. Part 1. 4°. Washington, 1860.

Reports on Observations of the total eclipse of the sun, August 7, 1869. 4°. Washington, 1869.

Fourth Meteorological Report of James P. Espy. [See also Documents of 3d session, 34th Congress.] 4°. Washington, 1857.

Results of Meteorological Observations, 1854 to 1859. Vol 1. [See also Documents of 1st session, 36th Congress.] 4°. Washington, 1861.

NOTE.—See under EXPLORATIONS AND SURVEYS, *post*.

BANKS.

Annual Reports on the condition of the banks throughout the Union, 1854 ; 1855 ; 1860 ; 1862. [See also Documents.] 4v.

CENSUS.

Fifth Census ; or enumeration of the inhabitants of the United States 1830. To which is prefixed a schedule of the whole number of persons within the several districts, taken according to the acts of 1790, 1800, 1810, 1820. Folio. Washington, 1832.

Sixth Census, 1840. Folio. Washington, 1841.

Statistics of the United States as collected and returned by the marshals under the 13th section of the act for taking the 6th Census. Folio. Washington, 1841.

Compendium of the enumeration of the Inhabitants and Statistics, from returns of the 6th Census. Folio. Washington, 1841.

Seventh Census, 1850. 4°. Washington, 1853.

Report of Joseph C. G. Kennedy, Superintendent of the Census, for December 1, 1852 ; with report for Dec. 1, 1851. Washington, 1853.

Statistical view of the United States ; being a compendium of the seventh census. With the results of every previous census, beginning with 1790. By J. D. B. De Bow. Washington, 1854.

Preliminary Report on the eighth Census, 1860. By J. C. G. Kennedy. Washington, 1862.

Population of the United States in 1860. Compiled from the the original returns of the 8th Census. By J. C. G. Kennedy. 4°. Washington, 1864.

Agriculture of the United States in 1860. Compiled from returns of the 8th Census. By J. C. G. Kennedy. 4°. Washington, 1864.

Manufactures of the United States in 1860. Compiled from returns of the 8th Census. 4°. Washington, 1866.

Statistics of the United States, including mortality, property, &c. Compiled from returns of the 8th Census. 4°. Washington, 1866.

UNITED STATES:

Ninth Census of the United States, 1870. Statistics of Population. Tables 1 to 8. 4°. Washington, 1872.

The same. Agriculture. Tables 3 to 7. 4°. Washington, 1872.

COAST SURVEY.

Annual Reports of the Superintendent of the Coast Survey, 1851 to 1868. [See also Documents.] 19v. [Report for 1851, 8°; vol. sketches accompanying the same, 4°; succeeding reports all 4°.] Washington, 1852–71.

COMMERCE.

Reports on the Commerce and Navigation of the United States for 1850; 1852; 1854 to 1864. [See also Documents.] 13v. Washington, 1851–65.

Report of Israel D. Andress on the Trade and Commerce of the British N. A. Colonies, and upon the Trade of the Great Lakes and Rivers. [See also Documents, 1st session, 32d Congress.] 1853.

Report on the Commercial Relations of the United States with all Foreign Nations. [See also Documents, 1st session, 34th Congress.] 4v. 4°. Washington, 1856–57.

Annual Reports of the Commercial Relations of the United States with Foreign Nations, for 1858 to 1861. [See also Documents.] 4v. 4°. Washington, 1860–62.

The same, for 1862; 1864; 1867: 1868. [See also Documents.] 4v. Washington, 1863–69.

COURT OF CLAIMS.

Reports, 1855–56, 2v.; 1857–58, 3v.; 1858–59; 1862–63. [See also Documents.] 7v.

EXPLORATIONS AND SURVEYS.

Geological Survey of Wisconsin, Iowa and Minnesota, Report of. By David Dale Owen. With 4° vol. of Illustrations. 4°. Philadelphia, 1852.

Geological Survey of Colorado and New Mexico, Preliminary Report. By F. V. Hayden. Washington, 1869.

Physics and Hydraulics of the Mississippi River, Report. By A. A. Humphreys and H. L. Abbot. 4°. Philadelphia, 1861.

United States Exploring Expedition, during the years 1838–42, under command of Charles Wilkes. 29v. 19v. 4° and 10v. folio. Philadelphia, 1844–58.

CONTENTS.

V. 1–5. Narrative. With an atlas. 6v. 4°. Philadelphia, 1844.
V. 6, Ethnography and Philology. By Horatio Hale. 4°, Philadelphia, 1846.
V. 7. Zoophytes. By James D. Dana. With Atlas, folio. 4°. Philadelphia, 1846–49.
V. 8. Mammalia and Ornithology. By Titian R. Peale. 4°.

UNITED STATES:

V. 8. Mammalogy and Ornithology. By John Cassin. With Atlas, folio. 4°. Philadelphia, 1858.

V. 9. Races of Man. By Charles Pickering. 4°.

V. 10. Geology. By James D. Dana. With Atlas, folio. 4°.

V. 11. Meteorology. By Charles Wilkes. 4°.

V. 12. Mollusca and Shells. By Augustus A. Gould. With Atlas, folio. 4°. Philadelphia, 1852.

V. 13—14. Crustacea. By James D. Dana. With Atlas, folio. 2v. 4°. Philadelphia, 1852–55.

V. 15. Botany. Part 1. Phanerogamia. By Asa Gray. With Atlas, folio. 4°. Philadelphia, 1856.

V. 16. Botany. Part 2. Cryptogamia-Filices, including Lycopodiaceæ and Hydropterides. By W. D. Brackenridge. With Atlas, folio. 4° Philadelphia, 1854–55.

V. 20. Herpetology. Prepared under the superintendence of S. F. Baird. With Atlas, folio. 4°. Philadelphia, 1858.

Atlas of Charts. From the surveys of the expedition. 2v. Folio. Philadelphia, 1858.

[There are two volumes numbered as Vol. 8. There are wanting for the completion of the work, Vols. 17, 18 and 19.]

Exploration of the Valley of the Amazon. Part 2. [See also Documents of 2d session, 32d Congress.] Washington, 1854.

United States Naval and Astronomical Expedition to the Southern Hemisphere, 1849–52. J. M. Gilliss, Superintendent. [See also Documents of 1st session, 33d Congress.] 6v. 4°. Washington, 1855–6. (Vols. 3, 4, 5 and 6 *wanting*).

Narrative of the Expedition of an American Squadron to the China Seas and Japan, 1852–54, under command of Commodore M. C. Perry. [See also Documents of 2d session, 33d Congress.] 2v. 4°. Washington, 1856. (Vol. 1 *wanting*).

Report on the U. S. and Mexican Boundary Survey. By Wm. H. Emory. [See also Documents of 1st session, 34th Congress.] 2v. 4°. Washington, 1857-59.

Reports of Explorations and Surveys to ascertain route for a Railroad from the Mississippi River to the Pacific Ocean, made 1853–55. [See also Documents.] 12v in 13. 4°. Washington, 1855–60.

FINANCE.

Reports of the Secretary of the Treasury of the United States [on the finances] in obedience to act of 10th May, 1800; to which are prefixed the reports of Alex. Hamilton on the Public Credit, a National bank, manufactures and the establishment of a mint. (1790 to 1828.) 2v. Washington, 1828–29.

Reports on the Finances, 1851 to 1863; 1866. [See also Documents.] 14v.

INDIAN AFFAIRS.

Abstracted Indian trust bonds, Report on. [See also Documents, 2d session, 36th Congress.] 1861.

Commissioner of Indian Affairs, Report of, 1851. [See also Documents].

Historical and Statistical Information respecting the Indian tribes. By H. R. Schoolcraft. 5v. 4°. Philadelphia, 1851. [See *General Library*, under SCHOOLCRAFT].

UNITED STATES:

LIBRARY OF CONGRESS.

Catalogue. 4°. Washington, 1861.

Alphabetical Catalogue. 4°. Washington, 1864.

Catalogue of Additions. 1863 to 1866. 4v.

The same, 1867 to 1870. 4v. 4°. Washington, 1868–71.

Report of Librarian on condition of the Library. 1866 to 1869. 4 (pamphlet) v.

MESSAGES AND DOCUMENTS.

Message of the President to the two Houses of Congress. [With Accompanying Documents.] 1852–3; 1853–4; 1855–6 to 1862–3. [See also Documents.] 36v.

The same; Abridgment. 1858–9 to 1870–71. 13v.

The same; Department of State. 1863–4 to 1867–8. [See also Documents.] 15v.

[Diplomatic Correspondence.] Papers relating to Foreign Affairs, 1861 to 1864; 1868. [See also Documents.] 10v.

Message and Documents; Department of Interior, 1863–4; 1864–5; 1866–7; 1867–8. [See also Documents.] 5v.

The same; Navy Department, 1862–3; 1864–5; 1866–7; 1867–8. [See also Documents.] 4v.

The same; Post Office Department, 1863–4; 1866–7, [with Navy]; 1867–8. [See also Documents.] 4v.

The same; War Department, 1863–4; 1866–7; 1867–8. [See also Documents.] 4v.

OBITUARIES.

Obituary Addresses on the death of—

Henry Clay, 1852;

Jacob Collamer, 1865;

Henry Winter Davis, 1866;

Stephen A. Douglas, 1861;

Wm. Pitt Fessenden, 1869;

Solomon Foot, 1866;

Wm. R. King, 1853;

Zachary Taylor, 1850;

Daniel Webster, 1852.

PATENTS.

Digest of Patents, issued, 1790 to 1839. Washington, 1840.

The same, issued, 1839 to 1841. Washington, 1842.

UNITED STATES:

Reports of the Commissioner of Patents, [on Agriculture,] for 1847 to 1852; 1854 to 1860. [See also Documents. For succeeding years see under AGRICULTURE, p. 60, *ante*.] 13v.

Reports of the Commissioner of Patents, [on Arts and Manufactures,] for 1850 to 1862; 1866 to 1868. [See also Documents.] 36v.

Specifications and Drawings of Patents issued from the U. S. Patent Office, [copies certified by Commissioner,] from the week ending July 4, 1871, to the week ending March 26, 1872. 39v. 4°. Washington, 1871–72.

PUBLIC LANDS.

General Public Acts of Congress respecting sale of public lands, with instructions and opinions. 2v. Washington, 1838.

Reports of the Commissioners of the General Land Office, for 1867; 1868. [See also Documents.] 2v.

Report of Commissioner, 1866. Parts 1 and 2. [Part 2, folio, Maps.] 2v.

SMITHSONIAN INSTITUTION.

Annual Reports of the Board of Regents, showing the operations, expenditures and condition of the Institution, for the years 1848; 1853 to 1859; 1861; 1863; 1864; 1867 to 1869. 14v.

Smithsonian Contributions to Knowledge. V. 1—17. 4°. Washington, 1848–71.

Smithsonian Miscellaneous Collections. V. 1—9. Washington, 1862–69.

MISCELLANEOUS.

Congressional Directory, 2d session of 41st Congress. By B. P. Poore. Washington, 1869.

Constitution, Manual and Rules, 1860–1. Compiled by John M. Barclay.

Digested Summary and list of Private Claims. [See also Documents.] 3v. 4°. Washington, 1853. (Vols. 2 and 3 *wanting*).

Duplicate Letters; Fisheries and the Mississippi. Documents relating to transactions at negotiation of Ghent. Collected by J. Q. Adams. Washington, 1822.

Instructions to Envoys and Ministers to the French Republic. 1798. Philadelphia.

Manual on the Cultivation of the Sugar Cane. Washington, 1833.

[Maps of.] Boundary under the Treaty of Washington of Aug. 9th, 1842. Sheets 1 to 30. Folio; in large case.

The same; Islands in the River St. John. Sheets 1 to 5. Folio.

The same; Side Work. Sheets 1 to 4. Folio.

Post Offices in the United States, with names of Postmasters. Washington, 1851.

UNITED STATES :

The same ; corrected to Oct. 20, 1867. 4°. Washington, 1868.

[Revolutionary Claims.] Resolutions, Laws and Ordinances relating to pay, &c., of the officers and soldiers of the Revolution. Washington, 1838.

Roll of Honor. Nos. 11 ; 14 ; 17 to 20 ; 22 ; 24 ; 25. 9v. Washington, 1866–70.

Trial of Andrew Johnson, [Acting] President of the United States, before the Senate, on Impeachment by the House for High Crimes and Misdemeanors. 3v. Washington, 1868.

NOTE. For the following Reports, see also Documents.

Battle of Murfreesboro, Report on. By W. S. Rosecrans. Washington, 1863.

Fort Pillow Massacre, Report of Joint Committee on. 1864.

Virginia Campaign, Report on. By John Pope. 1863.

Conduct of the War, Report of Joint Committee on. 1863 ; 1865. 6v.

Secretary of War, Annual Report of. 1864–5.

Construction of a Military Road from Fort Walla-Walla to Fort Benton, Report on. By John Mullan. Washington, 1863.

Chief of Engineers, Report of. 1868 ; 1871. 2v.

Chief Signal Officer, Report of. 1870.

Chinese Correspondence. 1867 to 1869, Report on.

Covode Investigation, 1860. Report.

Foreign and Domestic Commerce ; Statistics. 1864.

International Congress on prevention and repression of Crime, Preliminary Report of the Commissioner. Washington, 1872.

Inter-oceanic Railroads and Canals. 1866.

Investigation into causes of the Gold Panic. 1870.

Ku-Klux Committee, Report of. 1872.

Light Houses, Report on. 1852.

Mineral Resources west of Rocky Mountains. By J. Ross Browne. 1868.

Mining Statistics west of Rocky Mountains. By R. W. Raymond. 1870.

Paraguayan Investigation. 1870.

President's Message on Enlistments [for Great Britain] in the U. S. Washington, 1856.

Reconstruction, Report of Joint Committee on. 1866.

Troubles in Kansas, Report of Special Committee. 1856.

VERMONT.

JOURNALS.

NOTE. For Journals of the Council of Safety from August 15, 1777, to March 12, 1778, see Slade's Vermont State Papers, p. 197 to p. 237. For Journals of the General Assembly, March, June and October sessions, 1778, see Slade's Vermont State Papers, p. 257 to p. 285.

Journals of the General Assembly, 1784, February session; 1784, October session; 1785, June session; 1787, February session; 1788 to 1835. 54v. in 53. (Two copies of 1785, June session; 1794; 1797; and 1799. Three copies of 1795; 1798; 1802; and 1804, October session. Four copies of 1796; 1801; 1803; 1804, January session; and 1805 to 1835).

NOTE. The Journal of the February session of 1797 was never printed; see Journal of October session, 1797, p. 283. The Journals to 1799, except those for 1791, January session; 1793; 1797 and 1798 are small 4°.

Senate and House Journals, 1836 to 1870. 71v. (4 copies).

Capital of Vermont. Journal of the proceedings and debates of the General Assembly, at the Special session, Feb., 1857. Montpelier, 1857.

REPORTS OF STATE OFFICERS, ETC.

Adjutant General's Reports, 1862 to 1866. [Those after 1866 are found in Legislative Documents.] 5v. (4 copies).

Quarter-master General's Reports, 1863 to 1865. [Those after 1865 are found in Legislative Documents.] 3v. (4 copies).

Surgeon General's Report, 1865. [That for 1864 is in appendix to House Journal for that session, and those after 1865 are in Legislative Documents.] (4 copies).

Register of Commissioned Officers of Vermont Volunteers, June 1, 1863. (4 copies).

NOTE. The Adj. Gen's. Reports for 1862 and 1863; the Q. M. Gen's. Reports, 1863 to 1865; the Surgeon Gen's. Report for 1865 and the Register of Officers are bound in one volume entitled "Vermont Military Reports, 1862-5.'.

Auditor's Reports, 1842 to 1865. [Those after 1865 in Legislative Documents.] 24v. in 7. (4 copies of all except 1842; two copies of 1842).

NOTE. The Bank, Treasury, State Prison and Insane Asylum Reports are made to the Auditor, and are to be found printed in his Reports.

[Insurance Commissioners' Reports, 1869 and 1870, are to be found in Legislative Documents].

Railroad Commissioner's Reports, 1856 to 1865. [Those after 1865 in Legislative Documents.] 10v. in 2. (4 copies).

Report of Board of Commissioners for Common Schools, 1828. [This is bound with Reports of State Superintendent, 1846–51.] 16°. Woodstock, 1828. (3 copies).

Annual Reports of the State Superintendent of Common Schools, 1846 to 1851. 6v. bound in 1. (3 copies).

VERMONT:

Circular of State Superintendent of Common Schools to County Superintendents and Address to Teachers, Dec. 1, 1845. [Bound with Set "A" of Annual Reports of Superintendent, 1846 to 1851.] St. Albans. 1845.

Reports of the State Board of Education, with the Reports of the Secretary, 1857 to 1865. [Those after 1865 in Legislative Documents.] 9v. in 3. (4 copies).

Report of Commissioner under resolution of 1857 relating to establishment of a Reform School. [This with report of committee on subject of juvenile offenders, 1865, and first five pamphlet reports of Trustees of Reform School, 1866 to 1870, bound in one volume.] (4 copies).

[Reform School Reports, 1866 to 1870, are found in volume just named and in Legislative Documents].

[Reports of Trustees of Vermont University and State Agricultural College, 1866 to 1870, are found in Legislative Documents].

[Reports of Fish Commissioners are found in Legislative Documents].

Legislative Documents, 1866 to 1870. 5v. (4 copies).

ADDRESSES, ETC.

An Oration before the Re-Union Society of Vermont Officers, October 25th, 1866. By Col. W. G. Veazey. Rutland, 1866.

An Oration before the Re-Union Society of Vermont Officers, October 22d, 1868. By Gen. P. T. Washburn. Montpelier, 1869.

An Oration before the Re-Union Society of Vermont Officers, November 4, 1869. By Gen. W. W. Grout. Rutland, 1869.

NOTE. For the following addresses delivered before the Vermont Historical Society, and published by order of the Legislature, see *General Library* under VERMONT HISTORICAL SOCIETY PUBLICATIONS.

1848, Address by James Davie Butler;
1848, Address by George Frederick Houghton;
1850, Address by D. P. Thompson;
1858, Address by Pliny H. White;
1858, Address by A. D. Hager;
1866, Address by G. F. Edmunds;
1866, Address by J. E. Rankin.

CATALOGUES.

Catalogue of State Library, 1850. (4 copies).

The same, 1858. (4 copies).

VERMONT:

CONSTITUTIONAL CONVENTIONS.

Journal of the Constitutional Convention, 1814; 1822; 1828; 1836; 1843; 1850; 1857; 1870. [8 pamphlets bound in 1 vol.] Danville, Burlington, Royalton, St. Albans and Montpelier, 1814–70. (2 copies).

NOTE. With one copy of the above volume is bound a copy of each of the following pamphlets.

Constitution of the State of Vermont, as revised by the Council of Censors, and recommended for the consideration of the People. Windsor, 1785. [With this is reprinted the Constitution as established in 1778].

Constitution of the State of Vermont, as established by Convention in 1778, and revised by Convention in June, 1786. Windsor, 1786.

Constitution of Vermont, as revised and amended by the Council of Censors, 1792. Rutland.

Constitution of Vermont as adopted by the Convention holden at Windsor, 1793. Windsor, 1793.

Constitutionalist, or amendments proposed by the Council, supported by the writings and opinions of James Wilson and others. [Supposed to be by N. Chipman.] Montpelier, 1814.

Essay on amendments proposed by the Council. Delivered at Norwich, 22d Feb., 1814. By Charles Marsh. Hanover, 1814.

Speech of Hon. Daniel Chipman, delivered in Convention, Jan. 6, 1836. Middlebury, 1837.

Last Resort. By Harvey Howes. Fair Haven, 1870.

COUNCIL OF CENSORS.

NOTE. The original Journals of the Council of Censors, 1785–6 and 1792, are in the Library, together with the original Addresses of these Councils to the Freemen. Extracts from the Journal of the Council of 1785-6 may be found in Slade's State Papers, p. 511 to p. 516. The Address of this Council is reprinted in Slade's State Papers, p. 531 to p. 534; and that of the Council of 1792, pp. 547 and 548.

Journal of the Council of Censors, 1813–14; 1820–21; 1827; 1834–5; 1841–2; 1848–9; 1855–6; 1862; 1869. [9 pamphlets bound in 1 vol.] Middlebury, Danville, Burlington and Montpelier, 1814–69. (2 copies).

NOTE. With each copy of the above volume is bound a copy of the following pamphlets.

Proceedings of the Council of Censors of the State of Vermont. [1785–6.] Windsor, 1786. [This is the address reprinted in Slade, p. 531; with appendix on arrearage of taxes due January 1, 1786.]

Proceedings of the Council of Censors, 1792. Rutland, 1792. [This contains the address reprinted in Slade, p. 547; the Constitution as proposed by this Council in 1792; an account of arrearages of taxes due Nov. 26, 1792; and the Constitution as established in 1786].

Address of the Council of Censors, [Feb. 4, 1800.] Bennington, 1800.

VERMONT:

Address of the Council of Censors, [Dec., 1806.] Bennington, 1807.

DIRECTORIES.

[Directory, 1826.] On sheet. Folio.

Directory and Rules of the House of Representatives, 1832 to 1835. [4 pamphlets bound in 1 vol.] 16°. Montpelier, 1832–35.

Directory and Rules of the Senate and House of Representatives, 1837 to 1870. [34 pamphlets, 16°: those from 1837 to 1867 bound in 3 vols.] Montpelier, 1837–70.

Directory, Rules and Orders, with lists of officers and other Historical Information; and manual of Parliamentary Practice. 7v. 16°. Montpelier, 1864–70. (2 copies).

Manual of the Legislature of Vermont, 1859 to 1870. [12 pamphlets bound in 1 vol,] 12°. Montpelier, 1859–70.

NOTE. These Manuals are published by the Assistant Clerks of the House and not by the State. A Manual of the Legislature of 1858 is printed in the Appendix of the House Journal of that year. Bound with the above Manuals will be found the following three pamphlets.

Deming's Statistical View of the Legislature of Vermont, 1850. [By L. Deming.] 16°. Montpelier, [1850].

Description of the State Houses of Vermont. [By W. W. Avery and H. B. Davis.] 16°. Montpelier, 1859.

Vermont Legislative Compendium for 1864. [By P. Deming.] 12°. Montpelier, 1864.

See *General Library* under DEMING.

EARLY HISTORY.

Petitions to His Majesty King GEORGE the Third. [These are the original petitions, circulated and signed in Western Vermont in 1766, which were sent to England Dec. 25, 1766, by Samuel Robinson. They pray for a Confirmation of the New Hampshire Grants. Bound with them are signed Powers of Attorney by the Inhabitants to the said Samuel Robinson and others.] Small 4°. [See Vermont Historical Collections, Vol. 1, p. 271].

Vermont's Appeal to the candid and impartial World, containing a fair stating of the Claims of Massachusetts Bay, New Hampshire and New York. The Right the State of Vermont has to Independence. With an address, &c. By Stephen R. Bradley. 12°. Hartford, [1780].

Vindication of the Opposition of the Inhabitants of Vermont to the Government of New York, and of their right to form an Independent State. Humbly submitted to the consideration of the impartial world. By Ethan Allen. 12°. Windsor, 1779. [Bound with the above].

Copy of a Remonstrance of the Council of the State of Vermont against the Resolutions of Congress of the 5th of December last, which interfere with their internal police. 12°. Hartford, 1783.

VERMONT:

Vermont State Papers; being a collection of Records and Documents connected with the establishment of government by the People of Vermont. Compiled by William Slade, Jun. Middlebury, 1823. [See also *General Library* under SLADE].

NOTE.—For works treating of Vermont History, published by the authors and not by the State, see *General Library* under ALLEN (ETHAN, HEMAN and IRA); HALL, (B. H. and HILAND); THOMPSON, ZADOCK; WILLIAMS, SAMUEL; and others. See also VERMONT HISTORICAL SOCIETY and VERMONT HISTORICAL GAZETTEER.

ELECTION SERMONS.

By Samuel Shuttlesworth, October 13, 1791;
By William Forsyth, October 10, 1799;
By Tilton Eastman, October 13, 1808;
By George G. Ingersol, October 14, 1830;
By William S. Perkins, October 11, 1832;
By Tobias Spicer, October 10, 1833;
By Silas McKeen, October 9, 1857;
By C. A. Thomas, October 15, 1858.

GEOLOGY.

Annual Reports on the Geology of Vermont, by C. B. Adams, 1845 to 1848. 4v. (3 copies 1845 and 1847; 4 copies 1846; 2 copies 1848.)

Report on the Geology of Vermont, descriptive, theoretical, economical and scenographical. By E. Hitchcock, E. Hitchcock. Jr., A. D. Hager and C. H. Hitchcock. 2v. 4° Claremont, 1861. [See *General Library* under HAGER].

PRINTED BILLS.

Printed Bills, 1864 to 1870. 7v.

REGISTRATION REPORTS.

First to Twelfth Reports relating to the Registry and Returns of Births, Marriages and Deaths in this State, 1857 to 1868. 12v. Burlington, Rutland, &c., 1859—70. (4 copies).

MISCELLANEOUS DOCUMENTS

NOTE.—These consist mainly of Reports which are also to be found in the regular Documents of their respective years.

Remarks of Mr. [Heman] Allen's Counsel upon the Petition of Silas Hathaway [to the Legislature of Vermont], praying for a new trial, &c. 1822.

Memorial of the Legislature for the Repeal of Acts incorporating the Grand Lodge and Grand Chapter of Vermont. Presented October 23, 1830.

Proceedings and Instructions concerning the System of International Literary and Scientific Exchanges established by Alexandre Vattemare. Burlington, 1848.

Annual Reports in Relation to International Exchanges and the Vermont State Library. Montpelier, 1850.

VERMONT:

Report on the Claim of the Iroquois Indians upon the State of Vermont, for their "Hunting Ground." By T. P. Redfield. Montpelier, 1854.

Report of the Commissioners appointed by the Governor on the Claim of the Iroquois Indians. Montpelier, 1855.

Reports and Resolutions on Slavery, &c., by Select Committee of the Senate. Montpelier, 1855.

Reports of Select Committees of the Senate on Slavery and the Condition of Kansas, and on the Outrage on the Freedom of Debate in Congress. Burlington, 1856.

Preliminary Report on the Natural History of Vermont. By Augustus Young. Burlington, 1856.

Report on the Artificial Propagation of Fish. By George P. Marsh. Burlington, 1857.

Report of the Committee for Erection of Monument over the Grave of Ethan Allen. Montpelier, 1858.

Report of Select Committee on Slavery, the Dred Scott Decision, and Action of Federal Government thereon. Montpelier, 1858.

Report of the Geological Survey. By Edward Hitchcock. Burlington, 1858.

Preliminary Report on Geology. By Edward Hitchcock. Montpelier, 1859.

Report of the Committee on the Judiciary in regard to the late Decision of the Board of Education. Montpelier, 1860.

Report of Committee on Military Affairs on H. 39, 1862.

Report of Committee on Military Affairs relative to the Militia of this State. 1862.

Report of Commissioners relative to the Restoration of Sea Fish to the Connecticut River and its Tributaries. 1866; 1867; 1869.

Report of Commissioner to the Universal Exposition of 1867, at Paris, France. Rutland, 1867.

VIRGINIA.

Senate Journal and Documents, 1850–1; 1852; 1859–60 to extra session, September, 1863; 1865–6; 1866–7. [The Senate Documents are bound with the Journals.] 9v.

House Journals, 1849–50: 1850–1; 1852–3 to 1866–7. 12v.

Documents, 1847–8; 1849–50; 1850–51; 1852; 1852–3, Part 1; 1855–6 to 1866–7. [Those for 1866–7 are bound with House Journal.] 31v.

Journal, Acts and Proceedings of General Conventions, 1850–51; 1861. 2v.

Documents containing Statistics of Virginia, ordered to be printed by the State Conventions. 1850–51; 1861. 2v.

Constitution of the State and Ordinances adopted by the Convention at Alexandria, February, 1864. (Pamphlet).

WASHINGTON.

House and Council Journals, 1854–5 to 1860–1. (Council Journal, 1854–5, and House Journal, 1856–7, *wanting.*) 12v.

WEST VIRGINIA.

Senate and House Journals, 1865 to 1868, extra session ; 1870. (House Journal, 1865 and 1868, extra session, *wanting.*) 10v.

Message and Documents for the sessions of 1866 ; 1867 ; 1868 ; 1871. [1867 and 1868 bound with House Journals.] 2v.

Adjutant General's Reports, 1864 to 1868. [Those of 1866 and 1867 bound with House Journals of 1867 and 1868.] 3v.

Reports of Auditor, Regents of Normal School and Treasurer, for year ending Sept. 30, 1868. 3v., (pamphlet).

Fifth Annual Report of General Superintendent of Public Schools, 1868. [See also Documents].

WISCONSIN.

Senate and House Journals, 1856 to 1871. (1863 and House Journal, 1861, *wanting*). 33v.

Governor's Message and Accompanying Documents for the *sessions* of 1857 to 1861 ; 1863 ; 1865 to 1871. 17v.

Adjutant General's Reports, 1862 to 1865. [Those for 1863, 1864 and 1865 in separate volumes. That for 1862 in Documents of the session of 1863. Duplicates of those for 1864 and 1865 in Documents of 1865 and 1866.] 3v.

Report of the Secretary of State for the year 1852. [For reports of other years see Documents].

First Report of Insurance Department, 1870. [See also Documents].

Transactions of the Wisconsin State Agricultural Society, with abstract of returns of County Societies. Vols. 5, 6 and 9, 1858–59 ; 1860 ; 1870. 3v. Madison, 1860–71.

Journal of Conventions to form a Constitution, 1846 ; 1847–8. 2v.

Report on the Geological Survey of the State, made Dec., 1861. By James Hall and J. D. Whitney. Vol. 1. 4° [Albany,] 1862. [For Owen's Report on Geology see under UNITED STATES, p. 63, *ante*].

Reports and Collections of the State Historical Society of Wisconsin, 1854 to 1869. Vols. 1 to 5. 5v. in 4. Madison, 1854–68.

LAW REPORTS.

LAW REPORTS.

UNITED STATES REPORTS.

SUPREME COURT REPORTS.

	Date.	No. Vols.
Dallas' Reports,	1781—1806	4
Cranch's Reports,	1800—1815	9 in 8
Wheaton's Reports,	1816—1827	12
Peters' Reports,	1827—1842	16
Howard's Reports,	1843—1860	24
Black's Reports,	1861—1862	2
Wallace's Reports,	1863—1870	12

CIRCUIT COURT REPORTS.

Abbott's Circuit and Dist. Court Reports,	1865—1871	2

FIRST CIRCUIT.

Gallison's Reports,	1812—1815	2
Mason's Reports,	1816—1830	5
Sumner's Reports,	1830—1839	3
Story's Reports,	1839—1845	3
Woodbury & Minot's Reports,	1845—1847	3
Curtis' Reports,	1851—1856	2
Clifford's Reports,	1858—1867	2

SECOND CIRCUIT.

Paine's Reports,	1810—1840	2
Blatchford's Reports,	1845—1856	6

Cases decided in this Court are reported in vols. 20, 21, 22, 23, 24, 25 and 29 of Vermont Reports.

THIRD CIRCUIT.

Dallas' Reports, 2d, 3d and 4th vols., contain cases decided in this Court. See U. S. Supreme Court, *ante.*

Wallace's Reports. [Reprint of 2d edition,]	1801	1
Washington's C. C. Reports,	1803—1827	4
Peters' C. C. Reports,	1803—1818	1
Baldwin's Reports,	1829—1833	1
Wallace (Junior's) Reports,	1842—1862	3

(Vol. 2, Wallace, Jr., *wanting*).

UNITED STATES:

FOURTH CIRCUIT.	Date.	No. Vols.
Marshall's Decisions. By Brockenbrough,	1802—1833	2
Taney's Decisions. By J. Mason Campbell,	1836—1861	1
SEVENTH CIRCUIT.		
McLean's Reports,	1829—1854	6
EIGHTH CIRCUIT.		
Miller's Decisions, by Woolworth,	1863—1869	1
Dillon's Reports,	1870—1871	1
NINTH CIRCUIT.		
Hempstead's Reports,	1820—1826	1
DISTRICT OF COLUMBIA.		
Cranch's Reports,	1801—1842	6

DISTRICT COURT REPORTS-

DISTRICT OF MAINE.		
Ware's Reports, Ware's Reports, with cases in,	1822—1839 1854—1855	1
DISTRICT OF MASSACHUSETTS.		
Sprague's Decisions,	1841—1864	2
Lowell's Decisions,	1865—1871	1
DISTRICT OF VERMONT.		
Reported in Vermont Reports, Vols. 20 to 25.		
DISTRICT OF NEW YORK.		
Van Ness' Prize Cases,	1814	1
Blatchford and Howland's Reports. Betts' Decisions,	1827—1837	1
Olcott's Reports. Betts' Decisions,	1843—1850	1
Abbott's Reports. Betts' Decisions,	1847—1850	1
Blatchford's Prize Cases,	1861—1865	1
Benedict's Reports,	1865—1871	3
DISTRICT OF PENNSYLVANIA.		
Peters' Admiralty Decisions,	1792—1807	2
EASTERN DISTRICT OF PENNSYLVANIA.		
Crabbe's Reports,	1836—1846	1
DISTRICT OF SOUTH CAROLINA.		
Bee's Admiralty Reports,	1792—1805	1
TERRITORY AND DISTRICT OF ARKANSAS.		
Hempstead's Reports. See under Circuit Court Reports, *ante*.		

UNITED STATES :

DISTRICT OF MICHIGAN, OHIO, ETC.

	Date.	No. Vols.
Newberry's Admiralty Reports,	1842—1847	1

DISTRICT OF SOUTHERN OHIO.

Bond's Reports,	1856—1871	2

DISTRICT OF CALIFORNIA.

McAllister's Reports,	1855—1859	1

DISTRICT OF OREGON.

Deady's Reports,	1860—1870	1

TERRITORY AND DISTRICT OF KANSAS.

McCahon's Reports,	1858—1868	1

OPINIONS OF ATTORNEYS GENERAL.

Official Opinions of the Attorneys Gen'l,	1791—1869	12
Andrew's Digest of Opinions of the Attorneys General to 1857.		

COURT OF CLAIMS.

Devereux's Reports,	1856	1
Nott and Huntington's Reports,	1863—1870	6

DIGESTS.

Brightly's Digest of Federal Decisions,	1789—1870	2

NOTE. The following "United States Digest" is of the State as well as Federal Courts. The Annual Digest, beginning in 1847, is in fact a continuation of Putnam's Equity Digest as well of the Common Law and Admiralty Digest.

UNITED STATES DIGEST.

EQUITY.

Putnam's United States Equity Digest,		—1847	2

COMMON LAW AND ADMIRALTY.

Metcalf and Perkins,	(1)	—1847	1
Curtis,	(2-3)	—1847	2
Putnam,	(4-5)	—1847	2
Sanger's Table of cases to vols. 1-5	(6)	—1847	1

COMMON LAW, EQUITY AND ADMIRALTY.

Annual Digest. By J. P. Putnam,	(7-15)	1847—1855	9
Annual Digest. By Geo. S. Hale,	(16-19)	1856—1859	4
Annual Digest. By H. F. Smith,	(10-14)	1860—1864	5
Annual Digest. By H. W. Frost,	(25-29)	1865—1869	5

THE SAME. NEW SERIES.

Annual Digest. By B. V. Abbott,	(1)	1870	1

ENGLISH REPORTS.

ENGLISH COMMON LAW REPORTS, [containing a full reprint of all the Cases decided in Courts of King's and Queen's Bench, from 1819 to 1865; Court of Common Bench, from 1813 to 1865; Court of Nisi Prius, from 1814 to 1849.] 118v. Philadelphia.

CONTENTS.

Reports.	Vol. of E. C. L. R.
Adolphus and Ellis,	28 to 40
Adolphus & Ellis, new series, (or Queen's Bench,)	41 to 83
Barnewall and Adolphus,	20 to 27
Barnewall and Alderson,	5 to 7
Barnewall and Cresswell,	8 to 21
Best and Smith,	101 to 118
Bingham,	8 to 25
Bingham's New Cases,	27 to 37
Broderip and Bingham,	5 to 7
Carrington and Kirwan,	47 and 61
Carrington and Marshman,	41
Carrington and Payne,	12 to 38
Chitty,	18
Common Bench, (Manning, Granger & Scott,)	50 to 67
The Same. (J. Scott,)	70 to 86
The Same. New Series,	87 to 115
Deacon,	38
Douglas,	26
Dowling and Ryland,	16 and 22
Ellis and Blackburn,	72 to 92
Ellis, Blackburn and Ellis,	96
Ellis and Ellis,	102 to 107
Gow,	5
Holt,	3
Manning and Granger,	39 to 49
Manning and Ryland,	17
Marshall,	4
Moody and Malkin,	22
J. B. Moore,	4 to 22
Moore and Payne,	17
Moore and Scott,	28 and 30
Nevile and Manning,	28 to 36
Nevile and Perry,	36
Ryan and Moody,	21
Scott,	30 and 36
Starkie,	2 and 3
Taunton,	1 to 4

LAW REPORTS, [containing Decisions of English Courts subsequent to 1865.] 39v. Philadelphia.

CONTENTS.

Common Law Series.

Queen's Bench Reports. From Mich. T. 1865 to Trin. T. 1871. 6 vols.

Common Pleas Reports. From Mich. T. 1865 to Trin. T. 1871. 6 vols.

Exchequer Reports. From Mich. T. 1865 to Trin. T. 1871. 6 vols.

Admiralty and Ecclesiastical Reports. From Mich. T. 1865 to Trin. T. 1869. 2 vols.

Probate, Divorce and Matrimonial Causes. From Mich. T. 1865 to Trin. T. 1869. 1 vol.

Equity Series.

Chancery Appeal Cases. Including Bankruptcy and Lunacy Cases. 1865–1871. 6 vols.

Equity Cases. Before the Master of the Rolls and the Vice-Chancellors. 1865–1871. 12 vols.

Yelverton's Reports. First American edition, with notes by Theron Metcalf. Andover, 1820.

CANADIAN REPORTS.

UPPER CANADA.

King's Bench Reports. (Old Series.) 6 vols. (Vols. 1, 2 and 6 *wanting.*)

Queen's Bench Reports. (New Series.) [1844 to 1870.] 29 vols. (Vols. 4, 15 and 18 *wanting.*)

LOWER CANADA.

Stuart's Reports, King's Bench and Appeals to Privy Council, 1834. 1 vol.

Lower Canada Reports, [1851 to 1868.] 17 vols.

ALABAMA.

		Date.	Vols.
Minor's Reports.		1820—1826	1
Stewart's Reports,		1827—1831	3
Stewart and Porter's Reports,		1831—1834	5
Porter's Reports,		1834—1839	9
Alabama Reports, (Vol. 11 *wanting.*)	(1—11 Ala. N. S.)	1840—1847	11
Ormond's Reports,	(12—15 Ala. N. S.)	1847—1849	4
Cocke's Reports,	(16—18 Ala. N. S.)	1849—1851	3
Shephard's Reports,	(19—21 Ala. N. S.)	1851—1852	3
Alabama Reports,	(22—24 Ala. N. S.)	1853—1854	3
Shephard's Reports,	(25—41 Ala. N. S.)	1854—1868	17
Danner's Reports,	(42 Ala. N. S.)	1868	1
Jones's Reports,	(43—45 Ala. N. S.)	1868—1871	3

ARKANSAS.

Pike's Reports,	(1— 5 Ark.)	1837—1842	5
English's Reports,	(6—13 Ark.)	1843—1853	8
Barber's Reports,	(14—24 Ark.)	1853—1867	11
Cox's Reports,	(25—26 Ark.)	1867—1871	2

CALIFORNIA.

Bennett's Reports,	(1 Cal.)	1850—1851	1
Hepburn's Reports,	(2— 4 Cal.)	1852—1854	3
Morris' Reports,	(5 Cal.)	1855	1
Booraem's Reports,	(6— 8 Cal.)	1856—1857	1
Lee's Reports,	(9—12 Cal.)	1858—1859	4
Harmon's Reports,	(13—15 Cal.)	1859—1860	3
Bagley & Harmon's Reports,	(16—19 Cal.)	1860—1862	4
Hillyer's Reports,	(20—22 Cal.)	1862—1863	3
Tuttle's Reports,	(23—32 Cal.)	1863—1867	10
Hale's Reports,	(33—37 Cal.)	1867—1869	5
Johnson's Reports,	(38 Cal.)	1869	1
Thompson's Reports,	(39—40 Cal.)	1870—1871	2

DIGESTS.

Wood's Digest of Laws, with Judicial Decisions,	1857	1

CONNECTICUT.

		Date.	Vols.
Kirby's Reports,		1785—1788	1
Root's Reports,		1789—1798	2
Day's Reports,		1802—1813	5
Day's Reports,	(1—21 Conn.)	1814—1852	21
Matson's Reports,	(22—24 Conn.)	1852—1856	3
Hooker's Reports,	(25—36 Conn.)	1856—1870	12

DIGESTS.

Baldwin's Digest,		1785—1869	1

DELAWARE.

Harrington's Reports,		1832—1858	5
Houston's Reports,		1856—1858	1

FLORIDA.

Branch's Reports,	(1 Fla.)	1846	1
Archer's Reports,	(2 Fla.)	1847	1
Hogue's Reports,	(3—5 Fla.)	1848—1851	3
Papy's Reports,	(6—8 Fla.)	1852—1859	3
Galbraith's Reports,	(9-11 Fla.)	1860—1867	3
Galbraith & Meek's Reports,	(12 Fla.)	1868	1

DIGESTS.

Galbraith's Index to Reports,	(1—11)	1846—1866	1

GEORGIA.

Charlton's (T. U. P.) Reports,		1805—1810	1
Charlton's (R. M.) Reports,		1811—1837	1
Dudley's Reports,		1821—1833	1
Georgia Decisions,		1842—1843	1
Kelly's Reports,	(1— 3 Geo.)	1846—1847	3
Kelly and Cobb's Reports,	(4— 5 Geo.)	1848	2
Cobb's Reports,	(6—20 Geo.)	1849—1856	15
Martin's Reports,	(21—30 Geo.)	1857—1860	10
Lester's Reports, (Vol. 33 *wanting.*)	(31—33 Geo.)	1860—1863	3
Bleckley's Reports,	(34—35 Geo.)	1864—1866	2
Hammond's Reports,	(36—40 Geo.)	1867—1870	5

DIGESTS.

Bacon's Digest of Reports,	(21—30)	1857—1862	1

ILLINOIS.

		Date.	Vols.
Breese's Reports,	(1 Ill.)	1819—1831	1
Scammon's Reports,	(2— 5 Ill.)	1832—1843	4
Gilman's Reports,	(6—10 Ill.)	1844—1848	5
Peck's Reports,	(11—30 Ill.)	1849—1862	20
Freeman's Reports,	(31—54 Ill.)	1863—1870	24
DIGESTS.			
Wood and Long's Digest of Reports,		1819—1866	2
Henry and Read's Digest, vol. 3,		1854—1863	1

INDIANA.

Blackford's Reports,		1817—1847	8
Carter's Reports,	(1— 2 Ind.)	1848—1851	2
Porter's Reports,	(3— 7 Ind,)	1851—1857	5
Tanner's Reports,	(8—14 Ind.)	1857—1861	7
Harrison's Reports,	(15—17 Ind.)	1861—1862	3
Kerr's Reports,	(18—22 Ind.)	1862—1864	5
Harrison's Reports,	(23—29 Ind.)	1864—1868	7
Black's Reports,	(30—34 Ind.)	1869—1870	5

IOWA.

Morris' Reports,		1839—1845	1
Greene's Reports,		1847—1852	4
Clarke's Reports,	(1— 8 Iowa)	1855—1861	8
Withrow's Reports,	(9—21 Iowa)	1860—1867	13
Stiles' Reports,	(22—31 Iowa)	1867—1871	10
DIGESTS.			
Dillon's Digest of Reports,		1839—1859	1
Hammond's Digest of Reports,		1859—1866	1

KANSAS.

Banks' Reports,	(1—5 Kan.)	1862—1870	5
Webb's Reports,	(6 Kan.)	1870	1

KENTUCKY.

Hughes' Reports,	(Myers' Ed.)	1785—1801	1
Kentucky Decisions, (Sneed)	(Myers' Ed.)	1801—1805	1
Hardin's Reports,		1805—1808	1
Bibb's Reports,		1808—1817	4

KENTUCKY :

	Date.	Vols.
Marshall's (A. K.) Reports,	1817—1821	3 in 2
Littell's Reports,	1822—1824	6 in 3
Littell's Select Cases,	1795—1821	
Monroe's (T. B.) Reports,	1824—1828	7 in 3
Marshall's (J. J.) Reports,	1829—1832	7
Dana's Reports,	1833—1840	9 in 5
Monroe's (Ben.) Reports,	1840—1858	18
Metcalfe's Reports,	1859—1863	4
Duvall's Reports,	1864—1866	2
(Vol. 2, Duvall, *wanting.*)		
Bush's Reports,	1866—1870	7
DIGESTS.		
Monroe and Harlan's Digest of Reports,	1793—1853	2

LOUISIANA.

		Date.	Vols.	
Martin's Reports,		1809—1823	12	in 10
Martin's Reports, (*new series*),		1823—1830	8	
Miller's Reports,	(1— 5 La.)	1830—1833	5	in 10
Curry's Reports,	(6—19 La.)	1833—1841	14	
Robinson's Reports,		1841—1846	12	
Robinson's Reports,	(1— 4 La. An.)	1846—1849	4	
King's Reports,	(5— 6 La. An.)	1850—1851	2	
Randolph's Reports,	(7—11 La. An,)	1852—1856	5	
Ogden's Reports,	(12—15 La. An.)	1857—1860	4	
(Vol. 15 La. An. *wanting.*)				
Glenn's Reports,	(16—18 La. An.)	1861—1866	3	
Hawkins' Reports,	(19—21 La. An.)	1867—1869	3	

MAINE.

		Date.	Vols.
Greenleaf's Reports,	(1— 9 Maine)	1820—1832	9
Fairfield's Reports,	(10—12 Maine)	1833—1835	3
Shepley's Reports,	(13—18 Maine)	1836—1841	6
Appleton's Reports,	(19—20 Maine)	1841	2
Shepley's Reports,	(21—30 Maine)	1842—1849	10
Redington's Reports,	(31—35 Maine)	1849—1853	5
Heath's Reports,	(36—40 Maine)	1853—1855	5
Adams' Reports,	(41—42 Maine)	1856	2
Ludden's Reports,	(43—44 Maine)	1857—1858	2
Hubbard's Reports,	(45—51 Maine)	1859—1864	7
Virgin's Reports,	(52—58 Maine)	1865—1870	7

MAINE:

DIGESTS.

		Date.	Vols.
Virgin's Digest of Reports,	(27—43)	1847—1859	1
Virgin's Supplement,	(44—56)	1859—1869	1

MARYLAND.

LAW.

Harris and McHenry's Reports,		1700—1799	4
Harris and Johnson's Reports,		1800—1826	7
Harris and Gill's Reports,		1826—1829	2
Gill and Johnson's Reports,		1829—1843	12
Gill's Reports,		1843—1851	9
Magruder's Reports,	(1— 2 Md.)	1851—1852	2
Miller's Reports,	(3—18 Md.)	1852—1861	16
Brewer's Reports,	(19—26 Md.)	1862—1866	8
Stockett's Reports,	(27—34 Md.)	1867—1871	8

CHANCERY.

Bland's Chancery Reports,		1811—1832	3
Maryland Chancery Reports,	(Johnson)	1847—1854	4

(*This Court is now abolished.*)

DIGESTS.

Stockett, Merrick and Miller's Digest of Maryland Reports,	1843—1855	1
Cohen and Lee's Digest of Reports, Vols. 9—20,	1855—1866	1

MASSACHUSETTS.

Quincy's Reports,		1764—1771	4
Massachusetts Reports, (Vol. 1 by Williams; vols. 2 to 17 by Tyng,)		1804—1822	17
Pickering's Reports,		1822—1840	24
Metcalf's Reports,		1840—1847	13
Cushing's Reports,		1848—1860	12
Gray's Reports,		1854—1860	16
Allen's Reports,		1861—1867	14
Browne's Reports,	(97—104 Mass.)	1867—1870	8
Thatcher's Criminal Cases,		1823—1843	1

DIGESTS.

Supplement to Hilliard's Digest, (15 Pick. to 3 Met.)		1
Mass. Digest, Bennett and Heard, and Heard and Holland,	1804—1869	3

MICHIGAN.

LAW.

		Date.	Vols.
Douglass' Reports,		1843—1847	2
Manning's Reports,	(1 Mich.)	1847	1
Gibbs' Reports,	(2— 4 Mich.)	1848—1858	3
Cooley's Reports,	(5—12 Mich.)	1858—1864	8
Meddaugh's Reports,	(13 Mich.)	1864—1865	1
Jennison's Reports,	(14—18 Mich.)	1866—1869	5
Clarke's Reports,	(19—21 Mich.)	1869—1870.	3

CHANCERY.

Harrington's Chancery Reports,		1838—1842	1
Walker's Chancery Reports,		1842—1846	1

DIGESTS.

Cooley's Digest of Reports,		1838—1865	1

MINNESOTA.

Officer's Reports,	(1— 9 Minn.)	1851—1854	9
Spencer's Reports,	(10—15 Minn.)	1854—1870	6

MISSISSIPPI.

LAW.

Walker's Reports,	(1 Miss.)	1818—1832	1
Howard's Reports,	(2— 8 Miss.)	1834—1843	7
Smedes & Marshall's Reports,	(9—22 Miss.)	1843—1850	14
(Vol. 4, Smedes & Marshall, *wanting*.)			
Cushman's Reports,	(23—29 Miss.)	1850—1855	7
George's Reports,	(30—39 Miss.)	1855—1865	10
Reynolds' Reports,	(40 Miss.)	1866	1

CHANCERY.

Freeman's Chancery Reports,		1839—1843	1
Smedes and Marshall's Chancery Reports,		1840—1853	1

MISSOURI.

Missouri Reports,		1821—1852	16 in 11
Bennett's Reports,	(16—21 Mo.)	1852—1855	6
Jones' Reports,	(22—30 Mo.)	1855—1860	9
Jones' Barclay & Whittelsey	(31 Mo.)	1860—1862	1
Whittelsey's Reports,	(32—41 Mo.)	1862—1867	10
Post's Reports,	(42—48 Mo.)	1867—1871	7

NEBRASKA.

		Date.	Vols.
Woolworth's Reports,	(1 Neb.)		1

NEVADA.

		Date.	Vols.
Lewis' Reports,	(1 Nevada)	1865	1
Helm's Reports,	(2—7 Nevada)	1866—1872	6

NEW HAMPSHIRE.

		Date.	Vols.
New Hampshire Reports,		1816—1849	20
Foster's Reports,	(21—31 N. H.)	1850—1855	11
Fogg's Reports,	(32—37 N. H.)	1855—1859	6
Chandler's Reports,	(38—44 N. H.)	1859—1865	7
Hadley's Reports,	(45—48 N. H.)	1865—1869	4

DIGESTS.

		Date.	Vols.
Gilchrist's Digest of Reports,	(1-12 N. H.)	1816—1842	1
Bell's Digest of Reports,	(13-31 N. H.)	1842—1855	1
Morrison's Digest of Reports,		1816—1865	1

NEW JERSEY.

LAW.

		Date.	Vols.
Coxe's Reports,		1790—1795	1
Pennington's Reports,		1806—1813	1
Southard's Reports,		1816—1820	2
Halsted's Reports,		1821—1831	7
Green's Reports,		1831—1836	3
Harrison's Reports,		1837—1842	4
Spencer's Reports,		1842—1845	1
Zabriskie's Reports,		1847—1855	4
Dutcher's Reports,	(29 N. J. Law.)	1855—1863	5
Vroom's Reports,	(30—34 N. J. Law.)	1863—1870	5

CHANCERY.

		Date.	Vols.
Saxton's Chancery Reports,		1830—1832	1
Green's Chancery Reports,		1838—1846	3
Halsted's Chancery Reports,		1845—1852	4
Stockton's Chancery Reports,		1852—1859	3
Beasley's Reports,	(13 N. J. Eq.)	1859—1862	2
McCarter's Reports,	(14—15 N. J. Eq.)	1862—1866	2
Green's (C.E.) Reports,	(16—21 N. J. Eq.)	1866—1871	6

NEW YORK.

LAW.

	Date.	Vols.
Coleman and Caines' Cases,	1794—1805	1
Johnson's Cases,	1789—1803	3
Caines' Reports,	1803—1805	3
Caines' Cases,	1804—1805	2 in 1
Johnson's Reports,	1806—1823	20
Anthon's Nisi Prius Cases,	1808—1818	1
Yates' Select Cases,	1811	1
Cowen's Reports,	1823—1828	9
Wendell's Reports,	1828—1841	26
Hill's Reports,	1841—1845	7
Denio's Reports,	1845—1848	5
Lalor's supplement to Hill & Denio's Repts.,	1842—1844	1
Barbour's Supreme Court Reports,	1847—1871	61
Lansing's Supreme Court Reports,	1869—1871	3
Lockwood's Reversed Cases,	1799—1847	1

COURT OF APPEALS.

Comstock's Reports,	(1— 4 N. Y.)	1847—1851	4
Selden's Reports,	(5—10 N. Y.)	1851—1854	6
Kernan's Reports,	(11—14 N. Y.)	1854—1857	4
Smith's Reports,	(15—27 N. Y.)	1857—1863	13
Tiffany's Reports,	(28—39 N. Y.)	1863—1868	12
Hand's Reports,	(40—45 N. Y.)	1869—1871	6

SUPERIOR COURT.

Hall's Reports,	1828—1829	2
Sandford's (S. C.) Reports,	1847—1852	5
Duer's Reports,	1852—1856	6
Bosworth's Reports,	1856—1864	10
Robertson's Reports,	1863—1868	7
Sweeny's Reports,	1869—1870	2

COMMON PLEAS.

Smith's (E. D.) Reports,	1850—1854	4
Hilton's Reports,	1855—1860	2
Daly's Reports,	1859—1865	1

PRACTICE AND CODE REPORTS.

Howard's Practice Reports,	1844—1871	42

CHANCERY.

Johnson's Chancery Reports,	1814—1823	7
Hopkins' Reports,	1823—1826	1
Paige's Reports.	1828—1845	11

NEW YORK:

		Date.	Vols.
Barbour's Chancery Reports,		1845—1848	3
Edwards' Reports,		1831—1850	4
Hoffman's Reports,		1839—1840	1
Clarke's Reports,		1839—1841	1
Sandford's Chancery Reports,		1843—1847	4
	CRIMINAL.		
Roger's City Hall Recorder,		1816—1821	6
Parker's Criminal Reports.		1839—1868	6
Wheeler's Criminal Cases,		1776—1824	3
	SURROGATE.		
Bradford's Reports,		1849—1857	4
Redfield's Reports,		1857—1863	1
Tucker's Reports,		1864—1869	1
	DIGESTS.		
Abbott's Digest of Reports,		1794—1869	8
Tiffany's Court of Appeals Digest, vol. 1–27.			1

NORTH CAROLINA.

LAW.

Martin's Reports,	*(Battle's Ed.)*	1790—1796	2 in 1
Haywood's Reports,	*(Battle's Ed.)*	1789—1806	2
Taylor's Reports,	*(Battle's Ed.)*	1799—1802	2 in 1
Cameron & Norwood's Conference Rep'ts,		1800—1804	
Murphey's Reports,		1804—1819	3
(Vol. 1, Murphey, *wanting.*)			
Carolina Law Repository,	*(Battle's Ed.)*	1813—1816	2 in 1
North Carolina Term Reports,		1816—1818	
Hawks' Reports,		1820—1826	4
Devereux's Reports,		1826—1834	4
(Vol. 4, Devereux, *wanting.*)			
Devereux and Battle's Reports,		1834—1839	4
Iredell's Reports,		1840—1852	13
Busbee's Reports,		1852—1853	1
Jones' Reports,		1853—1862	8
Winston's Reports,		1863—1864	1
Phillips' Reports,		1866—1868	1
Phillips' Reports,	(63—64 N. C.)	1868—1870	2
McCorkle's Reports,	(65 N. C.)	1871	1

(The distinction of Law and Equity has been abolished. See vol. 63, *N. C.)*

NORTH CAROLINA:

EQUITY.

	Date.	Vols.
Devereux's Equity Reports,	1828—1834	2
Devereux and Battle's Equity Reports,	1834—1840	2
Iredell's Equity Reports,	1840—1852	8
Busbee's Equity Reports,	1852—1853	1
Jones' Equity Reports,	1853—1860	6
Phillips' Equity Reports,	1866—1868	1

DIGESTS.

Battle's Digest of Reports,	1789—1866	3

OHIO.

Tappan's Reports,		1816—1819	1
Hammond's Reports,	(1— 9 Ohio)	1821—1839	9
Wilcox's Reports,	(10 Ohio)	1840—1841	1
Stanton's Reports,	(11—13 Ohio)	1841—1844	3
Griswold's Reports,	(14—19 Ohio)	1845—1850	6
Lawrence's Reports,	(20 Ohio)	1851	1
McCook's Reports,	(1 Ohio State)	1852	1
Warden's Reports,	(2— 4 Ohio State)	1853—1855	3
Critchfield's Reports,	(5—20 Ohio State)	1855—1870	16
Wright's Nisi Prius Reports,		1831—1834	1
Disney's Cincinnati Superior Court Rep'ts,		1854—1860	2

DIGESTS.

Gholson and Okey's Digest of O. and O. St. Reports,	1867	1

OREGON.

Wilson's Reports,	(1—2 Oregon)	1853—1868	2

PENNSYLVANIA.

Dallas' Reports,	1754—1806	4
Addison's Reports,	1791—1799	1
Yeates' Reports,	1791—1808	4
Binney's Reports,	1799—1814	6
Browne's Reports,	1806—1814	6
Ashmead's Reports,	1808—1841	2
Sergeant and Rawle's Reports,	1814—1828	17
Rawle's Reports,	1828—1835	5
Penrose and Watts' Pennsylvania Reports,	1829—1832	3

PENNSYLVANIA:

		Date.	Vols.
Watts' Reports, (Vol. 5 Watts *wanting*.)		1832—1840	10
Miles' Reports,		1835—1840	2
Wharton's Reports,		1835—1841	6
Watts and Sargeant's Reports,		1841—1845	9
Brightly's Nisi Prius Reports,		1809—1851	1
Grant's Cases,		1852—1863	3
Pennsylvania Select Equity Cases,		1850	1
Philadelphia Reports, Common Pleas,		1850—1861	4
Barr's Reports,	(1—10 Penn. St.)	1845—1849	10
Jones' Reports,	(11—12 Penn. St.)	1849	2
Harris' Reports,	(13—24 Penn. St.)	1849—1855	12
Casey's Reports,	(25—36 Penn. St.)	1855—1860	12
Wright's Reports,	(37—50 Penn. St.)	1860—1865	14
Smith's Reports,	(51—67 Penn. St.)	1865—1871	17

RHODE ISLAND.

Angell's Reports,	(1 R. I.)	1835—1851	1
Durfee's Reports,	(2 R. I.)	1851—1853	1
Knowles' Reports,	(3 R. I.)	1853—1856	1
Ames' Reports,	(4—8 R. I.)	1856—1867	5

SOUTH CAROLINA.

LAW.

Bay's Reports,	1783—1804	2
Brevard's Reports,	1792—1816	3 in 2
Mills' Reports, (Constitutional.)	1817—1818	2
Nott and McCord's Reports,	1817—1820	2
McCord's Reports,	1820—1828	4 in 2
Harper's Reports,	1823—1824	1
Bailey's Reports,	1828—1832	2
Hill's Reports,	1833—1837	3 in 2
Riley's Reports, (Bound with Riley's Chan.)	1836—1837	1
Dudley's Reports,	1837—1838	1
Rice's Reports,	1838—1839	1
Cheves' Reports,	1839—1840	1
McMullan's Reports,	1835—1842	2
Speer's Reports,	1843—1844	2
Richardson's Reports, Vols. 1—4,	1844—1847	4
Strobhart's Reports,	1843—1850	5
Richardson's Reports, Vols. 5—12,	1850—1860	8

South Carolina:

		Date.	Vols.
Richardson's Reports, (13 Law and 12 Equity in 1 vol.,)		1860—1866	1
Richardson's Reports,	(1 S. C., N. S.)	1868—1869	1

(*The distinction between Law and Chancery is abolished. See* 1 *S. C., N. S.*)

Chancery.

	Date.	Vols.
Desaussure's Reports,	1785—1813	4
Harper's Chancery Reports,	1824	1
McCord's Chancery Reports,	1825—1827	2
Bailey's Chancery Reports,	1830—1831	1
Richardson's Cases,	1831—1832	1
Hill's Chancery Reports,	1833—1836	2 in 1
Riley's Chancery Reports,	1836—1837	1
Dudley's Chancery Reports,	1837—1838	1
Rice's Chancery Reports,	1838—1839	1
Cheves' Chancery Reports,	1839—1840	1
McMullan's Chancery Reports.	1840—1842	1
Speer's Chancery Reports,	1842—1844	1
Richardson's Chancery Reports, vols. 1—2,	1844—1846	1
Strobhart's Chancery Reports,	1846—1850	4
Richardson's Chancery Reports, vols. 3—14; [Vol. 12 is bound with Law Reports],	1850—1868	11

TENNESSEE.

		Date.	Vols.
Overton's Reports, (Tenn.)	(*Cooper's Ed.*)	1791—1815	2 in 1
Cook's Reports,	(*Cooper's Ed.*)	1811—1814	1
Haywood's Reports,	(*Cooper's Ed.*)	1816—1818	3 in 1
Peck's Reports,		1822—1824	1
Martin & Yerger's Reports,	(*Cooper's Ed.*)	1825—1828	1
Yerger's Reports,		1832—1837	10
Meigs' Reports,		1838—1839	1
Humphreys' Reports,		1839—1851	11
Swan's Reports,		1851—1853	2
Sneed's Reports,		1853—1857	5
Head's Reports,		1859—1860	3
Coldwell's Reports,		1860—1869	6
Heiskell's Reports,		1870	1

TEXAS.

		Date,	Vols.
Webb & Duval's Reports,	(1— 3 Texas)	1846—1848	3
Hartley's Reports,	(4—21 Texas)	1849—1858	18
Moore & Walker's Rep'ts,	(22—24 Texas)	1858—1860	3
Walker's Reports,	(25 Texas)	1860	1
Paschal's Reports,	(25 Texas Sup.)	1860	1
Robards & Jackson's Rep.	(26—27 Texas)	1861—1865	2
Paschal's Reports,	(28—31 Texas)	1866—1869	4
Wheelock's Reports,	(32—33 Texas)	1869—1871	2

DIGESTS.

Alexander's Digest of Texas Reports,	1854	1

VERMONT.

N. Chipman's Reports,		1789—1791	1
D. Chipman's Reports,		1789—1825	2 in 1
Tyler's Reports.		1801—1803	2
Brayton's Reports,		1815—1819	1
Aikens' Reports,		1826—1827	2
Reports by the Judges,	(1— 9 Vt.)	1827—1837	9
Shaw's (G. B.) Reports,	(10 Vt.)	1838	1
Shaw & Weston's Reports,	(11 Vt.)	1839	1
Weston's Reports,	(12—14 Vt.)	1840—1843	3
Slade's Reports,	(15 Vt.)	1843	1
Washburn's Reports,	(16—23 Vt.)	1844—1850	8
Deane's Reports,	(24—26 Vt.)	1851—1854	3
Williams' Reports,	(27—29 Vt.)	1854—1857	3
Shaw's (W. G.) Reports,	(30—35 Vt.)	1857—1864	6
Veazey's Reports,	(36—44 Vt.)	1865—1872	9

DIGESTS.

Washburn's Digest,	1789—1850	2

NOTE. The Library contains 1 copy of N. Chipman's Reports, and Vol. 2 of Aikens' Reports: 2 copies of Brayton's Reports; Vol. 1, Vermont Reports, and Vol. 1, Washburn's Digest: 3 copies of D. Chipman's Reports; Vol. 1, Aikens' Reports; Vols. 2, 7, 16, 25, Vermont Reports. It contains 4 copies of all other reports and digests in the preceding list under VERMONT.

VIRGINIA.

Wythe's Chancery Reports,	1788—1799	1
Washington's Reports,	1790—1796	2
Virginia Cases,	1789—1826	2 in 1
Call's Reports,	1797—1825	6
Hening and Munford's Reports,	1806—1809	4

VIRGINIA:

		Date.	Vols.
Munford's Reports,		1810—1820	6
Gilmer's Reports,		1820—1821	1
Randolph's Reports,		1821—1828	6
Leigh's Reports,		1829—1841	12
Robinson's Reports,		1842—1844	2
Grattan's Reports,		1844—1872	21
Patton, Jr., and Heath's Reports. Court of Appeals,		1855—1856	2
DIGESTS.			
Tate's Index to Virginia Reports.		1790—1846	2

WEST VIRGINIA.

Hagans' Reports,	(1—3 W. Va.)	1863—1869	3

WISCONSIN.

Burnett's Reports,		1842—1843	1
Chandler's Reports,		1849—1852	4
Smith's Reports,	(1—11 Wis.)	1853—1860	11
Spooner's Reports,	(12—15 Wis.)	1860—1862	4
Conover's Reports,	(16—25 Wis.)	1862—1870	10
DIGESTS.			
Simmons' Digest of Reports,		1842—1868	1

ELEMENTARY LAW.

ELEMENTARY LAW.

A.

Abbott, B. V. and A. A General Digest of the Law of Corporations. Presenting the American Adjudications upon Public and Private Corporations. With a selection of English Cases. New York, 1869.

——— A Treatise upon the United States Courts and their Practice ; and the modes of Pleading and Procedure in them. With numerous Practical Forms. 2v. New York, 1869-71.

Adams, John, Jr. The Doctrine of Equity, being a Commentary on the Law as administered by the Court of Chancery. 5th American edition. With additional Notes and References by G. T. Bispham. Philadelphia, 1868.

[Aikens, Asa.] Practical Forms; with notes and references explanatory of the law. Being a convenient manual. 12°. Windsor, 1823.

American Law Register. Vols. 1—10, 1861 to 1871. 10v. Philadelphia, 1862–71.

American Law Review. A Quarterly Periodical. Vols. 1—6, 1866–67 to 1871–72. 6v. Boston, 1867–72.

American Leading Cases. Select Decisions of American Courts, in several departments of law, with especial reference to Mercantile law. By J. I. Clarke Hare and H. B. Wallace. 5th edition. Philadelphia, 1871.

Angell, Joseph K. A Treatise on the Limitations of Actions at Law, and suits in equity. Boston, 1829.

——— A Treatise on the Limitations of Actions at Law and suits in Equity and Admiralty, with an Appendix containing the American and English Statutes of Limitations. 5th edition. By John W. May. Boston, 1869.

——— A Treatise on the Law of Water Courses, with an Appendix containing Statutes on Flowing, and Forms of Declarations. 6th edition. By J. C. Perkins. Boston, 1869.

——— and Ames, Samuel. A Treatise on the Law of Private Corporations Aggregate. 8th edition. By John Lathrop. Boston, 1866.

——— and Durfee, Thomas. A Treatise on the Law of Highways. Boston, 1857.

B.

Barton, Charles. History of a suit in Equity, from its commencement to its final termination. With Forms of Bills, &c. By James P. Holcombe. With an Appendix containing the Ordinances of Lord Bacon, Rules of Practice in Equity, in the Circuit Court of the United States, and the English Orders in Chancery. Cincinnati, 1859.

Bashford vs. Barstow. [Proceedings had on the information in the nature of a *quo warranto* upon the relation of Coles Bashford against William A. Barstow, contesting the right to the office of Governor of Wisconsin.] Madison, 1856.

Benet, Capt. S. V. A Treatise on Military Laws, and the Practice of Courts Martial. 2d ed. New York, 1862.

Bennett, E. H. and Heard, F. F. A Selection of Leading Cases in Criminal Law. 2v. Boston, 1857.

Bennett, M. L. The Vermont Justice, being a Treatise on the Civil and Criminal Jurisdiction of Justices of the Peace. Burlington, 1864.

Bible, The. In the Public Schools. Arguments in the case of John D. Minor, *et al.* vs. the Board of Education of the City of Cincinnati, *et al.*, in the Superior Court of Cincinnati, with the Opinions and Decision of the Court. Cincinnati, 1870.

Bigelow, M. M. A Treatise on the Law of Estoppel, and its application in practice. Boston, 1872.

——— See REDFIELD, I. F., *post.*

Bingham, Anson. A Treatise on the Law of Descents. Albany, 1870.

——— The Law of Executory Contracts for the sale of Real Property. Albany, 1872.

Bingham, Peregrine. The Law of Infancy and Coverture. 2d American ed. By E. H. Bennett. Burlington, 1849.

Bishop, Joel P. Commentaries on the Law of Marriage and Divorce, of Separations without Divorce, and of the Evidence of Marriage in all Issues; embracing also Pleading, Practice, and Evidence in Divorce Causes, with Forms. 4th edition. 2v. Boston, 1864.

——— Commentaries on the Criminal Law. 3d edition, revised and enlarged. 2v. Boston, 1865.

——— Commentaries on the Law of Criminal Procedure; or Pleading, Evidence and Practice in Criminal Cases. 2v. Boston, 1866.

——— The First Book of the Law, explaining the Nature, Sources, Books. and Practical Applications of Legal Science, and methods of Study and Practice. Boston, 1868.

Blackstone, Sir William. Commentaries on the Laws of England, in four books, with notes selected; Baron Field's Analysis, and additional notes, and a Life of the Author, by George Sharswood. 2v. Philadelphia, 1864.

Blackwell, R. S. A Practical Treatise on the Power to Sell Land for the Non-Payment of Taxes. 2d edition, revised and enlarged. Boston, 1864.

Boutwell, George S. A Manual of the direct and excise tax system of the United States. 4th edition. Boston, 1864.

Brightly, F. C. A Collection of Leading Cases on the Law of Elections in the United States. Philadelphia, 1871.

Broom, Herbert. A Selection of Legal Maxims. Classified and illustrated. 6th American, from the 4th London edition. Philadelphia, 1868.

Browne, Causten. A Treatise on the Construction of the Statute of Frauds, with an Appendix containing the existing English and American Statutes. 3d edition. Boston, 1870.

Buck, Edward. Massachusetts Ecclesiastical Law. 12°. Boston, 1866.

Burrill, Alexander M. A Law Dictionary and Glossary, containing full Definitions of the Principal Terms of the Common and Civil Law, embracing also all the Principal Common and Civil Law Maxims. 2d edition. 2v. New York, 1859.

C.

Caldwell, James S. Law of Arbitrations, with Precedents. 2d American edition. By Chauncey Smith. Burlington, 1853.

Chalmers, George. Opinions of Eminent Lawyers on various points of English Jurisprudence, chiefly concerning the Colonies, Fisheries and Commerce of Great Britain. Burlington, 1858.

Chipman. Daniel. An Essay on the Law of Contracts for the Payment of Specifick Articles. Middlebury, 1822.

Chipman, Nathaniel. Principles of Government; a Treatise on Free Institutions, including the Constitution of the United States. Burlington, 1833.

Chitty, Joseph. A Practical Treatise on Medical Jurisprudence. 2d American edition. Philadelphia, 1836.

——— A Treatise on Pleading and Parties to Actions, containing Precedents of Pleadings. 14th American edition, with additional notes and references to later Decisions, by J. C. Perkins. 3v. Springfield, 1859.

Conkling, A. A Treatise on the Organization, Jurisdiction and Practice of the Courts of the United States, with an Appendix of Practical Forms. 4th edition, corrected and enlarged, Albany, 1864.

——— The Admiralty Jurisdiction, Law and Practice of the Courts of the United States; with an Appendix containing the

New Rules of Admiralty Practice, and numerous Practical Forms of Process, comprising the entire progress of a Suit in Admiralty. 2d edition. 2v. Albany, 1857.

Cook, Robley D. Manual of the Highway Laws of the State of New York, with an Appendix of Forms. Albany, 1870.

Cooley, Thomas M. A Treatise on the Constitutional Limitations which rest upon the Legislative Power of the States of the American Union. Boston, 1868.

Cord, William H. A Treatise on the Legal and Equitable Rights of Married Women; as well in respect to their Property and Persons as to their Children. With an Appendix of the recent American Statutes and the Decisions under them. Philadelphia, 1861.

Crary, C. The Law and Practice in Special Proceedings, and in Special Cases within the Courts, etc., of the State of New York; with an Appendix of Forms. 2d edition. 2v. Albany, 1866.

Crocker, Uriel H. and Geo. G. Notes on the General Statutes of Massachusetts. Boston, 1869.

Cruise, William. A Digest of the Law of Real Property. Revised by H. H. White. Further revised with additions for American Statutes, by Simon Greenleaf. 3v. Boston, 1849–50.

Cushing, Luther S. Rules of Proceeding and Debate in Deliberative Assemblies. 16°. Boston, 1850.

——— Elements of the Law and Practice of Legislative Assemblies in the United States of America. 2d edition. Boston, 1859. (3 copies).

——— See REPORTS of Controverted Elections, *post*.

D.

Dean, Amos. Principles of Medical Jurisprudence, designed for the Professions of Law and Medicine. Albany, 1854.

Domat, Jean. The Civil Law in its Natural Order; together with the Public Law, translated into English by William Strahan; with remarks on some Differences between the Civil Law and the Law of England. Edited by Luther S. Cushing. 2v. Boston, 1853.

Drake, Charles D. A Treatise on the Law of Suits by Attachment in the United States. 3d edition, with an Appendix, containing the Leading Statutory Provisions of the several States and Territories. Boston, 1868.

Dwarris, Sir Fortunatus. A General Treatise on Statutes; their Rules of Construction, and the Proper Boundaries of Legislation and of Judicial Interpretation, with American notes and additions by Platt Potter. Albany, 1871.

E.

Edwards, Charles. On Receivers in Equity and under the New York Code of Procedure, with Precedents. 3d edition. New York, 1857.

Elwell, John J. A Medico-Legal Treatise on Malpractice and Medical Evidence, comprising the Elements of Medical Jurisprudence. New edition. New York, 1866.

F.

Flanders, Henry. A Treatise on the Law of Fire Insurance. Philadelphia, 1871.

Fleta; seu Commentarius Juris Anglicani. Editus, cum Dissertatione Historica ad eundem, per J. Seldenum. 4°. Londini, 1647.

Forsyth, William. Cases and Opinions on Constitutional Law and various points of English Jurisprudence. London, 1869.

——— History of Trial by Jury. London, 1852.

G.

Gibbs, Montgomery. Practical Forms and Precedents for Lawyers, Commissioners, Notaries, &c., with Forms and Instructions. 2d edition. New York, 1854.

Gordon, Thomas F. A Digest of the Laws of the United States, including an Abstract of the Judicial Decisions relating to the Constitutional and Statutory Law. Philadelphia, 1827.

Greenleaf, Simon. A Treatise on the Law of Evidence. 7th edition. 3v. Boston, 1854–59.

——— Edition of Cruise on Real Property. [See Cruise].

——— Examination of the Testimony of the Four Evangelists, by the Rules of Evidence administered in Courts of Justice; with an Account of the Trial of Jesus. Boston, 1846. [See *General Library.*]

Gregg, W. P. See Railroad Laws, *post.*

H.

Halleck, H. W. International Law; or Rules Regulating the Intercourse of States in Peace and War. New York, 1861.

Hamilton, Alexander. See *General Library.*

Hanover, M. D. A Practical Treatise on the Law of Horses. Cincinnati, 1872.

Hare, J. I. C., and H. B. Wallace. See American Leading Cases, *ante;* and Smith, J. W., and White, F. T., *post.*

Heard, F. F. See *General Library.*

Hill, James. A Practical Treatise on the Law relating to Trustees. 4th American edition, with notes and references, by Geo. T. Bispham. Philadelphia, 1867.

Hilliard, Francis. The Law of Bankruptcy and Insolvency. 2d edition. Philadelphia, 1867.

——— The Law of Injunctions. Philadelphia, 1865.

——— A Treatise on the Law of Mortgages of Real and Personal Property. 3d edition, revised and enlarged. 2v. Philadelphia, 1864.

——— The Law of New Trials, and other Rehearings. Philadelphia, 1865.

——— The Law of Sales of Personal Property. 3d edition greatly enlarged. Philadelphia, 1869.

——— A Treatise on the Law of Torts, or Private Wrongs. 3d edition, revised and enlarged. 2v. Boston, 1866.

——— A Treatise on Remedies for Torts, or Private Wrongs. Boston, 1867.

——— A Treatise on the Law of Vendors and Purchasers of Real Property. 3d edition, revised and greatly enlarged. Boston, 1868.

Hogan, Edmund. The Pennsylvania State Trials; containing the Impeachment, Trial and Acquittal of Francis Hopkinson [Judge], and John Nicholson [Comptroller-General]. Philadelphia, 1794.

Houck, Louis. A Treatise on the Law of Navigable Rivers. Boston, 1868.

Howard, Nathan, Jr. The Code of Procedure of Pleadings and Practice of the State of New York, 1862. 3d edition. New York, 1862.

Hurd, John C. The Law of Freedom and Bondage in the United States. 2v. Boston, 1858-62.

Hurd, Rollin C. A Treatise on the Right of Personal Liberty, and on the Writ of Habeas Corpus, and the Practice connected with it, with a view of the Law of Extradition of Fugitives. Albany, 1858.

J.

Jameson, John A. [A Treatise on the Principles of American Constitutional Law and Legislation.] The Constitutional Convention; its History, Powers, and Modes of Proceeding. New York, 1867.

——— The Same. 2d edition. Chicago, 1869.

Jefferson, Thomas. A Manual of Parliamentary Practice; composed originally for the Senate of the United States. Brought down to the practice of the present time. 12°. New York, 1858. (3 copies).

Justinian. The Institutes of. With English Introduction, Translation and Notes by Thomas Collett Sandars. 4th edition. London, 1869.

K.

Kent, James. Commentaries on American Law. 4th edition. 4v. New York, 1840.

Kerr, William W. A Treatise on the Law of Fraud and Mistake. With Notes to American Cases by O. F. Bump. New York, 1872.

Kinsman, J. Burnham. The Vermont Townsman; a compilation of the Laws of Vermont in relation to the powers, duties and liabilities of Town Officers and Towns. 12°. Boston, 1857.

L.

Law, Stephen D. Jurisdiction and Powers of the United States Courts, with Rules of Practice of Supreme and other Courts, etc. Albany, 1852.

Law Summary. See Oliver, B. L., *post.*

Lawrence, W. B. Visitation and Search; or an Historical Sketch of the British Claim to exercise a Maritime Police over the Vessels of all Nations, in Peace as well as in War, etc. Boston, 1858.

Leading Cases in Equity. See under White, F. T., *post.*

M.

Mackenzie, Lord. Studies in Roman Law, with comparative views of the Laws of France, England and Scotland. 2d edition. Edinburgh, 1865.

Maine, Henry S. Ancient Law; its connection with the early History of Society and its relation to Modern Ideas. With Introduction, by T. W. Dwight. New York, 1867.

Metcalf, Theron. Principles of the Law of Contracts, as applied by Courts of Law. New York, 1867.

Morris, P. P. A practical Treatise on the Law of Replevin in the United States, with an Appendix of Forms and a Digest of Statutes. 2d and revised edition. Philadelphia, 1869.

Morse, John T., Jr. A Treatise on the Law relating to Banks and Banking; with an Appendix containing the National Banking Act of June 3d, 1864, and Amendments thereto. Boston, 1870.

——— The Law of Arbitration and Award. Boston, 1872.

Moses, H. H. The Law of Mandamus and the Practice connected with it, with an Appendix of Forms. Albany, 1867.

O.

Oliver, B. L. The Law Summary ; a collection of legal tracts on subjects of general application in business. 2d edition. Hallowell, 1833.

Ordronaux, John. The Jurisprudence of Medicine, in its relations to the Law of Contracts, Torts, and Evidence, with a supplement on the Liabilities of Vendors of Drugs. Philadelphia, 1869.

P.

Parsons, Theophilus. A Treatise on the Law of Contracts. 5th edition. 3v. Boston, 1864.

——— The Elements of Mercantile Law. 2d edition. Boston, 1862.

——— A Treatise on the Law of Partnership. 2d edition revised and enlarged. Boston, 1870.

Perry, Jairus Ware. A Treatise on the Law of Trusts and Trustees. Boston, 1872.

Phillimore, Robert. Commentaries upon International Law. 3v. in 2. Philadelphia, 1854–57.

Phillips, S. March. A Treatise on the Law of Evidence, with Notes by E. Cowen and N. Hill, and additional Notes and References by Isaac Edwards. 5th American edition. 3v. New York, 1868.

Phillips, Willard. A Treatise on the Law of Insurance. 5th edition. 2v. New York, 1867.

Pomeroy, J. N. An Introduction to the Constitutional Law of the United States. Especially designed for Students, General and Professional. New York, 1868.

——— An Introduction to Municipal Law. Designed for General Readers and for Students. New York, 1864.

Potter, Platt. See Dwarris, *ante*.

R.

Railroad Laws and Charters of the United States, collated, arranged and published with Synopsis and Explanatory Remarks, by W. P. Gregg and B. Pond. Vols. 1–2, [containing Laws and Charters of the New England States.] Boston, 1851.

Ram, James. A Treatise on Facts, as Subjects of Inquiry by a Jury. 1st American edition, by John Townshend. New York, 1870.

——— The Science of Legal Judgment. A Treatise designed to show the materials whereof, and the process by which, Courts construct their judgments. With additions by John Townshend. New York, 1871.

Ray, I. A Treatise on the Medical Jurisprudence of Insanity. 5th edition. Boston, 1871.

Redfield, Isaac F. Practical Treatise upon the Law of Railways. 2d edition. Boston, 1858.

——— The Law of Railways; embracing Corporations, Eminent Domain, Common Carriers, Telegraph Companies, Constitutional Law, Investments, &c. 4th edition, greatly enlarged. 2v. Boston, 1869.

——— Leading American Railway Cases, arranged according to Subjects. With Notes and Opinions; being a Supplement to the author's work on Railways. Boston, 1870.

——— The Law of Carriers of Goods and Passengers, Private and Public, Inland and Foreign. Also, the Construction, Responsibility, and Duty of Telegraph Companies; the Responsibility and Duty of Innkeepers, and the Law of Bailments of every class, embracing Remedies. Cambridge, 1869.

——— The Law of Wills. Part I. Embracing the Jurisprudence of Insanity; the effect of extrinsic Evidence; the Creation and Construction of Trusts applicable to Wills, with Forms and Instructions for Preparing Wills. Boston, 1864.
Part II. Embracing Devises, Legacies, Charitable Trusts, and the Duties of Executors and Administrators, and other Testamentary Trustees. Boston, 1866.

——— and M. M. Bigelow. Leading and Select American Cases in Law of Bills of Exchange, Promissory Notes and Checks. Boston, 1871.

Reeve, Tapping. The Law of Baron and Femme, of Parent and Child, Guardian and Ward, Master and Servant, and of the Powers of the Court of Chancery; with an Essay on the terms, Heir, Heirs, Heirs of the Body. 2d edition, with Notes and References to English and American Cases, by L. E. Chittenden. Burlington, 1846.

——— The same, 3d edition, with Notes and References, by A. J. Parker and C. E. Baldwin, Albany, 1867.

——— A Treatise on the Law of Descents in the several United States of America.

Reeves, John. History of English Law, from the time of the Saxons to the end of the reign of Elizabeth. A new edition, with Notes, &c., by W. F. Finlason. 3v. London, 1869.

Reports of Controverted Elections in the House of Representatives of the Commonwealth of Massachusetts. By Luther S. Cushing, C. W. Storey, and L. Josselyn. Boston, 1853. [A State publication.]

Roberts, William. A Treatise on the Statutes relating to Voluntary and Fraudulent Conveyances. 3d American edition. Burlington, 1845.

S.

Saunders, Thomas William. A Treatise upon the Law applicable to Negligence, with Notes of American Cases by Henry Hooper. Cincinnati, 1872.

Schouler, James. The Law of the Domestic relations; embracing Husband and Wife; Guardian and Ward; Parent and Child; Infancy; and Master and Servant. Boston, 1870.

Scott, Wm. L., and Jarnagin, M. P. A Treatise upon the Law of Telegraphs; with an Appendix containing the General Statuttory Provisions upon the subject of Telegraphs. Boston, 1868.

Scribner, C. H. A Treatise on the Law of Dower; embracing the Common Law and the Statutory Provisions upon that subject. 2v. Philadelphia, 1864–67.

Sedgwick, Theodore. A Treatise on the Measure of Damages awarded by Courts of Justice. 4th edition, revised and annotated by Henry D. Sedgwick, New York, 1868.

——— A Treatise on the Rules which govern the Interpretation and Application of Statutory and Constitutional Law. New York, 1857.

Sharswood, George. See Blackstone, W., *ante*, and Smith, J. W., *post*.

Shearman, Thomas G. and Amasa A. Redfield. A Treatise on the Law of Negligence. New York, 1869.

Smith, E. F. Commentaries on Statute and Constitutional Law, and Statutory and Constitutional Construction. Albany, 1848.

Smith, John W. A Selection of Leading Cases on the various Branches of the Law. 6th American from the 3d London edition, by J. I. Clarke Hare and John Wallace. 2v. in 3. Philadelphia, 1866.

——— The Law of Contracts. 5th American from the 4th London edition, and additional notes and references to recent American Cases, by Geo. Sharswood. Philadelphia, 1869.

Smith, William L. The Practice and Proceeding in Probate Courts; with an Appendix of Forms. 2d edition. Boston, 1868.

Spence, George. Equitable Jurisdiction of the Court of Chancery, comprising its Rise, Progress, and final Establishment. 2v. Philadelphia, 1846–50.

Story, Joseph. Commentaries on the Law of Agency as a Branch of Commercial and Maritime Jurisprudence. 6th edition, revised by E. H. Bennett. 3v. Boston, 1863.

——— Commentaries on the Law of Bailments, with illustrations from the Civil and Foreign Law. 7th edition, revised by E. H. Bennett. Boston, 1863.

——— Commentaries on the Law of Bills of Exchange, Foreign and Inland, as administered in England and America. 4th edition, revised by E. H. Bennett. Boston, 1860.

Story, Joseph. Commentaries on the Conflict of Laws, Foreign and Domestic, in regard to Contracts, Rights and Remedies, and especially in regard to Marriage, Divorces, Wills, Successions and Judgments. 6th edition, revised and greatly enlarged by I. F. Redfield. Boston, 1865.

——— The Same. 4th edition. Boston, 1852.

——— Commentaries on the Constitution of the United States, with a Preliminary Review of the Constitutional History of the Colonies and States, before the adoption of the Constitution. 3d edition, revised by E. H. Bennett. 3v. Boston, 1833.

——— Commentaries on Equity Jurisprudence, as administered in England and America. 9th edition, with extensive additions, by I. F. Redfield. 2v. Boston, 1866.

——— Commentaries on Equity Pleadings, and the Incidents thereto. 7th edition, with large additions, by I. F. Redfield. Boston, 1865.

——— Commentaries on the Law of Partnership, as a Branch of Commercial and Maritime Jurisprudence. 6th edition, by J. C. Gray, Jr. Boston, 1868.

——— Commentaries on the Law of Promissory Notes, and Guaranties of Notes and Checks on Banks and Bankers. 6th edition, revised, by J. W. Perry. Boston, 1868.

Story, W. W. A Treatise on the Law of Contracts. 4th edition, revised and greatly enlarged. Boston, 1856.

T.

Taylor, John N. A Treatise on the American Law of Landlord and Tenant, with a selection of Precedents. 4th edition. Boston, 1866.

Thompson, Isaac Grant. The Assessors, Collectors and Town Clerks' Manual, with an Appendix of Forms. Albany, 1870.

———The Supervisor's Manual, with an Appendix of Forms. Albany, 1869.

Throop, M. H. A Treatise on the Validity of Verbal Agreements, as affected by the Legislative Enactments in England and the United States, commonly called the Statute of Frauds. Vol. 1. Albany, 1870.

Tomlins, Thomas Edlyne. The Law Dictionary, explaining the Rise, Progress and Present State of the British Law; defining and interpreting Words and Terms, with additions by T. C. Granger. 1st American edition, 3v. Philadelphia, 1836.

Townshend, John. A Treatise on the Wrongs called Slander and Libel, and on the Remedy by Civil Action for those Wrongs. New York, 1868.

——— See Voorhies, *post.*

Trial of Andrew Johnson, [Acting] President of the United States, on Articles of Impeachment. 3v. Washington, 1868. [See Journals and Documents, *ante*, under UNITED STATES].

Trials. See Bashford *v.* Barstow, and Hogan, *ante*, and Vallandigham and Wharton, *post.*

Tyler, Ransom H. A Treatise on the Remedy by Ejectment, and the Law of Adverse Enjoyment in the United States, in respect to the Action for the Recovery of Real Property. Albany, 1870.

V.

Vallandigham, Clement L. The Trial of, by a Military Commission; and the Proceedings under his Application for a Writ of Habeas Corpus in the Circuit Court. Cincinnati, 1863.

Van Santvoord, George. See *General Library.*

Vattel, Emerich. The Law of Nations. From the new edition by J. Chitty. With additional Notes and References by E. D. Ingraham. Philadelphia, 1852.

[Voorhies'] Code of Procedure, of the State of New York, as amended to 1860, 7th edition. By John Townshend. New York, 1860.

W.

Walker, Timothy. Introduction to American Law, designed as a First Book for Students. 4th edition, Boston, 1860.

Wallace, J. W. The Reporters. Chronologically arranged, with occasional Remarks on their respective Merits. 3d edition, revised. Philadelphia, 1855.

Washburn, Emory. A Treatise on the American Law of Real Property. 2v. Boston, 1862.

——— A Treatise on the American Law of Easements and Servitudes. 2d edition. Boston, 1867.

Waterman, Thomas W. A Treatise on the Law of Set-off, Recoupment and Counter Claims. New York, 1869.

Wharton, F. A Treatise on the Conflict of Laws, or Private International Law, including a Comparative View of Anglo-American, Roman, German and French Jurisprudence. Philadelphia, 1872.

——— A Treatise on the Criminal Law of the United States, embracing Pleading and Evidence; Trial and its Incidents. 6th and revised edition. 3v. Philadelphia, 1868.

——— State Trials of the United States during the Administration of Washington and Adams, with References, Historical and Professional, and Preliminary Notes on the Politics of the Times. Philadelphia, 1849.

Wheaton, Henry. Elements of International Law. 8th edition, revised, with Notes, by R. H. Dana, Jr. Boston, 1866.

——— The same. 3d edition. Philadelphia, 1846.

White, F. T., and Tudor, O. D. A Selection of Leading Cases in Equity, with Notes ; and with References to American Cases, by J. I. Clarke Hare and H. B. Wallace. 3d American edition. 3v. Philadelphia, 1859.

Whiting, William. War Powers under the Constitution of the United States. 10th edition. Boston, 1864.

Williams, Joshua. Principles of the Law of Personal Property. 4th American edition. By Benjamin Gerhard and S. Wetherill. Philadelphia, 1872.

——— Principles of the Law of Real Property. 4th American, from the 9th English edition. With Notes and References to American Decisions, by W. H. Rawle andJ. T. Mitchell. Philadelphia, 1872.

Wills, William. Essay on the Principles of Circumstantial Evidence, illustrated by numerous Cases. Edited by Alfred Wills. 5th American edition. Philadelphia, 1872.

GENERAL LIBRARY.

A.

Abbott, A. O. Prison Life in the South: at Richmond, Andersonville, etc., during 1864 and 1865. 12°. New York, 1865.

Adams, Abigail. Journal and Correspondence of, written in France and England in 1785. Edited by her daughter. 12°. New York and London, 1841.

Adams, Andrew N. History of the Town of Fair Haven, Vermont. Fair Haven, 1870.

Adams, C. B. See Gray, Alonzo; also under GEOLOGY, p. 72, *ante*.

Adams, John. Letters addressed to his wife. Edited by his grandson, Charles Francis Adams. 2v. 16°. Boston, 1841.

—— Works; with a Life of the Author, notes and illustrations, by his grandson, Charles Francis Adams. 10v. Boston, 1856.

CONTENTS.

Autobiography, v. 2—3.
Constitution of the U. S. Defence of, 1778, v. 4-5.
Constitution of the U. S. Three Letters on, v. 6.
Correspondence, General, v. 9—10.
Davila, Discourses on, v. 6.
Debates in the Continental Congress, 1775-6, v. 2.
Diary, v. 2—3.
Dissertation on Canon and the Feudal Law, v. 3.
Essays, v. 3.
Government, Four Letters on, v. 6.
Government, Thoughts on, v. 4.
Instruction of the Town of Braintree to their Representative, 1765, v. 3.
Instruction of the Town of Boston to their Representative, 1768-9. v. 3.
Judiciary, On the Independence of; a controversy between W. Brattle and J. Adams, 1773, v. 3.
Letters to John Taylor, of Caroline, (Va.,) in reply to strictures on the Defence, v. 6.
Life, by C. F. Adams, v. 1.
Notes on Debates in Senate of U. S., v. 3.
Novanglus; a History of the Dispute with America, from 1754, v. 4.
Official Letters, Messages and Public Papers, v. 7—9.
Report of a Constitution for Massachusetts, 1779, v. 4.
Review of Mr. Hillhouse's Proposition for Amending the Constitution, v. 6.

Adams, John Quincy and Charles Francis. Life of John Adams. 2v. 16°. Philadelphia, 1871.

——— See Duplicate Letters, p. 66, *ante*.

Adams, Nehemiah. Life of John Eliot. Boston, 1870. [Vol. 3, Lives of Chief Fathers of N. E.]

Addison, Joseph. Works. 6v. New York, 1859.

CONTENTS.

Cato ; a Tragedy, v. 1.
Dialogues on Medals, v. 2.
Drummer ; a Comedy, v. 1.
Freeholder, v. 3.
Guardian, v. 4.
Letters, v. 2.
Lover, The, v, 3.
Plebeian and the Old Whig, v. 3.
Poems, v. 1.
Present State of the War, v. 2.
Spectator, vols. 5 and 6.
Tatler, v. 4.
Whig Examiner, v. 2.

Address of the Inhabitants of the Towns of Plainfield, Lebanon, Enfield, (alias Pelham,) Canaan, Cardigan, Hanover, Lime, Orford, Haverhill, Bath and Landaff, to the Inhabitants of the several Towns in the Colony of New Hampshire. 16°. Norwich, 1776.

"Addresses on Agriculture." 1. Address by John A. King, of New York, in 1850. 2. Report on Agricultural Survey in South Carolina, by E. Ruffin, in 1843. 3. Lectures in New York by James F. W. Johnston, in 1850.

Adler, G. J. Dictionary of the German and English Languages. 10th edition. New York, 1866.

A Further Accompt of the Progress of the Gospel among the Indians of New England. Reprinted [from the edition of 1659.] 4°. New York, 1865. [Sabin's Reprints. No. 6.]

Agassiz, Elizabeth Carey and Alexander. Seaside Studies in Natural History. Marine Animals of Massachusetts Bay. Radiates. Boston, 1865.

Agassiz, Louis Jean Rodolphe and *Mrs.* E. C. Journey in Brazil. Boston, 1868.

Aiken, John. Works of the British Poets. From Ben Johnson to Croly. Selected and chronologically arranged. With biographical and critical notices. 3v. New York, 1854.

Akenside, Mark. Poetical Works. Edited by Alex. Dyce. 16°. Boston, 1854.

Albro, John A. Life of Thomas Shepard. Boston, 1870. [Vol. 4, Lives of Chief Fathers of N. E.]

Alexander, W. L. See Kitto, John.

Alger, William Rounseville. Critical History of the Doctrine of a Future Life ; with a complete bibliography of the subject. New York, 1867.

Alison, Archibald. History of Europe from 1789 to 1815. 4v. New York, 1855.

Alldridge, W. J. The Universal Merchant. Philadelphia, 1797.

Allen, Ethan. A Brief Narrative of the Proceedings of the government of New York, relative to their obtaining the jurisdiction of that large District of Land, to the westward from Connecticut River which had been patented by New Hampshire, etc. etc. 12°. Hartford, [1774.]

——— Animadversory Address to the Inhabitants of the State of Vermont, with remarks on a Proclamation of George Clinton. Hartford, 1778.

——— Present State of the Controversy between the States of New York and New Hampshire on the one part, and the State of Vermont on the other. 12°. Hartford, 1782.

——— Reason the only Oracle of Man. Bennington, 1784.

——— See under VERMONT, p. 71, *ante*.

Allen, Ira. Copies of Letters to the Governor of Vermont, and Address to the Legislature thereof respecting a conspiracy against the author, and respecting a Ship Canal from Lake Champlain to the St. Lawrence. [1811. Imperfect.]

——— Natural and Political History of the State of Vermont; to which is added an Appendix containing Answers to Sundry Queries addressed to the author. London, 1798. [The same is reprinted in Vol. I. Vermont Historical Society Collections.]

——— Vindication of the Conduct of the General Assembly of Vermont, held at Windsor in October, 1778. 12°. Dresden, [1779.]

Allen, William. American Bibliographical Dictionary. 3d edition. Boston, 1857.

Allen, Z. Philosophy of the Mechanics of Nature, and the source and modes of action of natural motive power. New York, 1852.

Allibone, S. Austin. Critical Dictionary of English Literature and British and American Authors, living and deceased, from the Earliest Accounts to the latter half of the Nineteenth Century. 3v. Philadelphia, 1870–71.

American Almanac, and Repository of Useful Knowledge, for 1830–1861. 32v. 12°. Boston, 1830–61.

American Annals of the Deaf and Dumb. Vols. 1–15, bound in 5v. Hartford, 1848–70.

American Annual Cyclopædia. See Appleton.

American Antiquarian Society. Minor Publications, Nos. 1 to 53 (except Nos. 3, 5 and 8). Including "Proceedings," &c., to April, 1870. 50 pamphlets bound in 5v. Boston [and] Worcester, 1813–1870.

——— See Archæologia Americana.

American Asylum for the Deaf and Dumb. Annual Reports, 1st to 54th, 1817 to 1870. 54 pamphlets bound in 4v. Hartford, 1817–1870.

American Geographical and Statistical Society. Bulletin, vols. 1 and 2. New York, 1852–7.

——— Journal. Vol. 1. Sm. 4° New York, 1859.

——— The same. Part 1 of vol. 2. New York, 1860.

——— Proceedings. Vols. 1 and 2. New York, 1862–5.

American Institute of the City of New York. Transactions. See under NEW YORK, p. 46, *ante*.

American Institute Library. Alphabetical and Analytical Catalogue. New York, 1852.

American Pharmaceutical Association. Proceedings, 1851; 1852; 1855; 1858 to 1870. 15v.

American Quarterly Journal of Agriculture and Science. Conducted by E. Emmons and A. J. Prime. No. 2 of vol. 2. Albany, 1845.

American Unitarian Association. Tracts, Army Series. Boston, 1865.

America, or a General Survey of the Political Situation of the Powers of the Western Continent. Philadelphia, 1827.

Ames, Fisher. Works. With a selection from his speeches and correspondence. Edited by his son, Seth Ames. 2v. Boston, 1854.

CONTENTS.

Essays, Political and Miscellaneous, v. 2
Letters, v. 1.
Memoir, by J. T. Kirkland, v. 1.
Speeches, v. 2.

Amory, Thomas C. Life of James Sullivan. With Selections from his Writings. 2v. Boston, 1859.

——— Military Services and Public Life of Major General John Sullivan, of the American Revolutionary Army. Boston, 1868.

Analectic Magazine; containing Selections from foreign Reviews and Magazines. Vols. 1–14. 14v. Philadelphia, 1813–19.

The same. New Series. Vols. 1–2. 2v. Philadelphia, 1820.

Anburey, Thomas. Travels through the Interior Parts of America; in a series of letters. 2v. London, 1791. (Vol. 1 *wanting*.)

Anderson, Adam. Historical and Chronological Deduction of the Origin of Commerce. 2v. 4°. London. 1764.

Andrews, Charles. The Prisoners' Memoirs or Dartmoor Prison. 12°. New York, 1852.

Andrews, Ethan Allen. Copious and Critical Latin-English Lexicon, founded on the larger Latin-German Lexicon of Dr. William Freund; with Additions and Corrections from the lexicons of Gesner, Facciolati, Scheller, Georges, etc. New York, 1860.

Andrews, John. History of the War with America, France, Spain, and Holland, commencing in 1775 and ending in 1783. 4v. London, 1785–86.

Andros Tracts. See Prince Society.

Annual of Scientific Discovery ; or Year-Book of Facts in Science and Art, for 1850-1870. 20v. 12°. Boston, 1851-70.

Anson's Voyage. See Richard Walter.

Anstey, Henry. See Chronicles.

Antietam National Cemetery. History ; including a list of soldiers buried therein ; with ceremonies and address on occasion of the Dedication, Sept. 17, 1867. Baltimore, 1869.

Appleton's Dictionary of Machines, Mechanics, Engine-Work, and Engineering. 2v. New York, 1852.

Appleton's New American Cyclopædia. A Popular Dictionary of General Knowledge. Edited by George Ripley and Charles A. Dana. 16v. New York, 1860-63.

——— American Annual Cyclopædia and Register of Important Events. Vols. 1—10 ; 1861 to 1870. New York, 1863—71.

Apocatastasis, The, or Progress Backwards. Burlington, 1854.

Arabian Nights Entertainments. New York.

Arago, Francis. Biographies of Distinguished Scientific Men, Translated by Admiral W. H. Smyth, the Rev. Baden Powell and Robert Grant. First Series, and Second Series. 2v. Boston, 1859.

Archæologia Americana. Transactions and Collections of the American Antiquarian Society. Vols. 1—4. Worcester, Cambridge and Boston, 1820—60.

Ariosto, Ludovico. Orlando Furioso. [Spanish Translation]. Madrid, 1851.

Army of the Cumberland. Report of the First Meeting of the Society of ; held February, 1867.

——— Annals. See Fitch, John.

Arnold, Josias Lyndon. Poems. 12°. Providence, 1797.

Arnold, Samuel Green. History of the State of Rhode Island and Providence Plantations, from 1636 to 1790. 2v. New York, 1859—60.

Arnold, Thomas. History of Rome [to the End of the Second Punic War]. New York, 1857.

Astor Library. Catalogue or Alphabetical Index. Part 1 : Authors and Books. 4v. 4°. New York, 1857—61.

——— Supplement to Catalogue. With Index of Subjects. 4°. New York, 1866.

Atlantic Monthly. A Magazine of Literature, Science, Art and Politics. Vols. 1—29. Boston, 1857—72.

Atlas of the United States. Printed for the Use of the Blind at the Expense of John A. Gray, under the Direction of S. G. Howe. Boston, 1837.

B.

Babson, John J. History of the Town of Gloucester, Cape Ann ; including the Town of Rockport. Gloucester, Mass., 1860.

Backus, Isaac. A History of New England, with particular reference to the Baptists. Vol. 1. Boston, 1777.

——— A Church History of New England, 1690 to 1784. Vol. 2. [A continuation of the above.] Providence, 1784.

Bacon, Francis, *Lord*. Works. Collected and Edited by James Spedding, Robert Leslie Ellis and Douglas Denon Heath. 15v. Boston, 1860–64.

CONTENTS.

Advancement of Learning, Eng., v. 6.
Advertisement touching a Holy War, Eng., v. 13.
Annales, Additions and Corrections inserted in Camden's. Eng., v. 12.
Answers to Questions touching the office of Constables, v. 15.
Aphorismi et Consilia, Lat., v. 7.
Apophthegms, Eng., v. 13.
Arguments of Law, Eng., v. 15.
Augmentis Scientiarum, De. Lat., v. 2-3 ; Eng. v. 8—9.
Calor et Frigus, Eng., v. 7.
Christian Paradoxes, Eng., v. 14.
Cogitata et Visa, Lat., v. 7.
Cogitationes de Scientia Humana, Lat., v. 5.
Colours of Good and Evil, Eng., v. 13.
Confession of Faith, Eng., v. 14.
Description of the Intellectual Globe, Lat., v. 7; Eng., v. 10.
Discourse upon the Commission of Bridewell, v. 15.
Ebb and Flow of the Sea, Lat., v. 5; Eng., v. 10.
Elizabethæ, in Felicem Memoriam, Lat. and Eng., v. 11.
Elogium in Henricum Principem Walliæ, Lat. and Eng., v. 12.
Essays ; or, Counsels Civil and Moral, Eng., v. 12.
Filum Labyrinthi, Eng., v. 6.
Fragment of Abecedarium Naturæ, Lat., v. 2.
Historia Soni et Auditus, Lat., v. 7.
History of Dense and Rare, Lat., v. 4 ; Eng. v. 10.
History of Great Britain, beginning of, Eng., v. 11.
History of Life and Death, Lat. v. 3 ; Eng. v. 10.
History of the Reign of Henry VII. and VIII., Eng., v. 11.
History of the Winds, Lat., v. 3 ; Eng., v. 9.
Imago Civilis Augusti Cæsaris, Lat. and Eng., v. 12.
Imago Civilis Julii Cæsaris, Lat. and Eng. v. 12.
Index—Philosophical Works, v. 10. Literary and Professional Works, v. 15.
Inquiry respecting the Magnet, Lat., v. 4 ; Eng. v. 10.
Inquisitio Legitima de Motu, Lat., v. 7.
Instauratio Magna, Lat. v. 1-4 ; Eng. v. 8-10.
Interpretatione (de) Naturæ Prœmium, Lat., v. 6.
Letter to Sir Henry Savill, touching helps for the intellectual powers, Eng., v. 13.
Life of Bacon, by William Rawley, v. 1.
Maxims of the Law, Eng., v. 14.
Meditationes Sacræ, Lat. and Eng., v. 14.
Natural and Experimental History, Lat. v. 3-4 ; Eng. v. 9-10.
New Atlantis, Eng., v. 5.
Novum Organum, Lat., v. 1 ; Eng. v. 8.
Ordinances in Chancery, Eng. v. 15.
Partis Instaurationis Secundæ Delineatio, et Redargutis Philosophiarium, Lat. v. 7.
Phænomena Universi, Lat., v. 7.
Physiological and Medical Remains, Eng., v. 7.
Prayers, Eng., v. 14.

Preparative towards a Natural and Experimental History. Lat. v. 2 ; Eng., v. 8.
Preparation for the Union of Laws, Eng., v. 15.
Principles and Origins, according to the Fables of Cupid and Cœlum, Lat. v. 5 ; Eng. v. 10.
Prodromi sive Anticipationes Philisophiæ Secundæ, Lat., v. 5.
Promus of Formularies and Elegancies, Eng., v. 14.
Scala Intellectus, Lat., v. 5.
Sententiæ XII. de Interpretatione Naturæ, Lat., v. 7.
Short Notes for Civil Conversation, Eng., v. 13.
Statute of Uses, Reading on, Eng., v. 14.
Sylva Sylvarum ; or, a natural history, Eng., v. 4–5.
Temporis Partus Masculus, Lat., v. 7.
Theory of the Heaven, Lat., v. 7 ; Eng., v. 10.
Thoughts on the Nature of Things, Lat., v. 5 ; Eng., v. 10.
Topics of Inquiry respecting Light and Luminous Matter, Lat., v. 4 ; Eng. v. 10.
Translation of certain Psalms into English Verse, v. 14.
True Greatness of Britain, Eng., v. 13.
Use of the Law, Eng., v. 14.
Valerius Terminus of the Interpretation of Nature, Eng., v. 6.
Wisdom of the Ancients, Lat., and Eng., v. 12–13.

——— Essays. With annotations, by Richard Whately. 4th Edition. New York, 1859.

——— Personal History of. See Dixon, W. H.

Bacon, Roger. See Chronicles.

Baird, Robert. Religion in America. New York, 1845.

Baird, Spencer F., John Cassin, and G. N. Lawrence. Birds of North America; the descriptions of species based chiefly on the collections in the Smithsonian Institution. Text and Atlas. 2v. 4°. Salem, 1860.

——— See under UNITED STATES, p. 64, *ante.*

Baker, Lafayette C. History of the United States Secret Service. Philadelphia, 1867.

Baldwin, John D. Ancient America, in Notes on American Archæology. 12°. New York, 1872.

Ballads, English and Scottish. Selected and edited by F. J. Child. 8v. 16°. Boston, 1857–59.

Ballard, Edward. Memorial Volume of the Popham Celebration, 1862; commemorative of the planting of the Popham Colony, 1607. Edited by Rev. E. Ballard. (This contains bound with it an address by John A. Poor on Sir Ferdinando Gorges, published in New York, 1862.) Portland, 1863.

Ballou, Hosea, 2d. Ancient History of Universalism, from the time of the Apostles to the fifth General Council, with an Appendix tracing the doctrine to the Reformation. With Notes by A. St. J. Chambre and T. J. Sawyer. 12°. Boston, 1872.

Ballou, Maturin M. A Treasury of Thought, forming an Encyclopædia of Quotations from Ancient and Modern Authors. Boston, 1872.

Bancroft, George. History of the United States, from the Discovery of the American Continent. Vols. 1–9. Boston, 1843–66.

——— Literary and Historical Miscellanies. New York, 1857.

Barber, John Warner. Historical Collections, relating to the History and Antiquities of every town in Massachusetts. Worcester, 1839.

—— Connecticut Historical Collections. 2d edition. New Haven.

—— History and Antiquities of New England, New York, New Jersey and Pennsylvania. 3d edition. New York, 1856.

—— Historical Collections of the State of New York. New York, 1851.

Baring-Gould, Sabine. Curious Myths of the Middle Ages. 16°. Philadelphia, 1869.

Barlow, Joel. The Columbiad, a Poem. 4°. Philadelphia, 1807.

Barnard, Henry. Discourses in commemoration of the Life, Character and Services of the Rev. Thomas H. Gallaudet, LL. D. Hartford, 1852.

Barry, John Stetson. History of Massachusetts. 4th edition. 3v. Boston.

Bartlett, David W. Life and Public Services of Abraham Lincoln. With biographical sketch of Hannibal Hamlin. 12°. New York, 1860.

Bartlett, John. Familiar Quotations; an attempt to trace to their source passages and phrases in common use; chiefly from English authors. 4th edition. Boston, 1864.

Bartlett, John Russell. Dictionary of Americanisms; a glossary of words and phrases usually regarded as peculiar to the United States. 2d edition. Boston, 1859.

—— See Records under RHODE ISLAND, p. 49, *ante*.

Barton, William. Memoirs of David Rittenhouse. Philadelphia, 1813.

Battle Roll. See Perce, Elbert.

Baylies, Francis. Historical Memoir of the Colony of New Plymouth. Edited by S. G. Drake. 2v. Boston, 1866.

Bayne, Peter. Life and Letters of Hugh Miller. 2v. 12°. Boston, 1871.

Bailey, Joseph. See Miscellanies.

Beard, John R. See L'Ouverture, Toussaint.

Beattie, James. Poetical Works. Edited by Alex. Dyce. 16°. Boston, 1854.

Beck, Lewis C. See Natural History under NEW YORK, p. 46, *ante*.

Beckley, Hosea. History of Vermont; with descriptions, physical and topographical. 12°. Brattleboro, 1846.

Bede, The Venerable. Ecclesiastical History of England. Also the Anglo-Saxon Chronicle. Edited by J. A. Giles. 3d edition. London, 1859.

Belknap, Jeremy. History of New Hampshire. 3v. Boston, 1813 and Dover, 1812.

—— The Same. With notes by John Farmer. Vol. 1. [All of Farmer's edition ever published and containing Vols. 1 and 2 of Belknap's original edition.] Dover, 1831.

—— Life of. By his grand-daughter. 18°. New York, 1847.

Bellows, Albert J. How not to be Sick; a sequel to the "Philosophy of Eating." 3d edition. 12°. New York, 1869.

—— Philosophy of Eating. 5th edition. 12°. New York, 1869.

Bellows Falls Intelligencer. [First edited by Thomas Green Fessenden; called *Vermont Intelligencer and Bellows Falls Advertiser* until Feb. 4, 1822.] Vol. 1 and first 23 numbers of Vol. 2, (Jan. 1, 1817 to June 1, 1818); and Vols. 6, 7, 8 and 9, (Dec. 24, 1821 to Dec. 12, 1825.)

Bellows, Henry W. The Old World in its New Face. Impressions of Europe, 1867–1868. 2v. 12°. New York, 1868.

Benedict, George Grenville. Battle of Gettysburg, and the part taken therein by the Vermont Troops. Burlington, 1867.

Bentham, Jeremy. Theory of Legislation. Translated from the French of Etienne Dumont by R. Hildreth. 12°. London, 1864.

Benton, Thomas H. Abridgment of the Debates of Congress, from 1789 to 1856. From Gales and Seaton's Annals of Congress and Register of Debates, and from the official reported Debates by J. C. Rives. 16v. New York, 1860–61.

—— ThirtyYears' View; a History of the Working of the American Government for thirty years, from 1820 to 1850. 2v. New York, 1859.

Bible. Biblia Sacra, vulgatæ editionis Sixti V. Pont. Max. jussu recognita; et Clementis VIII. auctoritate edita. Folio. Lugduni, 1684.

—— Holy Bible; containing the Old and New Testaments, translated out of the original tongues, and with the former transtions diligently compared and revised. The References and Marginal Readings of the Polyglott Bible, with numerous additions from Bagster's Comprehensive Bible. New York, 1842. (2 copies.)

—— New Testament. Cherokee. Translated mainly by S. A. Worcester, and revised by C. C. Torrey and another. 12°. New York, 1860.

—— See Cruden, Norton, and Noyes.

Bibliotheca Americana. See Sabin, Joseph.

Bigelow, Jacob. Modern Inquiries, classical, professional and miscellaneous. 12°. Boston, 1867.

Binney, Horace. Inquiry into the Formation of Washington's Farewell Address. Philadelphia, 1859.

Blaev, Joannes. Geographia, quæ est Cosmographiæ Blavianæ Pars prima, qua orbis terræ tabulis ante oculos ponitur, et descriptionibus illustratur. 11v. Folio. Amstelædami, 1662.

Blancheton, Andre-Antoine. Vues Pittoresques des Chateaux de France. 2v. Folio. Paris.

Bleeker, Leonard. See Hough, F. B.

Blennerhassett Papers, embodying the private journal of Herman Blennerhassett and correspondence of Burr, Alston, etc.; with an account of the "Spanish Association of Kentucky," and a Memoir of Blennerhassett by Wm. H. Safford. Cincinnati, 1864.

Bliss, George, Jr. See Annual of Scientific Discovery, of which he was assistant Editor in 1850–1851.

Blodget, Lorin. Climatology of the United States, and of the temperate latitudes of the North American Continent. Philadelphia, 1857.

Bloodgood, S. De Witt. The Sexagenary, or Reminiscences of the American Revolution. Albany, 1866.

Blue Laws, etc. See Hinman, R. R.

Boeckh, August. Public Economy of the Athenians. Translated from the German by Anthony Lamb. Boston, 1857.

Bohn, Henry G. Guide to the Knowledge of Pottery, Porcelain, &c. With Catalogue of the Bernal Collection of Works of Art. 12°. London, 1857.

Bonaparte, Charles Louis Napoleon. See Napoleon III.

[Boon Sale.] Catalogue of Books and Pamphlets principally relating to America. New York, 1870.

Bossu, J. A. Travels through that part of North America formerly called Louisiana. Translated by J. R. Forster. 2v. London, 1771.

Boston. Annals of Primary Schools, 1818 to 1855. By Joseph M. Wightman.

——— Annual Report of Superintendent of Public Schools, 1853.

——— Reports of School Commissioners, 1857 to 1861. 5v.

——— Rules of School Commissioners, 1857.

——— Annual Reports of Receipts and Expenditures, 1819 to 1856. [Bound in 6v.]

——— Auditor's Reports. 1863–4; 1865–6 to 1869–70. 6v.

——— Laws and Ordinances, 1863.

——— Public Library. Catalogue. 1854.

——— ——— Catalogue of the Prince Library deposited in the Public Library. 4°. 1870.

——— ——— Index to the Catalogue of Books in the Upper Hall. 4°. 1861.

——— ——— Index to the Catalogue of [Books] in the Lower Hall. 4°. 1858.

——— ——— 15th to 18th Annual Reports of Trustees, 1867 to 1870. 4v.

Boston Rail Road Jubilee. An account of the Celebration commemorative of the opening of Railroad Communication between Boston and Canada, 1852.

Boston Board of Trade. 1st to 13th Annual Reports of the Government, 1855 to 1867. 13v.

Boswell, James. Life of Samuel Johnson. With additions by John Wilson Croker, to which are added two supplementary volumes of Johnsoniana. 10v. 16°. London, 1853.

Botta, Carlo. History of the War of the Independence of the United States of America. Translated by G. A. Otis. 3v. Philadelphia, 1820–21.

Botta, Vincenzo. Dante as Philosopher, Patriot and Poet. With an analysis of the Divina Commedia, its plot and episodes. 12°. New York, 1867.

[Boudreaux, F. J.] Happiness of Heaven. 16°. Baltimore, 1871.

Bouton, Nathaniel. History of Concord from 1725 to 1853. With a History of the ancient Penacooks. Concord, 1856.

——— See Provincial Papers, under NEW HAMPSHIRE, p. 43, *ante*.

Boutwell, George S. Speeches and Papers relating to the Rebellion and the overthrow of Slavery. 12°. Boston, 1867.

Bovee, Marvin H. Christ and the Gallows; or Reasons for the Abolition of Capital Punishment. 12°. New York, 1869.

Bowditch. Nathaniel Ingersoll. Memoir of Nathaniel Bowditch. 4°. Boston, 1840.

——— Suffolk Surnames. Boston, 1858.

Bowen, Francis. Documents of the Constitution of England and America. Cambridge, 1854.

——— Principles of Political Economy. 2d edition. Boston, 1859.

Bower, Archibald. History of the Popes, from the foundation of the See of Rome to the present time. Vols. 1–2. 4°. London, 1748–50.

Boynton, Charles B. History of the Navy during the Rebellion. 2v. New York, 1867–68.

Boynton, Edward C. History of West Point, its Origin and Military Importance during the Revolution; and the Origin and Progress of the U. S. Military Academy. New York, 1863.

Bozman, John Leeds. History of Maryland, from its First Settlement in, 1633, to the Restoration, in 1660. 2v. Baltimore, 1837.

Brackenridge, W. D. See under UNITED STATES, p. 64, *ante*.

Bradford, Alden. History of Massachusetts, 1764 to July, 1775. Boston, 1822.

——— The same, from July, 1775 to 1789, inclusive. Boston, 1825.

Bradford, Alden. The same, from 1790 to 1820. Boston, 1829.

——— The same, from 1620 to 1820. Boston, 1835.

Bradley, Stephen R. See under VERMONT, p. 71, *ante*.

Brayton, Patience [Greene]. Life and Religious Labours. 12°. (Title page *wanting.*)

Bremer, Frederika. Life, Letters and Posthumous Works. Edited by her sister, Charlotte Bremer. From the Swedish by Fredr. Milow and Emily Nonnen. 12°. New York, 1869.

Brewster, Charles W. Rambles about Portsmouth. Portsmouth, 1859.

——— The same. Second series, with Sketch of the Author by Wm. H. Y. Hackett. Portsmouth, 1869.

Brewster, *Sir* David. Memoirs of the Life, Writings and Discoveries of Sir Isaac Newton. 2v. Edinburgh, 1855.

Bright, John. Speeches on the American Question, with an Introduction by Frank Moore. 12°. Boston, 1865.

British Dramatists. Works. Selected, with Notes, Biographies, etc., by John S. Keltie. New York, 1870.

British Museum. List of Books of Reference in the Reading Room, 1869.

British Poets. [Little, Brown & Company's Edition.] 128v. 16°. Boston, 1854–64.

CONTENTS.

Akenside,	1 vol.	Marvell,	1 vol.
Ballads,	8 vols.	Milton,	3 vols.
Beattie,	1 vol.	Montgomery,	5 "
Burns,	3 vols.	Moore,	6 "
Butler,	2 "	Parnell & Tickell.	1 vol.
Byron,	10 "	Pope,	3 vols.
Campbell,	1 vol.	Prior,	2 "
Chatterton,	2 vols.	Scott,	9 "
Churchill,	3 "	Shakespeare,	1 vol.
Coleridge,	3 "	Shelley,	3 vols.
Collins,	1 vol.	Skelton,	3 "
Cowper,	3 vols.	Southey,	10 "
Donne,	1 vol.	Spencer,	5 "
Dryden,	5 vols.	Surrey,	1 vol.
Falconer,	1 vol.	Swift,	3 vols.
Gay,	2 vols.	Thomson,	2 "
Goldsmith,	1 vol.	Vaughan,	1 vol.
Gray,	1 "	Watts,	1 "
Herbert,	1 "	White,	1 "
Herrick,	2 vols.	Wordsworth,	7 vols.
Hood,	4 "	Wyatt,	1 vol.
Keats,	1 vol.	Young,	2 vols.

(Vol. I., Milton, and Vol. I., Young *wanting.*)

NOTE.—See also under names of each of the above authors.

British Poets. See Aiken, John.

Brodhead, John Romeyn. History of the State of New York. Vol. 1. First Period, 1609–1664. 2d edition. New York, 1859.

——— The Same. Vol. 2. 1664–1691. New York, 1871.

——— See under NEW YORK, p. 46, *ante*.

Brougham, Henry, *Lord*. Life and times of; written by himself. V. 1–3. 12°. New York, 1871–72.

Brown, David Paul. The Forum; or forty years full practice at the Philadelphia Bar. 2v. Philadelphia, 1856.

Brown, John, *D. D.* See Miscellanies.

Brown, John, *M. D.* Spare Hours. First Series. 12°. Boston, 1866.

——— The same. Second Series. 12°. Boston, 1866.

Brown, *Rev.* William, *M. D.* History of the Propagation of Christianity among the Heathen since the Reformation. 2v. London, 1814.

Browne, Albert G., Jr. Sketch of the Official Life of John A. Andrew, as Governor of Massachusetts; to which is added the Valedictory Address of Governor Andrew. 16°. New York, 1868.

Browne, *Sir* Thomas. Religio Medici; letter to a friend; Christian Morals; Urn Burial and other papers. 12°. Boston, 1863.

Browning, Elizabeth Barrett. Essays on the Greek Christian Poets, and on the English Poets. 16°. New York, 1863.

——— Poems. 4v. 16°. New York, 1862–63.

Brunet, Jacques Charles. Manual du libraire, et de l'amateur de livres, contenant : 1° un nouveau dictionnaire bibliographique ; 2° une table en forme de catalogue raisonne. 3d edition. Vols. 1–3. Bruxelles, 1821.

Brush, George Jarvis. See Dana, J. D.

Bryant, William Cullen. Library of Poetry and Song, Being choice Selections from the best Poets. 4°. New York, 1872.

——— Poems. Collected and arranged by the Author. 2v. 12°. New York, 1857.

——— See Homer.

Buckingham, Joseph T. Personal Memoirs and Recollections of Editorial Life. 2v. 16°. Boston, 1852.

——— Specimens of Newspaper Literature; with personal memoirs, anecdotes and reminiscences. 2v. 12°. Boston, 1850.

Bulfinch, Thomas. Age of Chivalry. Part 1. Sir Arthur and his Knights. Part 2. The Mabinogeon; or Welsh Popular Tales. 12°. Boston, 1861.

Bulwer Lytton, *Sir* Edward. Godolphin. 2v. 12°. New York, 1840.

——— and Forbes, John. On Water Treatment. A compilation edited by Roland S. Houghton. 12°. New York, 1851.

Burgoyne, *Gen.* John. See Miscellanies.

Burke, Edmund. Account of the European Settlements in America. 2d edition. 2v. London, 1758.

——— Life of. See James Prior.

——— Speeches and Correspondence, [form vols. 7 and 8 of the following edition of his works.]

Burke, Edmund. Works. 8v. 12°. London, 1854–57.

CONTENTS.

Account of a Late Short Administration, v. 1.
Address to British Colonists in N. America, v. 5.
Address to the King, v. 5.
Affairs in Ireland, 1797, v. 6.
Appeal from New to the Old Whigs, v. 3.
Conduct of the Minority, v, 3.
Considerations on the Present State of Affairs, 1792, v. 3.
Correspondence, v. 8.
Essay on Abridgment of English History, v. 6.
Fragments and Notes of Speeches, v. 6.
Hastings, Articles of Charge against, v. 4 and 5.
Hastings, Report of Committee on Trial of, v. 6.
Hastings, Speeches on the Impeachment of, v. 7-8.
Hints for an Essay on the Drama, v. 6.
Letter on American Affairs, v. 2.
Letter on Duration of Parliaments, v. 6.
Letters on the Penal Laws against Irish Catholics, v. 3.
Letter to a Member of the National Assembly, v. 2.
Letter to a Noble Lord, v. 5.
Letter to Dundas, with Sketch of Negro Code, v. 5.
Letter to Empress of Russia, v. 5.
Letters and Reflections on Execution of Rioters, 1780, v. 5.
Letters on a Regicide Peace, v. 5.
Letters on Trade of Ireland, v. 2.
Letter to W. Elliot, v. 5.
Letters to Bingham, Fox, Rockingham, Perry, Burgh, Merlott, Smith, Langrishe, and R. Burke, v. 3, 5 and 6.
Observations on the Present State of the Nation, v. 1.
Policy of the Allies, v. 3.
Preface to M. Brissot's Address, v. 3.
Reflections on French Revolution, v. 2.
Reports from Committee of House of Commons on Affairs of E. India Co., v. 4.
Representation to his Majesty, v. 2.
Speeches at Bristol, v. 1 and 2.
Speech on American Taxation, v. 1.
Speech on Army Estimates, v. 3.
Speech on Conciliation with America, v. 1.
Speech on Fox's E. India Bill, v. 2.
Speech on the Independence of Parliament, v. 2.
Speech on the Nabob of Arcot's Debts, v. 3.
Sublime and Beautiful, v. 1.
Thoughts on French Affairs, v. 3.
Thoughts on Scarcity, v. 5.
Thoughts on the Cause of the Present Discontents, v. 1.
Tracts relative to Laws against Popery in Ireland, v. 6.
Vindication of Natural Society, v. 1.

Burlington, [Vermont]. Annual Reports, made Feb., 1867 to 1869 : 1872. 4v.

Burnet, Gilbert. History of the Reformation of the Church of England. 6v. London, 1820.

Burns, Robert. Poetical Works. With Sketch of the author's life. 3v. 16°. Boston, 1863.

Burr, Aaron. Trial for Treason and Misdemeanor in the Circuit Court of the U. S. for the District of Va. (Title page *wanting.*)

Burroughs, Stephen. Memoirs of. 16°. Amherst, 1858.

Burton, Robert. Anatomy of Melancholy, what it is; with all the kinds, causes, symptoms, prognostics, and several cures of it; in three main partitions, with their several sections, members, and subsections; philosophically, medically, historically, opened and cut up. By Democritus Junior. New ed., with translations of Classical Extracts. 3v. Boston, 1859.

Burton, William E. Cyclopædia of Wit and Humor; selections from the writings of the most eminent humorists of America, Ireland, Scotland, and England. 2v. New York, 1859.

Bushnell, Horace. Women's Suffrage; the reform against nature. 12°. New York, 1869.

Butler, James Davie and Houghton, George Frederick. See under ADDRESSES, p. 69, *ante*.

Butler, L. C. Memorial Record of Essex, Vermont. 12°. Burlington, 1866.

Butler, Samuel. Poetical Works. 2v. 16°. Boston, 1857.

Byfield, Nathaniel. Account of the late Revolution in New England. Reprinted [from edition of 1689.] 4°. New York, 1865. [Sabin's Reprints No. 1.]

Byron, George Gordon, *Lord*. Poetical Works. 10v. 16°. Boston, 1861.

C.

Calef, Robert. More Wonders of the Invisible World; or the Wonders of the Invisible World Displayed in Five Parts. London, 1700. [Reprint. Small 4°. Roxbury, 1866. With Drake's Witchcraft Delusion in New England, v. 2, 3.]

Calhoun, John Caldwell. Works. Edited by Richard K. Cralle. 6v. New York, 1854–59.

CONTENTS.

Constitution and Government of the United States, v. 1.
Disquisition on Government, v. 1.
Reports and Public Letters, v. 5—6.
South Carolina Exposition, v. 6.
Speeches in Congress, v. 2—4.

California Newspapers. 1v. [A volume of collections of various California Newspapers printed in 1849 and 1850.]

Calvert, George H. The Gentleman. 12°. Boston, 1863.

Cammann, Henry J. and Camp, Hugh N. Charities of New York, Brooklyn and Staten Island. New York, 1868.

Camp, Hugh N. See Cammann.

Campbell, John, *Lord*. Lives of the Lord Chancellors and Keepers of the Great Seal of England, from the earliest times till the reign of King George IV. 7v. Philadelphia, 1851.

Campbell, Maria. Revolutionary Services and Civil Life of General William Hull. With History of the Campaign of 1812 and Surrender of Detroit, by J. Freeman Clarke. New York, 1848.

Campbell, Thomas. Poetical Works. With notes by W. A. Hill. 16°. Boston, 1863.

Campbell, William W. Annals of Tryon County: or the border warfare of New York during the Revolution. New York, 1831.

——— Life and Writings of De Witt Clinton. New York, 1849.

Canniff, William. Manual of the Principles of Surgery. Philadelphia, 1866.

Canning, George. Select Speeches, with a Biographical Sketch, &c. Edited by Robert Walsh. Philadelphia.

Capgrave, Johannes. See Chronicles.

Carey, Henry C. Principles of Social Science. 3v. Philadelphia, 1858–59.

Carey, Mathew. Olive Branch; or Faults on both sides, Federal and Democratic. 7th edition. 12°. Middlebury, 1816.

Carlyle, Thomas. Critical and Miscellaneous Essays; collected and republished. 4v. Boston, 1860.

——— History of Friedrich the Second, called Frederick the Great. Vol. 2. 12°. New York, 1859.

——— Oliver Cromwell's Letters and Speeches; with supplement and elucidations. 2v. 12°. New York, 1860.

Carpenter, Francis B. Six months at the White House with Abraham Lincoln. New York, 1866.

Carpenter, Mary. Juvenile Delinquents, their condition and treatment. London, 1853.

——— Our Convicts. 2v. in 1. London, 1864.

Carpenter, William B. Vegetable Physiology and Systematic Botany. Edited by E. Lankester. 12°. London, 1858.

Carroll, B. R. Historical Collections of South Carolina; embracing many rare and valuable pamphlets and documents relating to the history of that State, from its discovery to 1776. 2v. New York, 1836.

Casgrain. See under JOURNAL DES JESUITES, *post.*

Cassin, John. See Baird and United States Explorations and Surveys.

Catlin, George. Letters and Notes on the Manners, Customs, and Condition of the North American Indians; written during eight years' travel amongst the wildest tribes in 1832 to 1839. 2v. Philadelphia, 1857.

Caustic, Christopher. *Pseudonyme.* See Fessenden, T. G.

Cazin, Achille. Phenomena and Laws of Heat. Translated and edited by Elihu Rich. 16°. New York, [1868.]

Certain Inducements to well minded people * * to transport themselves or some servants or agents for them into the West Indies. Reprinted. [From edition supposed to have been printed in 1643.] 4°. New York, 1865. [Sabin's Reprints, No. 4.]

Cervantes Saavedra, Miguel de. The history of the ingenious gentleman Don Quixote of La Mancha ; translated from the Spanish by Motteux. With notes and essay by John G. Lockhart. 4v. 12°. Boston, 1865.

Chambers, Robert. Cyclopædia of English Literature ; a history, critical and biographical, of British authors, from the earliest to the present times. 2v. Philadelphia, 1859–60.

Champlain, Samuel de. Œuvres ; publiees sous le patronage de L'universite Laval par L'Abbe C. H. Laverdiere. Seconde edition. 2v. 4°. Quebec, 1870.

Chandler, Richard, *D. D.* Travels in Asia Minor, or an account of a tour made at the expense of the Society of Dilettanti. 2d edition. 4°. London, 1776.

——— Travels in Greece. 4°. London, 1776.

Channing, William Ellery. Works. 16th Complete edition. 6v. in 3. Boston, 1859.

CONTENTS.

Abolitionists, The, v. 2.
Address delivered at Lenox, Aug. 1, 1842, v. 6.
Annexation of Texas to the United States, v. 2.
Associations, Remarks on, v. 1.
Calvinism, Moral Argument against, v. 1.
Catholicism, Letter on, v. 2.
Charges at Ordinations, v. 5.
Church, The ; a discourse, v. 6.
Creeds, Letters on, v. 2.
Duty of the Free States, v. 6.
Education, Remarks on, v. 1.
Elevation of Laboring Classes, Lectures on, v. 5.
Emancipation, v. 6.
Fenelon, Character and Writings, v. 1.
Follen, C., Discourse on the death of, v. 5.
Milton, John, Character and Writings, v. 1.
Miscellanies, v. 5.
Napoleon, Life and Character, v. 1.
National Literature, Remarks on, v. 1.
Present Age, The ; an address, v. 6.
Religious Discourses, v. 3-4.
Self-Culture, Address on, v. 2.
Slavery, v. 2.
Slavery Question, Remarks on, v. 5.
Temperance, Address on, v. 2.
Tuckerman, J., Life and Character of, v. 6.
Union, The, v. 1.
War, Lecture on, v. 5.
War, Two Discourses on, v. 3-4.

Chaplin, Jeremiah. Life of Henry Dunster, First President of Harvard College. 16°. Boston, 1872.

Chapman, George Thomas. Sketches of the Alumni of Dartmouth College, from 1771 to 1867, with a brief History of the Institution. Cambridge, 1867.

Charlevoix, Pierre Francois Xavier de. Histoire et Description Generale de la Nouvelle France ; avec le journal historique d'un voyage fait par ordre du Roi dans l'Amerique Septentrionale. 6v. 16°. Paris, 1744.

Charlevoix, Pierre Francois Xavier de. History and General Description of New France. Translated, with notes, by John Gilmary Shea. 6v. 4°. New York, 1871–72.

Charlton, Edwin A. See New Hampshire as it is.

Chase, Enoch. Tables of Interest. 4°. Boston, 1824.

Chase, George Wingate. History of Haverhill, Massachusetts. 1640 to 1860. Haverhill, 1861.

Chastellux, Francois Jean, *Marquis de*. Travels in North America, in the years 1780—82. From the French, with notes, by an English gentleman (J. Kent.) 2v. London, 1787.

Chateaubriand, Rene Francois Auguste de. Los Martires. [Spanish ; translated by M. M. Flamant]. Madrid, 1852.

——— Los Natchez. [Spanish ; translated by M. M. Flamant]. Madrid, 1853.

Chatterton, Thomas. Poetical Works. With notice of his Life. 2v. 16°. Boston, 1857.

Chaucer, Geoffrey. Poetical Works. Edited by Richard Morris. With Memoir by Sir Harry Nicolas. 6v. 16°. London, 1870.

Chesterfield, Philip Dormer Stanhope, *Earl of*. Letters written to his Son. 2d edition. 4v. London, 1774.

Chicago. [Municipal Laws.] Charter and Ordinances to September, 1856, with Acts of Assembly relating to the City. Chicago, 1856.

——— 7th, 13th, 15th and 16th Annual Reports of the Board of Education, 1861 ; 1867 ; 1869 ; 1870. 4v.

——— 7th and 8th Annual Reports of the Board of Public Works, 1868 ; 1869. 2v.

——— 15th Annual Report of the Chicago Reform School, 1871.

Chicago Board of Trade. 11th and 13th Annual Reports of the Trade and Commerce of the City, 1869 ; 1870. 2v.

Chicago Historical Society. Charter, Constitution and By-Laws. Chicago, 1871.

Chief Fathers of New England, Lives of. See Adams, N. ; Albro, John A. ; Hooker, E. W. ; McClure, A. W., and Pond, E.

Child, Francis James. See Ballads, p. 121, *ante*.

Chipman, Daniel. Life of Nathaniel Chipman, LL. D., formerly member of the U. S. Senate, and Chief Justice of Vermont. With selections from his papers. Boston, 1846. (2 copies.)

——— Memoir of Thomas Chittenden ; with history of the Constitution during his administration. 12°. Middlebury, 1849. (3 copies.)

——— Memoir of Colonel Seth Warner ; to which is added Spark's Life of Ethan Allen. 16°. Middlebury, 1848. (2 copies.)

Choate, Rufus. Works ; with Memoir of his Life, by Samuel Gilman Brown. 2v. Boston, 1862.

Christian Examiner, The. Vols. 1 to 87. Boston and New York, 1824–69. [The complete publication.]

Christie, Robert. History of the late Province of Lower Canada, parliamentary and political. 6v. 12°. Quebec, 1848–55. (Vol. 5 *wanting.*)

Chronicles. Rerum Britannicarum Medii Ævi Scriptores; or Chronicles and Memorials of Great Britain and Ireland during the Middle Ages. 23v. London, 1858–68.

CONTENTS.

Annales Cambriæ, Edited by John Williams Ab Ithel. London, 1860.

Bacon, Roger. Opera quædam hactenus Inedita. Edited by J. S. Brewer. V. 1. London, 1850.

Capgrave, John. Liber de Illustiibus Henricis. Edited by Francis C. Hingeston. London, 1858.

Chronicon Monasterii de Abingdon. Edited by Joseph Stevenson. 2v. London, 1858.

Eulogium, Historiarum sive Temporis. Chronicon ab orbe condito usque ad annum Domini M.CCCC.LXVI.; a Monacho quodam Malmesburiensi exaratum. Accedunt Continuationes duæ, quarum una ad annum 1413. altera ad annum 1490 perducta est. Edited by Frank S. Haydon. 2v. London, 1858-60.

Fasciculi Zizaniorum Magistri Johannis Wycliff, cum Tritico. Ascribed to Thomas Netter, of Walden. Edited by W. W. Shirley. London, 1858.

Giraldis Cambrensis. Opera. Vols. 1 and 3. Edited by J. S. Brewer. 2v. London, 1861-3.

Grosseteste, Robertus. Epistolæ. Edited by Henry R. Luard. London, 1861.

Hardy. Thomas D. Descriptive Catalogue of Materials relating to the History of Great Britain and Ireland, to the end of the reign of Henry VII. V. 1. Parts 1-2. 2v. London, 1862.

Henry III. Royal and other Historical Letters illustrative of the reign of Henry III. Edited by W. W. Shirley. 2v. London, 1862-6.

Hoveden, Roger de. Chronica. Edited by William Stubbs. Vol. 1. London, 1868.

Johannis de Oxenedes. Chronica. Edited by Sir Henry Ellis. London, 1859.

London. Munimenta Gildhallæ Londoniensis. Liber Albus. Liber Custumarum. Edited by Henry T. Riley. 2v. in 3. London, 1859-60.

Monumenta Franciscana; scilicet, I. Thomas de Eccleston de Adventu Fratrum Minorum in Angliam. II. Adæ de Marisco Epistolæ. III. Registrum Fratrum Minorum Londoniæ. Edited by J. S. Brewer. London, 1858.

Oxford. Munimenta Academica, or Documents illustrative of Academical Life and Studies at Oxford. Parts 1 and 2. By Henry Anstey. 2v. London, 1868.

Church, Benjamin. History of King Philip's War, [and] of the Eastern Expeditions of 1689, 1690, 1692, 1696 and 1704. 2v. 4°. Boston, 1865–67. [Library of N. E. History, Nos. 2 and 3.]

Churchill, Charles. Poetical Works; with Life of the Author, by W. Tooke. 3v. 16°. Boston, 1854.

——— Works. 5th edition. 4v. 12°. London, 1774.

Cincinnati. Mayor's Message, Inaugural, and Reports of City Departments, April 10, 1861. Cincinnati, 1861.

Clarke, *Mrs.* Cowden. Complete Concordance to Shakspere. Boston, 1870.

Clarke, James Freeman. Ten Great Religions; an essay in comparative Theology. Boston, 1871.

——— See Campbell, Maria.

Clarke, *Rev.* Samuel. Lives of Sundry Eminent Persons in this Later Age. 4°. London, 1683.

Clement, Clara Erskine. Hand-book of Legendary and Mythological Art. 12°. New York, 1871.

Cobden Club Essays. Second Series, 1871–2. 2d edition. London, 1872. [See Duff].

Cochin, Augustin. Results of Emancipation. Translated by Mary L. Booth. 12°. Boston, 1864.

——— Results of Slavery. Translated by Mary L. Booth. 12°. Boston, 1863.

Coffin, William F. 1812; the War and its Moral: a Canadian Chronicle. Montreal, 1864.

Coggeshall, George. History of the American Privateers and Letters of Marque during our War with England in the years 1812–14. New York, 1856,

Colden, Cadwallader. History of the Five Indian Nations depending on the Province of New York. [Reprint.] With notes by J. G. Shea. New York, 1866.

——— Life of Robert Fulton. New York, 1817.

Coleridge, Samuel Taylor. Aids to Reflection: edited by Henry Nelson Coleridge. With Preliminary Essay by James Marsh. Burlington, 1846.

——— The Friend. A Series of Essays to Aid in the Formation of Fixed Principles in Politics, Morals and Religion. With Literary Amusements interspersed. Burlington, 1831.

——— Poetical and Dramatic Works: with a Memoir. 3v. 16°. Boston, 1861.

——— Statesman's Manual; or, the Bible the Best Guide to Political Skill and Foresight: a Lay Sermon. 12°. Burlington, 1832.

Collier, John Payne. Bibliographical and Critical Account of the Rarest Books in the English Language. 4v. New York, 1866.

Collins, William. Poetical Works. 16°. Boston, 1859.

Colman, Henry. [European] Agricultural and Rural Economy. From Practical Observation. 2v. in 1. Boston, 1857.

Colnett, James. Voyage to the South Atlantic, and round Cape-Horn, into the Pacific Ocean. 4°. London, 1798.

Colwell, Stephen. Ways and Means of Payment; a Full Analysis of the Credit System, with its Various Modes of Adjustment. Philadelphia, 1859.

Combe, William. Three Tours of Dr. Syntax; in search of the picturesque, in search of consolation, and in search of a wife, with Life of the Author by John Camden Hotten and illustrations by T. Rowlandson. London.

Conant, Edward. A Drill Book in the elements of the English Language. 12°. Montpelier, 1871.

Concord, N. H. Fifteenth Annual Report of Receipts and Expenditures, February 1, 1868.

Congress. History of 1789 to 1793. [By George Gibbs?] Philadelphia, 1843.

Connecticut State Agricultural Society. Transactions, 1854 to 1858. 5v. Hartford, 1855–59.

Constitutional Text Book. Containing selections from Webster's Writings, Dectaration of Independence, Constitution and Washington's Farewell Address. [Compiled by Lemuel Blake ?] New York and Boston, 1854,

Conybeare, William John, and Howson, J. L. Life and Epistles of St. Paul. 2v. London, 1865.

Cooper, James Fenimore. Choice Works. 20v. 12°. New York, 1856. (Vol. 19 *wanting.*)

CONTENTS.

Bravo, v. 12.
Deerslayer, or the First War-Path, v. 2.
Headsman, or the Abbaye des Vignerons, v. 13.
Homeward Bound, or The Chase ; a tale of the sea, v. 14.
Home as Found, sequel to Homeward Bound, v. 15.
Last of the Mohicans. a narrative of 1757, v. 3.
Lionel Lincoln, or the Leaguer of Boston. v. 8.
Pathfinder, or the Inland Sea, v. 4.
Pilot, a tale of the Sea, v. 7.
Pioneers, or the Sources of the Susquehanna, v. 5.
Prairie, v. 6.
Red Rover, v. 9.
Sea Lions, or the Lost Sealers, v. 20.
Spy, a tale of the neutral ground, v. 1,
Two Admirals, v. 16.
Water Witch, or Skimmer of the Seas, v. 11,
Wept of Wish-Ton-Wish, v. 10.
Wing-and-Wing, or le Feu-Follet, v. 17.
Wyandotte, or the Hutted Knoll, v. 18.

——— History of the Navy of the United States of America. 2v. Philadelphia, 1840.

——— Jack Tier, or the Florida Reef. 12°. New York, 1864.

Cooper, S. Concise System of Instructions and Regulations for Militia and Volunteers of the United States. New edition. 12°. Philadelphia, 1846.

Copeland, R. Morris. Country Life: a hand-book of agriculture, horticulture, and landscape gardening. Boston, 1860.

Cornwallis, Charles, *Marquis*. Correspondence. Edited, with notes, by Charles Ross. 3v. London, 1859.

Cothren, William. History of Ancient Woodbury, Conn., from 1659 to 1854; including Washington, Southbury, etc. Waterbury, Conn., 1854.

Cowper, William. Poetical Works. 3v. 16°. Boston, 1856.

——— Translation of Iliad and Odyssey. See Homer.

Crabb, George. English Synonymes, with copious illustrations and explanations drawn from the best writers. 10th edition. New York, 1868.

Craik, George L. Compendious History of English Literature, and of the English Language, from the Norman Conquest: with numerous specimens. 2v. New York, 1864.

Croffut, W. A., and Morris, John M. Military and Civil History of Connecticut during the war of 1861–65, with account of the various regiments and batteries. 3d edition. New York, 1869.

Croker, Thomas Crofton. Fairy Legends and Traditions of the South of Ireland. 16°. London, 1838.

Crosby, Nathan. Annual Obituary Notices of Eminent Persons who have died in the United States. For 1857. 8°. Boston, 1858.

Cruden, Alexander. Complete Concordance to the Holy Scriptures of the Old and New Testaments. From the 10th London edition. 4°. New York.

Cultivator, The. A Monthly Journal devoted to Agriculture, &c. New Series, vols. 3, 5, 6, 7 and 9. 5v. Albany, 1846–52.

Currier, Edward. Political Text Book ; containing Declaration of Independence, Lives of Signers, Inaugural Addresses and first Annual Messages of the Presidents, from Washington to Tyler, &c. 12°. Worcester, 1842.

Curtis, George Ticknor. Life of Daniel Webster. 2d edition. 2v. New York, 1870.

——— and G. S. Hillard and others. Discussions on the Constitution proposed to the people of Massachusetts, 1853. Boston, 1854.

Curwen, Samuel. Journal and Letters of the late Samuel Curwen, Judge of Admiralty, &c., an American refugee in England, from 1775 to 1784. To which are added biographical notices of many American loyalists and other eminent persons, by G. A. Ward. New York, 1842.

Custis, George Washington Parke. Recollections and Private Memoirs of Washington ; by his adopted son. With a memoir of the author, by his daughter ; and illustrative and explanatory notes, by Benson J. Lossing. New York, 1860.

Cutts, Mary Pepperrell Sparhawk. Life and Times of Hon. William Jarvis, of Weathersfield, Vermont. By his daughter. New York, 1869.

Cyclopædia of Biography : a record of the Lives of Eminent Persons. By Parke Godwin ; with Supplement by George Sheppard. New York, 1867.

Cyclopædia of Commerce and Commercial Navigation. Edited by J. S. Homans and J. S. Homans, Jr. New York, 1859.

Cyclopædia (Standard Library) of Political, Constitutional, Statistical and Forensic Knowledge. 4v. 12°. London, 1853.

Cyclopædias. See American Annual Cyc., Appleton's New American Cyc., Duyckinck's English Cyc., Encyc. Americana, Encyc. Britannica, Kitto, Knight, *et als.*

D.

Dall, Caroline H. The College, the Market and the Court; or Woman's relation to education, labor and law. Boston, 1867.

Dall, William H. Alaska and its Resources. Boston, 1870.

Dallas, George Mifflin. Life and Writings of Alexander James Dallas. Philadelphia, 1871.

Dana, Charles A. See Appleton.

Dana, James Dwight and G. J. Brush. System of Mineralogy. Descriptive Mineralogy, comprising the most recent discoveries. New York, 1870.

——— See under UNITED STATES, p. 64, *ante.*

Dana, Richard Henry, Jr. Two years before the mast; a personal narrative. New edition, with subsequent matter. 12°. Boston, 1869.

Dante, Alighieri. The Divine Comedy. Translated by H. W. Longfellow. 3v. Small 4°. Boston, 1867.

CONTENTS.—V. 1, Inferno.
V. 2, Purgatorio.
V. 3, Paradiso.

——— The New Life. Translated by C. E. Norton. Small 4°. Boston, 1867.

——— See Botta, Vincenzo.

Darley, Felix O. C. Sketches Abroad with Pen and Pencil. New York, 1869.

Dartmoor Prison. See Andrews, Charles.

Dartmouth College. Catalogues of, 1866–67; 1868–69; 1869–70. 3v.

——— Catalogue of Library, 1868.

——— See Chapman, Farrar and Tenney.

Darwin, Charles. The Variation of Animals and Plants under domestication, with preface by Asa Gray. 2v. 12°. New York, 1868.

Davis, Matthew L. Memoirs of Aaron Burr. 2v. New York, 1836–7.

Davis, W. W. H. History of the 104th Pennsylvania Regiment, to Sept. 30, 1864. Philadelphia, 1866.

Dawson, Henry B. Assault on Stony Point by Gen. Anthony Wayne. Sm. 4°. Morrisania, 1863.

——— Sons of Liberty in New York. New York, 1859.

Day Breaking if not the Sun Rising of the Gospel with the Indians in New England. Reprinted [from edition of 1647.] 4°. New York, 1865. [Sabin's Reprints, No. 9.]

Deaf and Dumb. See American Annals; American Asylum.

Dean, Amos. History of Civilization. 7v. Albany, 1868–69.

Dean, John Ward. Memoir of Rev. Nathaniel Ward. Albany, 1868.

Deane, Charles. Biographical Essay on Governor Hutchinson's Historical Publications. 16°. Boston, 1857.

De Costa, B. F. Lake George : its Scenes and Characteristics, with glimpses of the Olden Times. With account of Ticonderoga, &c., and Notes on Lake Champlain. 16°. New York, 1868.

——— Northmen in Maine. Albany, 1870.

——— Pre-Columbian Discovery of America by the Northmen. Albany, 1868.

De Forest, John W. History of the Indians of Connecticut, from the earliest known period to 1850. Hartford, Conn., 1853.

De Kay, James E. See under NEW YORK, Natural History, p. 46, *ante*.

De Lolme, J. L. Constitution of England. London, 1777.

Deming, Leonard. Catalogue of the principal Officers of Vermont, as connected with its political history, from 1778 to 1851. Middlebury, 1851. (4 copies.)

De Peyster, John Watts. Decisive Conflicts of the late civil war, or Slaveholders' Rebellion. No. 3. New York, 1867.

——— History of the Life of Leonard Torstenson. Poughkeepsie, 1855.

——— Personal and Military History of Philip Kearney, Major General U. S. Volunteers. New York, 1869.

De Quincey, Thomas. Writings. 22v. 12°. Boston, 1855–60.

CONTENTS.

AUTOBIOGRAPHIC SKETCHES. The Affliction of Childhood — Dream Echoes on these Experiences— Dream Echoes Fifty Years Later— Introduction to the World of Strife— Infant Literature — The Female Infidel — I am introduced to the Warfare of a Public School — I Enter the World — The Nation of London — Dublin — First Rebellion in Ireland — French Invasion of Ireland, and Second Rebellion — Traveling — My Brother — Premature Manhood. 1v.

AVENGER, THE AND OTHER PAPERS. The Avenger — Additions to the Confessions of an Opium-Eater — De Quincey — Barbara Lewthwaite — The Daughter of Lebanon — The Essenes ; Supplementary — Aelius Lamia—China—Traditions of the Rabbins. 1v.

BIBLIOGRAPHICAL ESSAYS. Shakespeare — Pope — Lamb — Gœthe — Schiller. 1v.

CÆSARS, THE. 1v.

CONFESSIONS OF AN ENGLISH OPIUM EATER. The Confessions — Suspiria de Profundis. 1v.

ESSAYS ON PHILOSOPHICAL WRITERS AND OTHER MEN OF LETTERS. Hamilton—Mackintosh — Kant — Richter — Lessing — Herder — Bentley — Parr. 2v.

ESSAYS ON THE POETS AND OTHER ENGLISH WRITERS. The Poetry of Wordsworth —Percy Bysshe Shelley — John Keats — Oliver Goldsmith — Alexander Pope — William Godwin — John Foster — William Hazlitt – Walter Savage Landor. 1v.

HISTORICAL AND CRITICAL ESSAYS. Philosophy of Roman History — The Essenes — Philosophy of Herodotus — Plato's Republic — Homer and the Homeridæ — Cicero — Style — Rhetoric — Secret Societies. 2v.

LETTERS TO A YOUNG MAN, AND OTHER PAPERS. Letters — Greek Tragedy — Conversation — Language — French and English Manners — Ceylon — California and the Gold Mania — Presence of Mind. 1v.

LITERARY REMINISCENCES. Literary Novitiate—Sir Humphrey Davy—William Godwin—Mrs. Grant — Recollections of Charles Lamb — Walladmor — Coleridge — Wordsworth—Southey —Recollections of Grasmere—The Saracen's Head—Society of the Lakes —Charles Lloyd — Walking Stewart — Edward Irving—Talfourd — The London Magazine—Junius — Clare — Cunningham — Attack by a London Journal — Duelling. 2v.

LOGIC OF POLITICAL ECONOMY, THE, AND OTHER PAPERS. The Logic of Political Economy—Life of Milton—The Suliotes—The Fatal Marksman—The Incognito; or Count Fitz-Hum—The Dice—The King of Hayti. 1v.

MEMORIALS AND OTHER PAPERS. The Orphan Heiress, Laxton—The Orphan Heiress, The Priory—The Pagan oracles—The Revolution of Greece—Klosterheim—The Sphinx's Riddle—Templars' Dialogues. 2v.

MISCELLANEOUS ESSAYS. On the Knocking at the Gate in Macbeth—Murder, considered as one of the Fine Arts—Second Paper on Murder—Joan of Arc—The English Mail-Coach—The Vision of Sudden Death—Dinner, Real and Reputed—Orthographic Mutineers—Sortilege, &c. 1v.

NARRATIVE AND MISCELLANEOUS PAPERS. The Household Wreck—The Spanish Nun—Flight of a Tartar Tribe—System of the Heavens as revealed by the Telescope—Modern Superstition—Coleridge and Opium-Eating—Temperance Movement—On War—The Last Days of Immanuel Kant. 2v.

NOTE-BOOK OF AN ENGLISH OPIUM EATER. The Three Memorable Murders—The True Relations of the Bible to merely Human Science—Schlosser's Literary History of the Eighteenth Century—The Antigone of Sophocles—The Marquis Wellesley—Milton *vs.* Southey and Landor—Falsification of English History—A Peripatetic Philosopher—On Suicide—Superficial Knowledge—English Dictionaries—Dryden's Hexastich—Pope's Retort upon Addison. 1v.

THEOLOGICAL ESSAYS AND OTHER PAPERS. On Christianity as an Organ of Political Movement—Protestantism—On the Supposed Scriptural Expression for Eternity—Judas Iscariot—On Hume's Argument against Miracles—Casuistry—Greece under the Romans—Secession from the Church of Scotland—Toilette of the Hebrew Lady—Milton—Charlemagne—Modern Greece—Lord Carlisle on Pope. 2v.

De Stæl-Holstein, Anne Louise Germaine Necker *Baronne.* Germany, with notes and appendices by O. W. Wright. 2v. 12°. New York, 1864.

De Tocqueville, See Tocqueville.

Deux-Ponts, Willliam de. My Campaigns in America; a journal kept in 1780–81. Translated from the French manuscript by S. A. Green. Boston, 1868.

Dewey, Orville. Problem of Human Destiny, or the end of Providence in the World and Man. New York, 1864.

Dexter, Samuel, Reminiscences of. By Sigma. 18°. Boston, 1864.

Dexter, Timothy. A Pickle for the Knowing Ones. 4th edition. 16°. Newburyport, 1848.

Dibdin, Thomas Frognall. Library Companion; or, the Young Man's Guide, and the Old Man's Comfort, in the choice of a Library. (1v. in 2 parts.) London, 1824.

Dickens, Charles. Works. (Globe edition.) 14v. 16°. New York, 1869.

CONTENTS.

Barnaby Rudge, and vol. 2, Sketches by Boz.
Bleak House.
Christmas Stories, and Pictures from Italy, and American Notes.
David Copperfield.
Dombey and Son.
Little Dorrit.
Martin Chuzzlewit.
Nicholas Nickleby.
Old Curiosity Shop, and vol. 1 Sketches by Boz.
Oliver Twist and Great Expectations.
Our Mutual Friend.
Pickwick Papers.
Tale of Two Cities, Hard Times, and Reprinted Pieces.
Uncommercial Traveller, Master Humphrey's Clock, Additional Christmas Stories, and General Index of Characters, Places, and Sayings.

Dickeson, Montroville Wilson. American Numismatical Manual of the Currency or Money of the Aborigines, and Colonial, State and United States Coins; with notices of each coin or series. 3d edition. 4°. Philadelphia, 1865.

Dictionaries. See Adler, Allen, Allibone, Andrews, Bartlett, Gardner, Gouldman, Haydn, Hole and Wheeler, Liddell, Lippincott, Richardson, Riddle, Scott, Smith, Spiers, Webster, Worcester, and others.

Dillon, John B. History of Indiana. Indianapolis, 1859.

Dimsdale, Thomas J. Vigilantes of Montana. 16°. Virginia City, 1866.

D'Israeli, Isaac. Amenities of Literature; consisting of Sketches and Characters of English literature. 2v. 12°. New York, 1841.

——— Calamities and Quarrels of Authors. With inquiries concerning their characters. Edited by his son, the Right Hon. B. D'Israeli. 2v. 12°. New York, 1868.

——— Curiosities of Literature. With a view of the life and writings of the author, by his son. 4v. Boston, 1860.

——— Literary Characters. or History of Men of Genius; Literary Miscellanies; and an Inquiry into the Character of James I. Edited by his Son. 12°. New York, 1868.

Disturnell, J. Influence of Climate. 4°. New York, 1866.

Dix, John A. Speeches and Occasional Addresses. 2v. New York, 1864.

Dixon, George, Voyage Round the World; particularly to the North-West Coast of America; performed in 1785–88, in the King George and Queen Charlotte, Captains Portlock and Dixon. 4°. London, 1789.

Dixon, William Hepworth. Personal History of Lord Bacon. From unpublished Papers. Boston, 1861.

Documentary History of the Protestant Episcopal Church in the Diocese of Vermont, including the Journal of the Conventions, from 1790 to 1832. Compiled by Rev. C. R. Batchelder, Rev. Geo. B. Manser and Rev. Albert H. Bailey. New York, 1870.

Dodd, William. See Miscellanies.

Dodonæus, Rembertus. Stirpium Historæ pemptades sex sive libri XXX. Folio. Antverpiæ, 1616.

Donne, John. Poetical Works. With a Memoir. 16°. Boston, 1855.

Dorchester. Taxable Valuation of Polls and Estates, and Amount of Tax for 1855. Boston, 1855.

Doton, Hosea. See Vermont Almanac.

Douglas, Stephen Arnold. Addresses in Congress on Occasion of his Death. Washington, 1861.

——— Life; with his most important Speeches and Reports. By a Member of the Western Bar. 12°. New York, 1860.

Douglas, Stephen Arnold. Political Debates with Abraham Lincoln. See Lincoln.

Dow, Lorenzo. [Exemplified Experience, or Lorenzo's Journal.] (*Title page wanting.*) 12°. pp. 704.

Downing, Andrew Jackson. Rural Essays. Edited, with Memoir of Author, by George William Curtis. New York, 1857.

Dowse, Thomas. Catalogue of the Private Library of. Boston, 1870.

Drake, Francis S. Dictionary of American Biography, including men of the time. 4°. Boston, 1872.

Drake, Samuel Gardner. Annals of Witchcraft in New England and elsewhere in the U. S. ; drawn from unpublished and other well authenticated records. Sm. 4°. Boston, 1869. [Woodward's Historical Series No. 8.]

——— Book of the Indians, or Biography and History of the Indians of North America. 7th edition. Boston, 1837.

——— History and Antiquities of Boston, from its settlement in 1630 to 1770. Boston, 1856.

——— History of the Indian Wars in New England to 1677 ; from the original work by Rev. William Hubbard ; with extensive notes. 2v. in 1. Sm. 4°. Roxbury, 1865. [Woodward's Historical Series Nos. 3 and 4.]

——— Result of Researches for Information relative to the Founders of New England. 4°. Boston, 1860.

——— Old Indian Chronicle ; a collection of rare tracts written and published in the times of King Philip's War. With illustrations and notes. Small 4°. Boston, 1867.

——— Particular History of the Five Years French and Indian War in New England and parts adjacent from 1744 to 1749 ; sometimes called Governor Shirley's War. Small 4°. Albany, 1870.

——— Witchcraft Delusion in New England ; its rise, progress and termination, as exhibited by Cotton Mather and Robert Calef, with preface, introduction and notes. 3v. Small 4°. Roxbury, 1866. [Woodward's Historical Series, Nos. 5, 6, 7.]

Draper, John William. History of the American Civil War. 3v. New York, 1867–70.

Drawing Room Portrait Gallery. Engraved on steel by D. J. Pound. With Memoirs. Folio. London,1859.

Dryden, John. Poetical Works. 5v. 16°. Boston, 1859.

Dublin Quarterly Journal of Science. Containing Papers read before the Royal Dublin Society, the Royal Irish Academy, the Geological Society of Dublin and the Natural History Society of Dublin. Edited by Samuel Haughton. Vol. 1—6. Dublin and London, 1861–1866.

Duche, Jacob. Discourses on various subjects. 3d edition. 2v. London, 1790.

Dudley Observatory. Correspondence between Board of Trustees and the Director. Albany, 1858.

——— Defence of Dr. Gould by the Scientific Council. Albany, 1858.

——— The Dudley Observatory and the Scientific Council. Statement of Trustees. Albany, 1858.

——— Reply to the Statement of the Trustees. By B. A. Gould. Albany, 1859.

Duer, William Alexander. Course of Lectures on the Constitutional Jurisprudence of the United States. 2d edition. Boston, 1856.

Duff, Grant. On the Teachings of Richard Cobden, Dec. 20, 1871. 12°. London.

Dunton, John. See Prince Society.

Du Puy, Henry W. Ethan Allen and the Green Mountain Heroes of '76. 12°. Boston, 1853.

Durfee, Calvin. History of Willams College. Boston, 1860.

——— Williams Biographical Annals. Boston, 1871.

Duyckinck, Evert A. and George L. Cyclopædia of American Literature ; embracing personal and critical notices of authors, and selections from their writings ; from the earliest period to the present day ; with portraits, autographs, and other illustrations. 2v. New York, 1856.

——— Supplement to the same ; containing obituaries of authors, notices omitted, &c. New York, 1866.

Dwight, Theodore. History of the Hartford Convention. New York, 1833.

Dyer, David. History of the Albany Penitentiary. Albany, 1867.

Dymond, Jonathan. Inquiry into the accordancy of War with the principles of Christianity. New York, 1847.

E.

Eastman, Charles Gamage. Poems. 16°. Montpelier, 1848.

Eaton, *Gen.* William. Life of; principally collected from his correspondence and other manuscripts. Brookfield, [Mass.,] 1813.

Ecce Deus ; Essays on the Life and Doctrine of Jesus Christ. With controversial notes on "Ecce Homo." 16°. Boston, 1867.

Ecce Deus Homo. See Parsons, T.

Ecce Homo : a Survey of the Life and Work of Jesus Christ. 16°. Boston, 1866.

Eclaireur, The. Vol. 1. Aug., 1853 to July, 1854. Hyde Park, New York, 1853–54.

Edinburgh Annual Register, for 1808–26. 19v. in 24. Edinburgh, 1810–28.

Edwards, Bryan. History, Civil and Commercial, of the British Colonies in the West Indies. 3v. London, 1801.

Edwards, Edward. Lives of the Founders of the British Museum. London, 1870.

——— Memoirs of Libraries; including a hand-book of Library Economy. 2v. London, 1859.

Edwards, Jonathan. Memoirs of the Rev. David Brainerd, Missionary to the Indians, chiefly taken from his own diary. Including his journal incorporated with the rest of his diary by Sereno Edwards Dwight. New Haven, 1822.

Edwards, Ninian W. History of Illinois from 1778 to 1833; and Life and Times of Ninian Edwards. Springfield, 1870.

Elliot, John. Brief Narration of the Progress of the Gospel amongst the Indians in New England in 1670. With notes by W. T. R. Marvin. Boston, 1868. [Reprint from London edition of 1671.]

Elliot, Jonathan. Debates on the adoption of the Federal Constitution; in the several State Conventions and in the General Convention at Philadelphia in 1787. With Journal of the Federal Convention, Martin's Letter, Yates' Minutes, Virginia and Kentucky Resolutions of '98–'99, etc. 5v. Philadelphia, 1859.

Elliott, Charles W. New England History; from the discovery of the continent by the Northmen, A. D. 986, to 1776. 2v. New York, 1857.

Ellis, George E. Life of Sir Benjamin Thompson, Count Rumford. Philadelphia.

Emerson, George B. Report on the Trees and Shrubs growing naturally in the forests of Massachusetts. Boston, 1846.

Emmons, Ebenezer. See under NEW YORK and NORTH CAROLINA, pp. 46 and 47, *ante*.

Encyclopædia Americana; a popular Dictionary of Arts, Sciences, Literature, History, Politics, and Biography. Edited by Francis Lieber, assisted by E. Wigglesworth. 13v. Philadelphia, 1842.

Encyclopædia Britannica; or Dictionary of Arts, Sciences, and General Literature. 8th edition. 21v. 4°. Boston, 1853–60.

——— Index to. 4°. Boston, 1860.

English Cyclopædia. A new Dictionary of Universal Knowledge. Conducted by Charles Knight. Second division; being that of Natural History. 4v. 4°. London, 1854–56.

Epictetus. Works; consisting of his Discourses, the Enchiridion, and Fragments. Translation based on that of Elizabeth Carter, by Thos. Wentworth Higginson. Boston, 1866.

Everett, Edward. Life of George Washington. 12°. New York, 1860.

——— Memorial of, from the city of Boston. Boston, 1865.

——— Orations and Speeches on various occasions. 4v. Boston, 1859–68.

Ewbank, Thomas. Descriptive and Historical Account of Hydraulic and other Machines for Raising Water, ancient and modern. 14th edition. New York, 1858.

Examination of Canon Liddon's Bampton Lectures on the Divinity of our Lord and Saviour Jesus Christ. By a clergyman of the Church of England. 12°. Boston, 1872.

F.

Fair Harvard; a Story of American College Life. 12°. New York, 1869.

Falconer, William. Poetical Works. With a Life by John Milford. 16°. Boston, 1854.

Farmer, John and Moore, J. B. Collections, Topographical, Historical and Biographical relating principally to New Hampshire; and Monthly Literary Journal. V. 1–2. Concord, N. H., 1831–23.

——— Gazetteer of the State of New Hampshire. 12°. Concord, 1823.

Farmer, The Complete Practical. New York, 1835.

Farmer's Herald. [St. Johnsbury.] Vols. 1 and 2; July 8, 1828 to June 30, 1830. (*No.* 1 *of Vol.* 1 *wanting.*)

Farrar, Timothy. Report of the Case of the Trustees of Dartmouth College against William H. Woodward. Portsmouth, [1819.]

Federalist, on the new Constitution, written in 1788 by Mr. Hamilton, Mr. Madison and Mr. Jay; with appendix containing the letters of Pacificus and Helvidius on the Proclamation of Neutrality in 1793. Washington, 1818.

——— The Same. A collection of essays written in favor of the New Constitution, as agreed upon by the Federal Convention, September 17, 1787. Reprinted from the original text, under the editorial supervision of Henry B. Dawson. University edition. New York, 1865.

——— The Same. Edited by John C. Hamilton. Philadelphia, 1871.

Felt, Joseph B. Historical Account of Massachusetts Currency. Boston, 1839.

Felton, C. C. Greece, Ancient and Modern. Lectures delivered before the Lowell Institute. 2v. Boston, 1867.

Ferguson, Adam. History of the Progress and Termination of the Roman Republic. 3v. Philadelphia, 1805.

Ferris, John Alexander. Financial Economy of the United States, Illustrated, and some causes which retard the progress of California demonstrated. 12°. San Francisco, 1867.

Fessenden, Thomas Green. Democracy Unveiled, or Tyranny Stripped of the Garb of Patriotism. By Christopher Caustic. 3d edition. 12°. New York, 1806.

Feuchtwanger, Lewis. Popular Treatise on Gems; a guide for the Lapidary, &c. 12°. New York, 1859.

Fisher, Richard Swainson. See A. J. Johnson.

Fitch, John. Annals of the Army of the Cumberland; with Biographies, Police Record, Anecdotes, Official Reports, &c. 5th edition. Philadelphia, 1864.

Flanders, Henry. Lives and Times of the Chief Justices of the Supreme Court of the United States. John Jay—John Rutledge. Philadelphia, 1858.

——— The same. Second series. William Cushing—Oliver Ellsworth—John Marshall. Philadelphia, 1859.

Fletcher, J. C. See Kidder, D. P.

Fleurieu, Charles Pierre Claret, *Comte de.* Discoveries of the French in 1768 and 1769, to the south east of New Guinea; with the subsequent visits to the same lands by English navigators, who gave them new names. From the French. 4°. London, 1791.

Flint, Austin, [Editor]. Contributions relating to causation and prevention of disease, and to camp diseases. New York, 1867.

Flint, Charles L. Grasses and Forage Plants; their natural history, comparative nutritive value, methods of cultivating, cutting, &c. Boston, 1860.

——— Milch Cows and Dairy Farming; with treatise upon the dairy husbandry of Holland; and Horsfall's system of dairy management. 12°. Boston, 1860.

——— See Agriculture under MASSACHUSETTS, p. 39, *ante*.

Fonvielle, W. de. Thunder and Lightning. Translated and Edited by T. L. Phipson. 16°. New York, 1869.

Force, Peter. Tracts and other Papers relating principally to the origin, settlement, and progress of the Colonies of North America, from the discovery of the country to the year 1776. 4v. Washington, 1836–46.

Forester, Frank. *Pseudonyme.* See Herbert, H. W.

Forster, John. Life and Times of Oliver Goldsmith. 5th edition. 2v. London, 1871.

——— Statesmen of the Commonwealth of England, with a treatise on the popular progress in English History. New York, 1858.

Forsyth, William. Life of Marcus Tullius Cicero. 2v. 12°. New York, 1865.

Foster, John Y. New Jersey and the Rebellion: a history of the services of the troops and people of New Jersey in aid of the Union Cause. Newark, 1868.

Foulke, William Parker. Remarks on Cellular Separation. Philadelphia, 1861.

——— Remarks on the Penal System of Pennsylvania. Philadelphia, 1855.

Fownes, Joseph. See Miscellanies.

Franklin, Benjamin. Works. Containing several political and historical tracts not included in any former edition, and many letters official and private not hitherto published; with notes and life, by Jared Sparks. 10v. Philadelphia.

CONTENTS.

Autobiography; and Life continued, by J. Sparks, v. 1.
Bagatelles, v. 2.
Constitution and Government of Pennsylvania, v. 3.
Correspondence, v. 7-10.
Essays and Tracts, Historical and Political, before the American Revolution, v. 3-4.
Essays on Politics, Commerce, and Political Economy, v. 2.
Essays on Religious and Moral Subjects, and the Economy of Life, v. 2.
Letters and Papers on Electricity, v. 5.
Letters and Papers on Philosophical Subjects, v. 6.
Political Papers during and after the American Revolution, v. 5.

——— Memorial of the Inauguration of the Statue of. Boston, 1857.

Franklin Society of the City of Chicago. Publications. II. Early Newspapers in Illinois. By Henry R. Ross. 4°. Chicago, 1870.

French, B. F. Historical Collections of Louisiana. 3v. New York, 1846–1851.

French, Henry F. Farm Drainage. Principles, processes and effects of draining land with stones, wood, plows, ditches, and especially with tiles. 12°. New York, 1859.

Freneau, Philip. Poems relating to the American Revolution. With Memoir and Notes by Evert A. Duyckinck. New York, 1865.

Frezier, Amadee Francois. Voyage to the South Sea, and along the coasts of Chili and Peru, 1712–14. Sm. 4°. London, 1717.

Frisbie, Barnes. History of Middletown, Vt., in Three Discourses. Rutland, 1867.

Froissart, *Sir* John. Chronicles of England, France, Spain, and the adjoining countries, from the latter part of the Reign of Edward II. to the Coronation of Henry IV. Translated from the French editions, by Thos. Johnes. 2v. London, 1839.

Frothingham, Richard, Jr. History of the Siege of Boston. Boston, 1849.

——— Life and Times of Joseph Warren. Boston, 1865.

Froude, James Anthony. History of England from the fall of Wolsey to the defeat of the Spanish Armada. 12v. 12°. New York, 1867–70.

——— Short Studies on Great Subjects. 12°. New York, 1868.

Furst Fonetic Redur. 16°. Sinsinati, 1851.

Further Queries upon the present state of New English Affairs, by S. E. Reprinted [from edition of 1689 or 1690.] 4°. New York, 1865. [Sabin's Reprints, No. 8.]

G.

Gallup, Joseph A. Outlines of the Institutes of Medicine. 2d edition. 2v. New York, 1845.

Gardner, D. P. Farmer's Dictionary; with Compendium of Practical Farming. 12°. New York, 1854.

Garland, Hugh A. Life of John Randolph of Roanoke. 2v. in 1. New York, 1860.

Garrard, Lewis H. Chambersburg, in the Colony and the Revolution. Philadelphia, 1856.

Gay, John. Poetical Works. With Life of the Author by Dr. Johnson. 2v. 16°. Boston, 1854.

Gayarre, Charles. History of Louisiana. French Domination. 2v. in 1. New York, 1866.

——— The Same. The American Domination. New York, 1866.

Gentleman's Magazine and Historical Chronicle. Vols. 1—103; 1731 to 1833. 103v. in 154. London, 1731–1833.

——— The Same. New Series. Vols. 1—45; 1834–56. 45v. London, 1834–56.

——— The Same. A New Series. Vols. 1—3; 1856–7. 3v. London, 1856–7.

——— General Index to the Same. 1731 to 1818. 5v. London, 1789–1821.

George, N. J. T. Pocket Gazetteer of the State of Vermont. 16°. Haverhill, N. H., 1823.

Gibbon, Edward. History of the Decline and Fall of the Roman Empire. With variorum notes. Edited by an English Churchman. 7v. 12°. London, 1854–66.

——— Miscellaneous Works. With Memoirs by John, *Lord* Sheffield. London, 1837.

Gibbs, George. Memoirs of the Administrations of Washington and John Adams, edited from the papers of Oliver Wolcott. 2v. New York, 1846.

——— See Congress.

Gihon, John H. Governor Geary's Administration in Kansas. 16°. Philadelphia, 1857.

——— See Soule, Frank.

Gilbart, James William. Practical Treatise on Banking. With View of American Banking Systems, &c., by J. S. Homans; and "Money," a Lecture, by H. C. Carey. Philadelphia, 1860.

Gillet, Ransom H. The Federal Government; its Officers and their Duties. 12°. New York, 1871.

Gillett, E. H. Life and Times of John Huss. 3d edition. 2v. Boston, 1871.

Gillies, John, *D. D.* Historical Collections relating to remarkable periods of the Success of the Gospel, and eminent instruments employed in promoting it. 2v. Glasgow, 1754.

Gillies, John, *LL. D.* History of Ancient Greece, its Colonies and Conquests, from the earliest accounts till the Division of the Macedonian Empire in the East. 2v. 4°. London, 1786.

Gilpin, William. Observations made in 1776 on several parts of Great Britain, particularly the Highlands of Scotland. Vol. 1. London, 1789.

——— Remarks on Forest Scenery and other Woodland Views. Volume 2. London, 1791.

Giraldus Cambrensis [or Gerald de Barri.] See Chronicles.

Gladstone, William Ewart. Juventus Mundi; the Gods and Men of the Heroic Age. Boston, 1869.

Godwin, Parke. See Cyclopædia of Biography.

Goethe, Johann Wolfgang Von. Faust. Translated by Bayard Taylor. 2v. Sm. 4°. Boston, 1871.

Goldsmith, Oliver. Poetical Works. With a Life by T. B. Macaulay. 16°. Boston, 1859.

——— See Forster, John.

Gonzalez, Manuel Fernandez y. El Condestable D Alvarado de Luna. Madrid, 1851.

Goodrich, Chauncey. Apocatastasis; or progress backwards. A new "tract for the times." Burlington, 1854.

——— Northern Fruit Culturist, or Farmer's Guide to the Orchard and Fruit Garden. 12°. Burlington, 1850.

Goodrich, S. G. History of the Indians of North and South America. 12°. Boston, 1848.

Gordon, William, *D. D.* History of the Rise, Progress, and Establishment of the Independence of the United States of America. 4v. London, 1788.

Gospels. See Norton, Andrews.

Gouin, L. F. New System of French and English Pronunciation. 16°. Montreal, 1859,

Gould, Augustus A. See under UNITED STATES, p. 64, *ante*.

Gould, Benjamin Apthorp. Investigations in the Military and Anthropological Statistics of American Soldiers. (Sanitary Memoirs of the War of the Rebellion). New York, 1869.

——— See Dudley Observatory.

Gouldman, Francis. Copious Dictionary in three parts. I. English-Latin. II. Latin-English. III. Proper Names and Places, with additions by W. Robertson, and further additions "by the skill and pains of Dr. Scattergood." 4°. Cambridge, 1678.

Graham, J. A. Descriptive sketch of the present state of Vermont. One of the United States of America. London, 1797.

Grahame, James. History of the United States of North America, from the plantation of the British Colonies till their assumption of National Independence. 2v. Philadelphia, 1852.

Grant, Anne, *Mrs.* Essays on the Superstitions of the Highlanders of Scotland. 2v. 16°. London, 1811.

Gray, Alonzo, and C. B. Adams. Elements of Geology. 12°. New York, 1855.

Gray, Asa. See under UNITED STATES, p. 64, *ante.*

Gray, John C. Essays, Agricultural and Literary. 12°. Boston, 1856.

——— See Atlas, p. 119, *ante.*

Gray, Thomas. Poetical Works. Edited, with a Life, by John Mitford. 16°. Boston, 1859.

Greeley, Horace. American Conflict ; a history of the Great Rebellion, 1860–65. Its causes, incidents and results ; exhibiting the drift and progress of American opinion respecting Human Slavery from 1776 to 1865. 2v. Hartford, 1864–66.

——— Recollections of a Busy Life ; including reminiscences of American Politics and Politicians ; with Miscellanies and a discussion on Law of Divorce. New York, 1868.

Green, Samuel Abbott. See Deux-Ponts.

Greene, George Washington. Historical View of the American Revolution. 12°. Boston, 1865.

——— Life of Nathaniel Greene, Major-General in the Army of the Revolution. 3v. New York, 1871.

Greenleaf, Moses. Statistical View of the District of Maine. Boston, 1816.

——— Survey of the State of Maine, in reference to its Geographical features, statistics and political economy. Portland, 1829.

——— Atlas accompanying the above. Folio.

Greenleaf, Simon. Examination of the Testimony of the Four Evangelists, by the rules of evidence administered in courts of justice ; with an account of the trial of Jesus. Boston, 1846.

Green Mountain Poets. Edited by A. J. Sanborn. 12°. Claremont, 1872.

Greenwood, F. W. P. History of King's Chapel in Boston ; the first Episcopal Church in New England. 12°. Boston, 1833.

Greenwood, James. Seven Curses of London. 12°. Boston, 1869.

Greg, William Rathbone. Literary and Social Judgments. London, 1868.

Gregory I. Sancti Gregorii Magni Papæ primi opera. Vols. 3, 4, 5 and 6 in 1. Folio. Parisiis, 1640.

Grosseteste, Robertus, [or Robert Greathead, Bishop of Lincoln.] See Chronicles.

Grote, George. History of Greece. 12v. 12°. New York, 1859.

——— Plato, and the other Companions of Sokrates. 3v. London, 1867.

Guillemin, Amedee. The Sun. From the French by A. L. Phipson. 16°. New York, 1869.

Guizot, Francois Pierre Guillaume. History of Civilization from the Fall of the Roman Empire to the French Revolution. Translated by William Hazlitt. 4v. 12°. New York, 1854.

H.

Hager, Albert D. Report on the Economical Geology, Physical Geography and Scenery of Vermont. Being a portion of the Geological Report made by Professor Hitchcock and his assistants. To which is added a description of some of the Lower Silurian Fossils of Northern Vermont and Canada, by E. Billings. 4°. Claremont, 1862.

——— See under GEOLOGY, p. 72 *ante*.

Hale, Horatio. See under UNITED STATES, p. 63, *ante*.

Hale, Sarah Josepha. Woman's Record, or Sketches of all Distinguished Women, from the Creation to A. D. 1854. With selections from Female Writers. 2d edition. New York, 1860.

Hall, Benjamin H. History of Eastern Vermont, from its earliest settlement to the close of the eighteenth century. With a Biographical Chapter and Appendixes. New York, 1858.

Hall, Hiland. History of Vermont from its discovery to its admission into the Union in 1791. Albany, 1868. (4 copies.)

Hall, James. See under IOWA, NEW YORK and WISCONSIN, pp. 36, 46, 74, *ante*.

Hallam, Henry. Constitutional History of England, from the accession of Henry VII. to the death of George II. 3v. Paris, 1841.

——— Introduction to the Literature of Europe in the fifteenth, sixteenth and seventeenth centuries. 4v. Paris, 1839.

——— View of the state of Europe during the Middle Ages. 2v. Paris, 1840.

Halleck, Henry Wager. Elements of Military Art and Science. 3d edition. 12°. New York, 1862.

Halliwell, James Orchard. Dictionary of Archaic and Provincial Words. 2d edition. 2v. London, 1850.

——— Historical Sketch of the Provincial Dialects of England. Albany, 1863.

Hamilton, Alexander. The Federalist. A Commentary on the Constitution of the United States. Edited by John C. Hamilton. Philadelphia, 1871.

——— See Federalist.

Hamilton, James Alexander. Reminiscences; or, Men and Events, at home and abroad, during three quarters of a century. New York, 1869.

Hamilton, John C. History of the Republic of the United States of America as traced in the writings of Alexander Hamilton and of his contemporaries. Vol. 1-6. New York, 1857-60.

——— See Hamilton, Alexander.

Hardee, Wm. J. Rifle and Infantry Tactics. 2d edition. 24°. Mobile, first year of the Confederacy.

Hardy, Thomas Duffus. See Chronicles.

Harleian Miscellany. Collection, of scarce, curious, and entertaining Pamphlets and Tracts, found in the Earl of Oxford's Library; interspersed with historical, political and critical notes. 12v. London, 1808-11.

Harmon, Daniel Williams. Journal of Voyages and Travels in the Interior of North America. Andover, Ms., 1820.

Harris, James. Hermes; or a Philosophical Inquiry concerning Universal Grammar. London, 1765.

——— Three Treatises. The first concerning Art. The second concerning Music, Painting, and Poetry. The third concerning Happiness. London, 1765.

Harris, Thaddeus William. Report on the Insects of Massachusetts injurious to Vegetation. Cambridge, 1841.

——— Treatise on some of the Insects injurious to Vegetation. Enlarged edition. Edited by C. L. Flint. Boston, 1862.

Hasted, Frederick. Appeals, Letters, Poems, Writings, &c. 1863.

Hawks, Francis L. Narrative of the Expedition of an American Squadron to the China Seas and Japan, performed in the years 1852—1854, under Command of Commodore Perry, by Order of the Government of the United States. New York, 1857.

Hawkesworth, John. Account of the Voyages undertaken by the Order of His Present Majesty, for making Discoveries in the Southern Hemisphere, and successively performed by Commodore Byron, Capt. Wallis, Capt. Cartaret, and Capt. Cooke, in the Dolphin, the Swallow, and the Endeavour. 2v. London, 1775.

Haydn, Joseph. Dictionary of Dates relating to all Ages and Nations; for universal reference. Revised by Benj. Vincent. London, 1860.

Haynes, Gideon. Pictures from Prison Life. Historical Sketch of the Massachusetts State Prison; with Narratives, Incidents and Suggestions on Discipline. 16°. Boston, 1869.

Hayes, Isaac I. Arctic Boat Journey, in the Autumn of 1854. 12°. Boston, 1860.

Heard, Franklin Fiske. Curiosities of the Law Reporters. 16°. Boston, 1871.

Heath, William. Memoirs; containing Anecdotes and Military Events of the American War. Boston, 1798.

Hedge, Frederic Henry. Primeval World of Hebrew Tradition. 16°. Boston, 1870.

——— Reason in Religion. 12°. Boston, 1865.

Heeren, Arnold Hermann Ludwig. History of the Political Systems of Europe and its Colonies. Translated by George Bancroft. 2v. Northampton, 1829.

Helps, Arthur. Spanish Conquest in America, and its Relation to the History of Slavery and to the Government of the Colonies. 4v. New York, 1856—68.

Hemenway, Abby Maria. Vermont Historical Gazetteer; embracing a History of Each Town. Vols. 1—2. Burlington, 1867—71.

——— See Poets and Poetry of Vermont.

Henry III. See Chronicles.

Herbert, George. Poetical Works. With Memoir and Notes by R. A. Wilmott. 16°. Boston, 1855.

Herbert, Henry William. Frank Forester's Horse and Horsemanship of the United States and British Provinces of N. A. 2v. New York, 1857.

Herodotus. History. New English version, edited with copious notes embodying the chief results, historical and ethnographical, obtained in the progress of cuneiform and hieroglyphical discovery. By George Rawlinson, H. Rawlinson and J. G. Wilkinson. 4v. London, 1856–60.

Herrick, Robert. Hesperides, or Works both Human and Divine. 2v. 16°. Boston, 1858.

Higginson, Thomas Wentworth. See Epictetus.

Hildreth, Richard. History of the United States of America; 1497 to 1821. 6v. New York, 1854–55.

Hinman, Royal Ralph. Blue Laws of New Haven Colony, usually called Blue Laws of Connecticut; Quaker Laws of Massachusetts; Blue Laws of New York, Maryland, Virginia and South Carolina. 12°. Hartford, Conn., 1838.

——— Historical Collection, from official records, &c., of the part sustained by Connecticut during the War of the Revolution. Hartford, Conn., 1842.

——— Letters from the English Kings and Queens, Charles II, James II, William and Mary, Anne, George II, etc., to the Governors of the colony of Connecticut, together with answers, from 1635 to 1749; and other ancient, literary and curious documents. 12°. Hartford, Conn., 1836.

Hind, Henry Youle. Narrative of the Canadian Red River Exploring Expedition of 1857, and of the Assiniboine and Saskatchewan Exploring Expedition of 1858. 2v. London, 1860.

Historical Account of all the Voyages Round the World, performed by English Navigators; extracted from the Journals of the Voyagers. 4v. London, 1774–3.

Historical Magazine, and Notes and Queries concerning the Antiquities, History and Biography of America. 10v. Small 4°. Boston, New York and Morrisania, 1857-66.

——— The Same. New Series. Vols. 1—6. Small 4°. Morrisania, 1867-69. (Vol. 4 not complete.)

Historical Register, containing an impartial relation of all Transactions, Foreign and Domestic, for the years 1716-1738. Vols. 1—23. London, 1717-38.

——— For the first seventeen months of the Reign of King George, 1714-15. 2v. London, 1724.

History (a complete) of the late War, or annual register of its rise, progress and events. With additions taken from Capt. John Knox's Historical Journal of the War in America. 6th edition. Dublin, 1774.

Hitchcock, Edward. Religious Truth, illustrated from Science, in Addresses and Sermons on special occasions. 12°. Boston, 1857.

——— See under MASSACHUSETTS and VERMONT, pp. 39 and 72, *ante*.

Hoadly, Charles J. Records of the Colony and Plantation of New Haven from 1638 to 1649. Hartford, 1857.

——— Records of the Colony or Jurisdiction of New Haven, from May, 1653 to the Union. With the New Haven Code of 1656. Hartford, 1858.

——— Public Records of the Colony of Connecticut from 1689 to 1706. Hartford, 1868.

——— Ditto, 1706 to 1716. Hartford, 1870.

Hole, Charles. Brief Biographical Dictionary. With additions and corrections by William Adolphus Wheeler. 12°. New York, 1866.

Holland, Josiah Gilbert. History of Western Massachusetts. 2v. 12°. Springfield, 1855.

Hollis, Thomas. Memoirs. 2v. 4°. London, 1780.

Hollister, Hiel. Pawlet for one hundred years. 12°. Albany, 1867.

Holm, Thomas Campanius. Short Description of Province of New Sweden, now called Pennsylvania. Translated from the Swedish, with notes, by Peter S. Du Ponceau. Philadelphia, 1834.

Holmes, Abiel. Annals of America, from 1492 to 1826. 2d edition. 2v. Cambridge, 1859.

——— Life of Ezra Stiles. Boston, 1798.

Holmes, Nathaniel. Authorship of Shakespeare. 2d edition. 12°. New York, 1867.

Homans, J. Smith and J. S., Jr. See Cyclopædia of Commerce.

Homer. The Iliad. Translated into English blank verse by W. C. Bryant. 2v. Small 4°. Boston, 1870.

Homer. The Iliad and Odyssey translated into English blank verse by W. Cowper. 2v. 4°. London, 1791.

——— The Iliad. Translated by A. Pope. 6v. 12°. London, 1813.

——— The Odyssey. Translated into English blank verse by William Cullen Bryant. 2v. Small 4°. Boston, 1871-72.

Homespun. See Lackland, Thomas.

Hood, Thomas. Poetical Works. With some Account of the Author. 4v. 16°. Boston, 1859.

Hooker, Edward W. Life of Thomas Hooker. Boston, 1870. [Vol. 6, Lives of Chief Fathers of New England.]

Hoopes, Josiah. Book of Evergreens; a Practical Treatise on the Coniferae, or Cone-bearing Plants. 12°. New York, [1868].

Hopkins, John Henry. Essay on Gothic Architecture. With Plans and Drawings for Churches. 4°. Burlington, 1836.

Hopkins, Samuel. The Puritans, or, the Church, Court and Parliament of England, during the Reigns of Edward VI. and Queen Elizabeth. 3v. Boston, 1860—61.

Horne, Thomas Hartwell. Introduction to the Study of Bibliography; to which is prefixed a Memoir on the Public Libraries of the Antients. 2v. London, 1814.

Horton, R. G. Life and Public Services of James Buchanan. 12°. New York, 1856.

Hosack, David. Memoir of De Witt Clinton. 4°. New York, 1829.

Hoskins, Nathan. History of the State of Vermont, from its Discovery and Settlement to 1830. 12°. Vergennes, 1831.

Hospinianus, Rodolphus. Historia Sacramentaria. 2v. 4°. Tiguri, 1598—1602.

Hotten, John Camden. Slang Dictionary; or the Vulgar Words, Street Phrases and Fast Expressions of High and Low Society. London, 1867.

Hough, Franklin B. History of Jefferson County in New York. Albany, 1854.

——— History of Lewis County in New York. Albany, 1860.

——— History of St. Lawrence and Franklin Counties, New York. New York, 1853.

——— Northern Invasion of October, 1780. Small 4°. New York, 1866.

——— Order Book of Capt. Leonard Bleeker, Campaign of 1779. 4°. New York, 1865.

——— Proceedings of a Convention of Delegates from several N. E. States, held at Boston 1780. Small 4°. Albany, 1867.

——— Proclamations for Thanksgiving. Small 4°. Albany, 1858.

Hough, Franklin B. Results of Meteorological Observations made at sundry Academies in the State of New York, from 1826 to 1850. Compiled from thc original returns. 4°. Albany, 1855.

——— Siege of Charleston by the British Fleet and Army, 1780. Small 4°. Albany, 1867.

——— Siege of Savannah by combined American and French Forces, 1779. Small 4°. Albany, 1866.

——— Washingtoniana, or Memorials of the Death of George Washington. 2v. 4°. [Albany,] 1865.

——— See Pouchot.

Houghton, George F. See Butler, James D.

Hoveden, Roger de. See Chronicles.

Hovey, Alvah. Memoir of the Life and Times of Isaac Backus. 12°. Boston, 1859.

Howe, Henry. Historical Collections of Virginia. Charleston, S. C., 1856.

Howe, S. G. See Atlas, p. 119, *ante*.

Howson, John Saul. See Conybeare, W. J.

Hoyt, Epaphras. Antiquarian Researches; a history of the Indian Wars in the country bordering Connecticut River, &c. Greenfield, Mass., 1824.

Hubbard, William. Present State of New England, being a narrative of the troubles with the Indians from 1607 to this present year, 1677. To which is added a discourse about the war with the Pequods in 1637. London, 1677. [Reprint, small 4°. Roxbury, 1865. With Drake's History of the Indian Wars, v. 1, 2].

Hughes, Thomas. Alfred the Great. 12°. Boston, 1871.

——— School Days at Rugby. By an Old Boy. 12°. Boston, 1861.

——— Tom Brown at Oxford; a sequel to School Days at Rugby, 2v. 12°. Boston, 1861.

Humboldt, Alexander Von. Sketch of a Physical Description of the Universe. Translated by E. C. Otte, E. H. Paul and W. S. Dallas. 5v. 12°. New York, 1855-60.

——— Personal Narrative of Travels in the Equinoxial Regions of the New Continent, during the years 1799-1804, by A. de Humboldt and Aime Bonpland; with maps, plans, &c. Translated by Thomasina Ross. 3v. 12°. London, 1852-53.

Hume, David. History of England from the Invasion of Julius Cæsar to the Abdication of James the Second, in 1688. 6v. 12°. New York, 1854-55.

Humphreys, David. Historical Account of the Incorporated Society for the Propagation of the Gospel in Foreign Parts. [Reprint, 1852.]

Hunnewell, James F. The Lands of Scott. 12°. Boston, 1871.

Hunt, Charles Havens. Life of Edward Livingston. With an introduction by George Bancroft. New York, 1864.

Hunter, W. S., Jr. Eastern Townships Scenery. Canada East. 4°. Montreal, 1860.

Hutchinson, Thomas. History of Massachusetts, from 1628 to 1750. 3d edition. 2v. Salem, 1795.

——— The Same, 1750 to 1774. [Being Vol. III.] London, 1828.

——— See Prince Society.

I.

Illustrated Library of Wonders. 13v. 16°. New York, 1869–70.

CONTENTS.

Egypt 3300 years ago.
Glass Making.
Great Hunts.
Human Body.
Intelligence of Animals.
Italian Art.
Sublime in Nature.
Wonders of Architecture.
" " Heat.
" " Optics.
" " Pompeii.
" " the Sun.
Thunder and Lightning.

NOTE.—See under respective authors.

Irving, Washington. Works. 16v. 12°. New York, 1859–60.

CONTENTS.

Alhambra, v. 15.
Astoria, v. 8.
Bonneville's Adventures, v. 10.
Bracebridge Hall, v. 6.
Columbus, Life of, v. 3—5.
Crayon Miscellany, v. 9.
Goldsmith, Oliver, Life of, v. 11.
Granada, Conquest of, v. 14.
Knickerbocker's New York, v. 1.
Mahomet and his Successors, v. 12—13.
Sketch Book, v. 2.
Tales of a Traveller, v. 7.
Wolfert's Roost, v. 16.

——— Life of George Washington. 5v. New York, 1859.

——— Spanish Papers and other Miscellanies. Arranged and edited by Pierre M. Irving. 2v. 12°. New York, 1866.

Items (in Life of an Usher) on Travel, Anecdote and Popular Errors. By one in retirement. 2d edition. 12°. Quebec, 1855.

J.

James, George Payne Rainsford. Life and Adventures of John Marston Hall. 2v. 12°. New York, 1834.

Jameson, *Mrs.* Anna [Murphy]. History of Our Lord as exemplified in Works of Art. Completed by Lady Eastlake. 2d edition. 2v. London, 1865.

——— Legends of the Madonna, as represented in the Fine Arts. Forming the Third Series of Sacred and Legendary Art. 4th edition. London, 1867.

——— Legends of the Monastic Orders, as represented in the Fine Arts. Forming the Second Series of Sacred and Legendary Art. 4th edition. London, 1867.

——— Sacred and Legendary Art. 6th ed. 2v. London, 1870.

Jarves, James Jackson. The Art-Idea: Part Second of Confessions of an Inquirer. 16°. New York, 1864.

Jarvis, Edward. Primary Physiology for Schools. 12°. Philadelphia, 1850.

—— Practical Physiology for the Use of Schools and Families. 12°. Philadelphia, 1848.

Jarvis, William. See Cutts, Mary P. S.

Jay, William, *Judge*. Life of John Jay. With selections from his Correspondence and Miscellaneous Papers. 2v. New York, 1833.

—— Review of the Causes and Consequences of the Mexican War. 2d edition. 12°. Boston, 1849.

Jeaffreson, John Cordy. Book about Lawyers. 12°. New York, 1867.

Jefferson, Thomas. Writings; being his autobiography, correspondence, reports, messages, addresses, and other writings, official and private. Published from the original MSS. deposited in the Department of State. With notes, &c., by the editor, H. A. Washington. 9v. Washington, 1853–54.

CONTENTS.

Autobiography, v. 1.
Anas, The. v. 9.
Biographical Sketches, v. 8.
Correspondence, v. 1—7.
Inaugural Addresses and Messages, v. 8.
Indian Addresses, v. 8.
Manual of Parliamentary Practice, v. 9.
Miscellaneous Papers, v. 9.
Replies to Public Addresses, v. 8.
Virginia, Notes on. v. 8.

Jefferys, Thomas. American Atlas; a Geographical Description of the whole American Continent; and chiefly the British Colonies. Folio. London, 1776.

Johnson, Andrew. Speeches. With Biographical Introduction by Frank Moore. 12°. Boston, 1866.

Johnson, A. J. New Illustrated Family Atlas. By R. S. Fisher. Maps compiled, &c., under supervision of J. H. Colton and A. J. Johnson. Folio. New York, 1865.

Johnston, J. F. W. See Addresses on Agriculture.

Jomini, *Baron* de. The Art of War. Translated from the French by G. H. Mendell and W. P. Craighill. 12°. Philadelphia, 1862.

Josephus, Flavius. Works. With a Life written by himself. Translated from the Greek by William Whiston. 4v. New York, 1869.

Journal des Jesuites, publie d'apres le manuscrit original conserve aux archives du Seminaire de Quebec par M M. les abbes Laverdiere et Casgrain. 4°. Quebec, 1871.

Journal of Prison Discipline and Philanthropy. Vol. 1, 1845; Vol. 5, No. 1, January, 1850; New Series, No. 5, 1866. Philadelphia, 1845—66.

Juan y Santacilia, Jorge, and Antonio de Ulloa. Voyage to South America. Translated from the Spanish, with notes, and an Account of the Brazils, by John Adams. 3d edition. 2v. London, 1772.

Junius. Letters. [Reprinted from Woodfall's edition.] 2v. in 1. New York.

Jussieu, Adrien de. Elements of Botany. Translated with additions by Jas. H. Wilson. 12°. London.

K.

Kalm, Peter. Travels in North America. Translated [from the German translation] by John Reinhold Forster. 2v. London, 1772.

Kay, Joseph. Social Condition and Education of the People in England. 12°. New York, 1863.

Keats, John. Poetical Works, with a Life. 16°. Boston, 1864.

Keltie, John S. See British Dramatists.

Kennedy, John P. Memoirs of the Life of William Wirt, Attorney General of the United States. 2v. Philadelphia, 1849.

——— Mr. Ambrose's Letters on the Rebellion. 16°. New York, 1865.

Kenzie, *Mrs.* John H. Wau-Bun, the "Early Day" in the North-West. New York, 1856.

Kidder, Daniel P. and J. C. Fletcher. Brazil and Brazilians, portrayed in historical and descriptive sketches. Philadelphia, 1857.

Kidder, Frederic. Expeditions of Capt. John Lovewell, and his encounters with the Indians, including account of the Pequauket battle, and reprint of Rev. Thomas Symmes's Sermon. Small 4°. Boston, 1865.

——— History of the Boston Massacre, March 5, 1770. Albany, 1870.

——— History of the first New Hampshire Regiment in the War of the Revolution. Albany, 1868.

——— Military Operations in Eastern Maine and Nova Scotia, during the Revolution. Albany, 1867.

King, John A. See Addresses on Agriculture.

Kinglake, Alexander William. Invasion of the Crimea; its origin and an account of its progress down to the death of Lord Raglan. V. 1—2. 12°. New York, 1868.

Kitto, John. Cyclopædia of Biblical Literature. 3d edition; edited by William Lindsay Alexander. 3v. 4°. Edinburgh, 1869–70.

Kneeland, Samuel. See Annual of Scientific Discovery, of which he was editor for 1867–1869 and assistant editor for 1870.

Knight, Charles. A History of England, 55 B. C. to A. D. 1867. 8v. London.

——— See English Cyclopædia.

Knowles, James D. Memoir of Roger Williams. 12°. Boston, 1834.

Knox, Capt. John. See History of the Late War.

Kohl, Johann George. See Maine Historical Society.

Kossuth, Louis. Life of. With his Public Speeches in the U. S. 12°. New York, 1852.

Kreil, Karl. Jahrbuecher der K. K. Central-Anstalt fuer Meteorologie und Erdmagnetismus. VII. and VIII. Baenden. 2v. 4°. Wien, 1860–61.

L.

Lackland, Thomas. *Pseudonyme?* Homespun; or five and twenty years ago. 12°. New York, 1867.

Lacroix, Jacques Vincent de. Review of the Constitutions of the principal States of Europe and of the United States of America. 2v. London, 1792.

Ladd, William. See Prize Essays.

Lamb, Charles. Works. 5v. 12°. New York, 1868.

CONTENTS,

Adventures of Ulysses, v. 5.
Album Verses, etc., v. 4.
Elia, v. 3.
——Last Essays of, v. 3.
Essays, v. 4.
Essays and Sketches, v. 5.
Final Memorials of Lamb, v. 2.
Letters, v. 1–2–5.
Letters under assumed signatures, v. 4.
Pawnbroker's Daughter, v. 5.
Poems, v. 4–5.
Rosamund Gray, v. 4.
Sketch of Lamb's Life, by T. N. Talfourd, v. 1.
Tales, v. 5.

Lamon, Ward H. Life of Abraham Lincoln; from his birth to his inauguration as President. 4°. Boston, 1872.

Lamont, James. Seasons with the Sea-horses; or sporting adventures in the Northern seas. New York, 1861.

Lander, Richard and John. Journal of an Expedition to explore the course and termination of the Niger. 3v. 16°. London, 1832.

Lanoye, Ferdinand. Rameses the Great; or Egypt 3300 years ago. 16°. New York, 1869.

——— Sublime in Nature, compiled from descriptions of travelers and celebrated writers. 16°. New York, 1870.

Lardner, Henry Dionysius. Popular Lectures on Science and Art. 2v. New York, 1859.

La Rochefoucauld-Liancourt, Francois Alexandre Frederic, *Duc* de. Voyage dans les Etats-Unis D'Amerique, fait en 1795, 1796 et 1797. 8v. 12°. Paris. L'an VII de la republique.

Laverdiere. See Journal des Jesuites, *ante*.

Lavington, Samuel. Sermons and other Discourses. 2d edition. London, 1810.

Lawrence, George N. See Baird, S. F.

Leake, Isaac Q. Memoir of the Life and Times of General John Lamb. Albany, 1857.

Lechford, Thomas. Plain Dealing, or News from New England. 4°. Boston, 1867. [Library of N. E. Hist. No. 4.]

Lecky, William Edward Hartpole. History of European Morals from Augustus to Charlemagne. 2v. New York, 1870.

Lee, Henry. Memoirs of the War in the Southern Department. Washington, 1827.

Lee, John S. Nature and Art in the Old World, or Sketches of Travel. 12°. Cincinnati, 1871.

Lee, Richard Henry, Jr. Memoir of the Life of Richard Henry Lee. With his correspondence. 2v. Philadelphia, 1825.

Lefevre, M. Wonders of Architecture. With a chapter on English Architecture, by R. Donald. 16°. New York, 1870.

Leggett, William. Collection of Political Writings. Selected by Theodore Sedgwick, Jr. 2v. in 1. 12°. New York, 1840.

Legion of Liberty and Force of Truth. 12°. 10th edition. 1847.

Lemay, Leon Pamphile. Essais Poetiques. Quebec, 1865.

Le Moine, J. M. Ornithologie du Canada. 16°. Quebec, 1861.

Le Pileur, A. Wonders of the Human Body. 16°. New York, 1870.

Lewis, *Rev.* John. History of the Life and Sufferings of the Reverend and Learned John Wicliffe, D. D., Warden of Canterbury, &c. London, 1720.

"Liberty"; [or the Liberty Bell.] 12°. 1839.

Library of New England History; containing Mourt's Relation; Church's Philip's War, &c.; and Lechford's Plain Dealing. 4v. 4°. Boston, 1865–67.

Liddell, Henry George. History of Rome from the earlier times to the establishment of the Empire. 12°. New York, 1864.

——— and Robert Scott. Greek-English Lexicon, based on the German work of Francis Passow, with additions by H. Drisler. New York, 1860.

Lidell, John A. Surgical Memoirs of the War of the Rebellion. Edited by Frank Hastings Hamilton. New York, 1870.

Liebig, Justus von. Letters on Modern Agriculture. Edited by John Blyth. 12°. New York, 1859.

Lincoln, Abraham. Life and Speeches. See Bartlett, D. W.

——— Political Debates between Hon. Abraham Lincoln and Hon. S. A. Douglas, in the Campaign of 1858, in Illinois. Columbus, O., 1860.

——— State Papers. Speeches, etc. See Raymond, H. J.

Lippincott's Complete Pronouncing Gazetteer; or, Geographical Dictionary of the World. Edited by J. Thomas, T. Baldwin, etc. 2v. Philadelphia, 1859.

Lippincott's Universal Pronouncing Dictionary of Biography and Mythology. By J. Thomas, M. D. 2v. Philadelphia, 1870.

Low, David. Domesticated Animals of the British Islands, London, 1845.

Lowell, James Russell. Poems. 7th edition. 2v. 12°. Boston, 1857.

Lowell, John Amory. Reply to a Pamphlet recently circulated by Mr. Edward Brooks. Boston, 1848.

Lowndes, William Thomas. Bibliographer's Manual of English Literature. New edition, revised and enlarged by Henry G. Bohn. 10 parts and appendix. 11v. 12°. London, 1857—64.

Lowth, Robert. See Miscellanies.

L'Ouverture, Toussaint. A Biography and Autobiography. The Biography by J. R. Beard, revised by James Redpath. 12°. Boston, 1863.

Lossing, Benson J. History of the United States. New York, 1860.

——— Pictorial Field-Book of the Revolution. 2v. New York, 1859.

——— Pictorial Field-Book of the War of 1812. New York, 1869.

Lodge, G. Henry. See Winckelmann.

Long, Moses. Historical Shetches of the Town of Warren, N. H. Reprinted. 1870.

Longfellow, Henry Wadsworth. Golden Legend. 12°. Boston, 1852.

New England Tragedies. 12°. Boston, 1868.

——— Poems. New edition. 2v. 12°. Boston, 1860.

——— See Dante.

Long Island Historical Society. 4th Annual Report. Brooklyn, 1867.

Lord, John. Old Roman World : the Grandeur and Failure of its Civilization. 2d edition. New York, 1868.

Loring, James Spear. The Hundred Boston Orators, appointed by the Municipal Authorities and other Public Bodies, from 1770 to 1852. Boston, 1855.

Lydius, John Henry. See Some Reflections, *post.*

Lyell, *Sir* Charles. Manual of Elementary Geology. New York, 1860.

Lyman, Theodore, 3d. Papers relating to the Garrison Mob. Boston, 1870.

M.

Macaulay, Thomas Babington, *Lord.* Critical and Miscellaneous Essays. 6v. 12°. New York, 1860—57. (Vols. 2 and 3 *wanting*).

——— History of England, from the Accession of James I. 5v. 12°. New York, 1853—61.

——— Speeches and Poems; with Report and Notes on the Indian Penal Code. 2v. 12°. New York, 1867.

McClellan, George B. Regulations and Instructions for the Field Service of the U. S. Cavalry in Time of War. 12°. Philadelphia, 1861.

McClure, A. W. Life of John Cotton. Boston, 1870. [Vol. 1, Lives of Chief Fathers of N. E.]

——— Lives of John Wilson, John Norton and John Davenport. Boston, 1870. [Vol. 2, Lives of Chief Fathers of N. E.]

McCrie, Thomas. Life of John Knox; with additions by Andrew Crichton. 12°. London, 1847.

Mackenzie, Alexander. Voyages from Montreal, on the River St. Lawrence, through the Continent of North America, to the Frozen and Pacific Oceans, in the years 1789 and 1793. With an account of the Fur Trade. 4°. London, 1801.

Mackenzie, William L. Lives and Opinions of Benj. Franklin Butler and Jesse Hoyt. Boston, 1845.

Mackintosh, Robert James. Memoirs of the Life of the Right Hon. Sir James Mackintosh. 2v. Boston, 1853.

McPherson, Edward. Political History of the United States of America during the Great Rebellion, from November 6, 1860, to July 4, 1864. Washington, 1864.

McRee, Griffith J. Life and Correspondence of James Iredell. 2v. New York, 1857-8.

Madden, Frederic W. History of Jewish Coinage and Money, in the Old and New Testaments. London, 1864.

Madison, James. Letters and other Writings. 1769—1836. Published by order of Congress. 4v. Philadelphia, 1865.

——— Papers, purchased by order of Congress; being his Correspondence and Reports of Debates during the Congress of the Confederation, and his Reports of Debates in the Federal Convention. Published under superintendence of H. D. Gilpin. 3v. Washington, 1840.

Mahan, Dennis H. Elementary Course of Civil Engineering, for the use of Cadets of the U. S. Military Academy. New York, 1868.

Maine Historical Society. Collections. Vol. 1 (reprint), Portland, 1865. Vols. 2—6, Portland, 1847—59.

——— The same, Second Series. Documentary History of the State of Maine, edited by William Willis. Vol. 1, containing a history of the Discovery of Maine. By J. G. Kohl. With appendix on Voyages of the Cabots, by M. d'Avezac. Portland, 1869.

Maison Rustique du XIX. Siecle. Vols. 4 and 5. Paris, 1849.

Mallet, Paul Henri. Northern Antiquities, or Historical Account of the manners, customs, religion, laws, expeditions and language of the ancient Scandinavians. Translated by Bishop Percy. New edition. Edited by I. A. Blackwell. 12°. London, 1859.

Mann, Heman. The Female Review. Life of Deborah Sampson, the Female Soldier in the War of the Revolution. [Reprint, with notes, &c., by J. A. Vinton.] 4°. Boston, 1866.

Mann, Mary. Life of Horace Mann, by his wife. Boston, 1865.

Mansfield, Edward D. Life of General Winfield Scott. 12°. New York, 1846.

Mantell, Gideon Algernon. Wonders of Geology. 7th edition. Revised and augmented by T. Rupert Jones. 2v. 12°. London, 1857–58.

Marana, Giovanni Paolo. The eight volumes of Letters writ by a Turkish Spy, who had lived five-and-forty years undiscover'd at Paris, giving an impartial Account to the Divan at Constantinople of the most remarkable transactions of Europe, and discovering intrigues and secrets of Christian Courts, (especially of France.) Continued from 1637 to 1682. 8v. 16°. London, 1753.

Mariners' Dictionary, or American Seaman's Vocabulary of Technical Terms and Sea Phrases. 16°. Washington, 1805.

Marion, F. Wonders of Optics. Translated and edited by Charles W. Quin. 16°. New York, 1869.

Marmont, *Marshal.* Spirit of Military Institutions, or Essential Principles of the Art of War. With notes by Henry Coppee. 12°. Philadelphia, 1862.

Marsh, George P. The Camel; his organization, habits and uses, considered with reference to his introduction into the United States. 12°. Boston, 1856.

——— Lectures on the English Language. New York, 1860.

——— Man and Nature; or Physical Geography as modified by Human Action. New York, 1864.

——— Origin and History of the English Language, and of the early literature it embodies. New York, 1867.

Marsh, *Mrs.* George P. Wolfe of the Knoll, and other Poems. 12°. New York, 1860.

Marsh, James. Remains. 3d edition. Boston, 1852.

CONTENTS.

Discourses.
Letter on the Will.
Memoir of Marsh, by J. Torrey.
Outlines of a Philosophical Arrangement.
Remarks on Physiology.
Remarks on Psychology.
Tract on Eloquence,
Tract on Evangelism.

NOTE. See Coleridge, S. T.

Marshall, Humphrey. History of Kentucky. 2v. Frankfort, 1824.

Marshall, John, *Chief Justice.* Life of George Washington. Compiled under the inspection of the Hon. Bushrod Washington, from original papers. 5v. Philadelphia, 1804–1807.

Martin, Luther. See Yates, Robert.

Martin, Robert Montgomery. Hudson's Bay Territories and Vancouver's Island, with an exposition of the chartered rights, conduct and policy of the Hudson's Bay Corporation. London, 1849.

Martineau, Harriet. Biographical Sketches. 12°. New York, 1869.

——— History of the Peace; being a history of England from 1816 to 1854. With an introduction, 1800 to 1815. 4v. Boston, 1865–66.

Marvell, Andrew. Poetical Works. With a Memoir of the Author. 16°. Boston, 1857.

Massachusetts General Hospital. Report of Board of Trustees, January, 1851. Boston, 1851.

Massachusetts Historical Society. Collections. 41v. 1st series, 10v. Boston, 1792–1846. 2d series, 10v. Boston, 1814–46. 3d series, 10v. Boston, 1830–49. 4th series, 10v. Boston, 1852–71. 5th series, V. 1. Boston, 1871.

——— Proceedings, 1855 to 1870. 9v. Boston, 1859–71.

——— Lectures delivered before the Lowell Institute, on Early History of Massachusetts. Boston, 1869.

——— Library. Catalogue. Boston, 1811.

——— The Same. 2v. Boston, 1859–60.

Mason, John. Brief History of the Pequot War. With introduction and notes by Thomas Prince. Reprinted. New York, 1869. [Sabin's Reprints No. 7.]

Masson, David. Life of John Milton; narrated in connection with the political, ecclesiastical and literary history of his time. V. 1-2. Boston, 1859 and London, 1871.

Mather, Cotton. Magnalia Christi Americana; or, the Ecclesiastical History of New England, from its first planting in the year 1620, unto the year of our Lord 1698. With notes, by Thos. Robbins, and translations of the Hebrew, Greek, and Latin quotations, by L. F. Robinson. 2v. Hartford, 1855—53.

——— Wonders of the Invisible World; being an account of the tryals of several witches lately executed in New-England. With observations upon the Nature, Number and Operations of the Devils: narrative of outrage committed by a knot of witches in Swede-Land; councels; brief discourse. London, 1693. [Reprint. Small 4°. Roxbury, 1866. With Drake's Witchcraft Delusion in N. E., v. 1.]

Mather, Increase. Remarkable Providences illustrative of the earlier days of American colonization: with preface by George Offor. 12°. London, 1856.

Mather, William W. See Natural History under NEW YORK, p. 46, *ante.*

Matthews, Lyman. History of the Town of Cornwall, Vermont. Middlebury, Vt., 1862.

Maury, Matthew Fontaine. Physical Geography of the Sea. New edition. New York, 1859.

Maury, Sarah Mytton. Statesmen of America in 1846. London, 1847.

May, Thomas Erskine. Constitutional History of England since the Accession of George III. 1760—1860. 2v. Boston, 1863.

Mayer, Brantz. Mexico ; Aztec, Spanish and Republican. 2v. in 1. Hartford, 1851.

—— Tah-Gah-Jute ; or Logan and Cresap. Albany, 1867.

Mayhew, Ira. Popular Education : for use of parents, teachers and young persons. 3d edition. 12°. New York, 1855.

Meares, John. Voyages made in the years 1788 and 1789, from China to the North-West Coast of America. With a narrative of a voyage in 1786, from Bengal, in the ship Nootka, &c. With observations on the probable existence of a North-West Passage. 4°. London. 1790.

Menault, Ernest. Intelligence of Animals, with illustrative anecdotes. 16°. New York, 1870.

Mercantile Library of the City of New York. 1st and 2d Supplement to Catalogue of Books, 1866 to 1872. New York, 1869–72.

—— Constitution. 16°. New York, 1870.

—— Annual Reports, 1863–4 ; 1867 ; 1869–70.

Merivale, Charles. Conversion of the Northern Nations. New York, 1866.

—— Conversion of the Roman Empire. New York, 1865.

—— History of the Romans under the Empire. 7v. New York, 1863–65.

Metropolitan Board of Health for the State of New York. 3d annual report, 1868.

Meunier, Victor. Adventures on the Great Hunting Grounds of the World. 16°. New York, 1870.

Middletown. See Frisbie, Barnes.

Military Gazette. Devoted to Military Literature. Jan. 1, 1860 to April 1, 1861. Vol. 3 and first 7 Nos. of Vol. 4. New York, 1860–61.

Mill, John Stuart. Dissertations and Discussions : Political, Philosophical and Historical. 3v. Boston, 1865.

—— Examination of Sir William Hamilton's Philosophy, and of the principal philosophical questions discussed in his writings. 2v. Boston, 1865.

—— On Liberty. 12°, Boston, 1864.

—— Principles of Political Economy ; with some of their applications to social philosophy. 2v. New York, 1864.

—— Subjection of Women. 12°. New York, 1869.

Miller, Hugh. Cruise of the Betsey; a ramble among the fossiliferous deposits of the Hebrides. With rambles of a geologist over the fossiliferous deposits of Scotland. 12°. Boston, 1859.

——— First Impressions of England and its People. 12°. Boston, 1859.

——— Foot-Prints of the Creator; or the Asterolepis of Stromness. 12°. Boston, 1860.

——— My Schools and Schoolmasters; or the story of my education. 12°. Boston, 1860.

——— Old Red Sandstone; or new walks in an old field. 12°. Boston, 1860.

——— Popular Geology; a series of lectures. With introduction by Mrs. Miller. 12°. Boston, 1860.

——— Testimony of the Rocks; or geology in its bearing on the two theologies, natural and revealed. 12°. Boston, 1859.

Mills, Frederick James. Life of John Carter. 12°. New York, 1868.

Milman, Henry Hart. History of Latin Christianity; including that of the Popes to the pontificate of Nicholas V. 8v. New York, 1859–61.

——— History of the Jews. 3v. 12°. New York, 1867.

Milton, John. Poetical Works. With Life of the Author, by John Mitford. 3v. 16°. Boston, 1859. (Vol. 1 *wanting.*)

——— Prose Works. 5v. 12°. London, 1853.

CONTENTS.

Accedence commencing Grammar, v. 5.
Animadversions upon the Remonstrants' Defence against Smectymnuus, v. 3.
Apology for Smectymnuus, v. 3,
Areopagitica. a speech for the Liberty of unlicensed Printing, v. 2.
Biographical Introduction, v. 1.
Brief notes on a Sermon, titled, "The fear of God and the King," v. 2.
Colasterion, v. 3.
Declaration for the election of John III., King of Poland, v. 3.
Defence of the People of England, in answer to Salmasius, v. 1.
Doctrine and Discipline of Divorce, v. 3.
Education, v. 3.
Eikonoclastes, v. 1.
Familiar Letters, v. 3.
History of Britain to the Norman Conquest, v. 5.
History of Moscovia, v. 5.
Judgment of Martin Bucer concerning Divorce, v. 3.
Letter to a Friend concerning Ruptures of the Commonwealth, v. 2.
Letter to General Monk, v. 2.
Letters of State to Sovereign Princes and Republics of Europe, v. 2.
Likeliest Means to remove Hirelings out of the Church, v. 3.
Manifesto of the Lord Protector against the Spaniards, v. 2.
Observations on Ormond's Peace, v. 2.
Posthumous Treatise on the Christian Doctrine, v. 4 and 5.
Prelatical Episcopacy, v. 2.
Reason of Church Government argued against Prelaty, v. 2.
Reformation in England. v. 2.
Tenure of Kings and Magistrates, v. 2.
Tetrachordon, v. 3,
Treatise of Civil Power in Ecclesiastical Causes, v. 2.
True Religion, Heresy, Schism, Toleration, against the growth of Popery, v. 2.
Way to establish a Free Commonwealth, v. 2.

Minnesota Historical Society. Collections for the year 1864. St. Paul, 1865.

Minot, George Richards. Continuation of [Hutchinson's] History of Massachusetts, 1748 to 1765. 2v. in 1. Boston, 1798–1803.

——— History of the Insurrections in Massachusetts in 1786, and the Rebellion consequent thereon. 2d edition. Boston, 1810.

Miscellanies. [Bound Pamphlets.] 6v.

CONTENTS.

VOL. I. 1. [John Brown, D. D.] Letter to the Rev. Dr. Lowth. Newcastle upon Tyne, 1766.

2. Letter from the Lord Bishop of London, [Thomas Sherlock,] on occasion of the late Earthquake. London, 1750.

3. William Dodd. Sermon preached April 26, 1759. 2d Edition. London.

4. Hard Case of a Country Vicar in respect of Small Tythes. (Title page *wanting*.)

5. Address relating to Balls. London, 1761.

6. Gen. John Burgoyne. Substance of [his] Speeches, 26th and 28th May, 1778, with Gen. Washington's Letter. London, 1778.

VOL. II. 1. Robert Lowth. Letter to Author of Divine Legation of Moses demonstrated. 4th edition. London, 1766.

2. Thomas Patten. Sufficiency of the External Evidence of the Gospel. Oxford, 1757.

3. State of the British and French Colonies in North America. London, 1755.

VOL. III. 1. Richard Price. Discourse on the Love of our Country; with Appendix. London, 1790.

2. Joseph Smith. Letter to William Pitt on Toleration and Church Establishment. London, 1787.

3. Joseph Bealey. Observations upon Mr. Owen's Sermon. Warrington, 1790

4. Danger of Repealing the Test Act London, 1790.

5. Episcopal Opinions on the Test and Corporation Acts delivered in 1718, London, 1790.

VOL. IV. 1. Enthusiasm of Methodists and Papists Compared. Parts 1 and 2. London, 1749.

2. Charge to the Clergy in 1741 by Richard, Lord Bishop of Lichfield. London, 1741.

VOL. V. 1. Sackville, Lord George. Proceedings of a General Court-Martial upon trial of. London, 1760.

2. Joseph Fownes. Enquiry into the Principles of Toleration. 3d edition London, 1790.

VOL. VI. 1. Evidence of the Resurrection cleared. London, 1744.

2. Nature of Patronage and duty of Patrons. London, 1735.

3. Daniel Waterland. Discourse of Fundamentals. Cambridge, 1735.

Missionary Voyage. See William Wilson.

Mitchell, S. Augustus. New Universal Atlas. Folio. Philadelphia, 1848.

Mitford, Mary Russell. Life. Told by herself in Letters to her Friends. Edited by A. G. K. L'Estrange. 2v. 12°. New York, 1870.

Monnier, Marc. Wonders of Pompeii. 16°. New York, 1870.

Montaigne, Michel de. Works; comprising his essays, journey into Italy, and letters, with notes from all the commentators, &c. By W. Hazlitt. New edition, edited by O. W. Wight. 4v. 12°. New York, 1859.

CONTENTS.

Bibliographical Notice of the Editions of Montaigne's Essays, by Dr. Payen, v. 3.

Biography of Montaigne, by B. St. John, v. 4.

Diary of a Journey through Switzerland, Germany and Italy, v. 4.

Essays, v. 1—3.

Letters, v, 4.

Life of Montaigne, v. 1.

Montgomery, James. Poetical Works. With a Memoir of the Author. 5v. 16°. Boston, 1860.

Montpelier, History of. See D. P. Thompson.

Monthly Magazine ; or, British Register, 1796—1804. Vols. 1—17. 17v. London, 1796—1804.

Moore, Frank. American Eloquence. Speeches and Addresses by the most Eminent Orators of America. 2v. New York, 1859.

——— Diary of the American Revolution, from newspapers and original documents. 2v. New York, 1863.

——— See Andrew Johnson, and Rebellion Record.

Moore, George Henry. "Mr. Lee's Plan—March 29, 1777." The Treason of Charles Lee, Major-General, Second in Command in the American Army of the Revolution. New York, 1860.

——— Notes on the History of Slavery in Massachusetts. New York, 1866.

Moore, Hugh. Memoir of Col. Ethan Allen. 12°. Plattsburgh, 1834.

Moore, Thomas. Epistles, Odes, and other Poems. 4°. London, 1806.

——— Poetical Works ; collected by himself. With a Memoir. 6v. 16°. Boston, 1856.

Moravian Historical Society. See Reichel, W. J.

Morgan, Lewis H. League of the Ho-De-No-Sau-Nee, or Iroquois. Rochester, 1851.

Morse, Jedidiah. The American Universal Geography. Part I. 3d edition. Boston, 1796.

——— and Parish, Elijah. Compendious History of New England. 2d edition. 16°. Newburyport, 1809.

Morton, Nathaniel. New England's Memorial ; or, the most memorable Passages of the Providence of God manifested to the Planters of New England ; with special reference to New Plymouth. 6th edition. With Governor Bradford's History and Dialogue, Portions of Prince's Chronology, etc. Boston, 1855.

Mosheim, Johann Lorenz von. Commentaries on the Affairs of the Christians before the time of Constantine the Great. Vol. 1, translated by R. S. Vidal ; Vol. 2, by James Murdoch. 2v. New York, 1853.

——— Institutes of Ecclesiastical History, Ancient and Modern. Translated by James Murdoch. 3v. New York, 1858.

Motley, John Lothrop. History of the United Netherlands from the Death of William the Silent to the Twelve Years, Truce, 1709. 4v. New York, 1861—68.

——— Rise of the Dutch Republic. 3v. New York, 1859.

Mourt, G. [Geo. Morton ?] Relation or Journal of the Plantation at Plymouth. 4°. Boston, 1865. [Lib. of N. E. Hist., No. 1.]

Mueller, Max. Chips from a German Workshop. 2v. 12°. New York, 1869.

Mulford, E. The Nation: the Foundations of Civil Order and Political Life in the United States. New York, 1870.

Murray, J. B. C. History of Usury from the Earliest Period to the Present Time; with Statement of Principles concerning Conflict of and Examination into Policy of Laws on Usury. Philadelphia, 1866.

N.

Napier, Mark. Life and Times of Montrose. 12°. Edinburgh, 1840.

Napoleon III. History of Julius Cæsar. 2v. New York, 1865–66.

Nashua. Charter and Ordinances, etc., with City Government for 1862–3. Nashua, 1862.

Nashville City and Business Directory for 1860–61. Vol. 5. Nashville, 1860.

Nason, Elias. Sir Charles Henry Frankland, Baronet; or Boston in the Colonial Times. Albany, 1865.

National Almanac and Annual Record for the years 1863 and 1864. 2v. 12°. Philadelphia, 1863–64.

National Insurance Convention of the United States. Official Report of the Proceedings, October, 1871. Compiled by Henry S. Olcott. New York, 1872.

National Police Convention. Official Proceedings, at Saint Louis, October, 1871. St. Louis, [1871.]

National Popular Education. 1st to 7th Annual Reports of the General Agent of the Board, 1848 to 1854. [Bound in 1v.]

Neal, Daniel. History of New England to the year 1700. 2v. 12°. London, 1720.

——— History of the Puritans, or Protestant Non-Conformists, 1517 to 1688. With notes by John O. Choules. 2v. New York, 1871–63.

Nettle, Richard. Salmon Fisheries of the St. Lawrence and its Tributaries. 12°. Montreal, 1857.

New American Cyclopædia. See Appleton.

New England Historical and Genealogical Register, for the years 1847–71. William Cogswell, Samuel G. Drake and others, editors. V. 1—25. Boston, 1847–71. (Vols. 16, 17 and 18 *wanting.*)

New England's First Fruits. Reprinted [from edition of 1643.] 4°. New York. 1865. [Sabin's Reprints, No. 7.]

New Hampshire as it is. A Historical Sketch, Gazetteer and General View of New Hampshire. Compiled by Edwin A. Charlton. Claremont, 1856.

New Hampshire. Festival of the Sons of, with Speeches. Boston, 1850.

——— Second Festival. Boston, 1854.

——— Gazetteer. See Farmer, John.

——— Historical Society. Collections. 8v. Concord, 1824–66.

——— Provincial Papers. Documents and Records Relating to the Province of New Hampshire from 1623 to 1722. Compiled and edited by Nathaniel Bouton. 3v. Manchester, 1867–69.

New Orleans. Laws and General Ordinances. Revised by Henry J. Leovy. New Orleans, 1857.

Newport. City Documents for the Municipal year 1867–68. Newport, 1868.

Newspapers. See Bellows Falls Intelligencer; California Newspapers; Cultivator; Eclaireur; Farmer's Herald; Military Gazette; Niles' Register; North Star; Port Folio; Reporter; Spooner's Vermont Journal, [with Vermont Journal]; Vermont Intelligencer; Vermont Journal; Vermont Mercury; Vermont Republican; Vermont Stock Journal; Weekly Wanderer; Windsor Federal Gazette; Wisconsin Farmer; Woodstock Observer.

New York City. Manual. See Valentine, D. T.

——— Report on Central Park. See Viele, E. T.

——— 14th Annual Report of the Board of Education, 1856.

New York County. Statistics of Population of the City and County of New York, 1865. Prepared by F. B. Hough. New York, 1866.

New York Society Library. Alphabetical and Analytical Catalogue. New York, 1850.

Nichols, W. R. See Annual of Scientific Discovery, of which he was an assistant editor in 1870.

Niles' [Weekly and National] Register. Vols. 8; 10 to 12; 16; 17; 19 to 30; 39; 41; 43; 49; 51 to 54; 56 to 63; 65; 69. 36v. Baltimore, 1815–46.

——— General Index to the first 12 volumes, 1811 to 1817. Baltimore, 1818.

Nisbet, James. See Soule, Frank.

North American Review. Vols. 1 to 113. Boston, 1815–71.

North, James W. History of Augusta, with notices of the Plymouth Company and Settlements on the Kennebec. Augusta, 1870.

North Star. [Danville. By Ebenezer Eaton.] Vols. 11 and 12, (Jan. 25, 1817 to Jan. 22, 1819); and Vols. 15 and 16, (Jan. 25, 1821 to Jan. 9, 1823.)

Norton, Andrews. Internal Evidences of the Genuineness of the Gospels; with particular reference to Strauss' "Life of Jesus." Boston, 1856.

——— Translation of the Gospels; with notes. 2v. Boston, 1856.

Norton, Charles Eliot. See Dante.

Notes upon Canada and the United States; from 1832 to 1840. By a Traveller. (This book contains also addenda to the above, and a Manual of Orthoepy. With notes upon the origin and abuse of words, printed in 1833.) 2d edition. 12°. Toronto, 1840.

Noyes, George Raphall. New Translation of the Hebrew Prophets. With introduction and notes. 3d edition. 2v. 12°. Boston, 1866.

——— New Translation of Job, Ecclesiastes and the Canticles; wiih introduction and notes. 3d edition. 12°. Boston, 1867.

——— New Translation of the Book of Psalms and of the Proverbs; with introductions and notes. 3d edition. 12°. 1867.

Noyes, John Humphrey. History of American Socialisms. Philadelphia, 1870.

O.

Official Reports of Battles, as published by order of the Confederate Congress at Richmond. New York, 1863.

Ohio Historical Society. Transactions of the Historical and Philosophical Society of Ohio. V. 1. Cincinnati, 1839.

Olcott, Henry S. See National Insurance Convention.

Old and New. Vols. 1 to 4. Boston, 1870–1.

Olin, Stephen. Travels in Egypt, Arabia Petræa and the Holy Land. 2v. 12°. New York, 1854. (Vol. 1 *missing.*)

Oliver, Peter. The Puritan Commonwealth; an historical review of the Puritan Government of Massachusetts. Boston, 1856.

Olmsted, Frederick Law. Walks and Talks of an American Farmer in England. 12°. Columbus, 1859.

Onderdonk, Henry, Jr. Documents and Letters intended to illustrate the Revolutionary Incidents of Queens County. 12°. New York, 1846.

Ormsby, Robert McKinley. History of the Whig Party. 12°. Boston, 1860.

Ormsby, W. L. Description of Bank Note Engraving. 4°. New York, 1852.

Orthoepy. Manual of. See Notes upon Canada, &c.

Osborn, A. Field Notes of Geology. 12°. New York, 1858.

Our Country. See Phelps, A. L.

Overman, Frederick. Treatise on Metallurgy; comprising mining and metallurgical operations, with a description of furnaces, &c. New York, 1855.

P.

Paine, Martyn. Discourse on the Soul and Instinct, physiologically distinguished from materialism. 12°. New York, 1849.

——— Institutes of Medicine. New York, 1847.

——— The Same. 8th edition. New York, 1867.

——— Medical and Physiological Commentaries. 3v. New York, 1840–44.

Paine, Robert Troup. Memoir of Robert Troup Paine, by his parents. 4°. New York, 1852.

Palfrey, John Gorham. History of New England during the Stuart Dynasty. 3v. Boston, 1859–64.

Palgrave, Francis Turner. Essays on Art. 12°. New York, 1867.

Palmer, Charles John. History and Illustrations of a House in the Elizabethan Style in Yarmouth. Folio. London, 1838.

Palmer, Edwin F. The Second Brigade; or Camp Life. 12°. Montpelier, 1864.

Palmer, Peter S. History of Lake Champlain from the first exploration in 1609 to 1814. Albany, 1866.

Pamphlets. Fifteen Cases Pamphlets. See indices to the same.

Panoplist, The, and Missionary Herald. Vols. 1—16. 16v. Boston, 1805—20.

Parish, Elijah. See Morse, Jedidiah.

Parker, Theodore. Historic Americans. 12°. Boston, 1871.

Parkman, Francis. History of the Conspiracy of Pontiac, and the War of the North American Tribes against the English Colonies after the Conquest of Canada. Boston, 1863.

——— Pioneers of France in the New World. Boston, 1865.

——— Jesuits in North America in the Seventeenth Century. Boston, 1867.

——— Discovery of the Great West. Boston, 1870.

Parnell, Thomas. Poetical Works of. With a Life by Oliver Goldsmith. [See Tickell.] 16°. Boston, 1854.

Parsons, Theophilus. Deus Homo; God-Man. 2d edition. Chicago, 1867.

——— Essays. 3d series. 12°. Boston, 1862.

——— Memoir of Theophilus Parsons, Chief Justice of the Supreme Judicial Court of Massachusetts. By his son. 12°. Boston, 1859.

Parton, James. Famous Americans of Recent Times. Boston, 1867.

——— General Butler in New Orleans; history of the Department of the Gulf in 1862. New York, 1864.

Parton, James. Life and Times of Aaron Burr. 3d edition. New York, 1860.

——— Life of Andrew Jackson. 3v. New York, 1860.

——— Life of Benjamin Franklin. 2v. New York, 1864.

Pascal, Blaise. Provincial Letters. A new translation, with introduction and notes by Thomas McCrie. Edited by O. W. Wight. 12°. New York, 1866.

Patten, Thomas. See Miscellanies.

Paul, Hiland. History of Wells, Vermont, with biographical sketches by Robert Parks. 12°. Rutland, 1869.

Pausanias. Description of Greece. Translated, with notes, by Thomas Taylor. New edition. 3v. London, 1824.

Pauw, Cornelius de. Recherches Philosophiques sur les Americains. Avec une Dissertation sur l'Amerique et les Americains, par Dom Pernety ; et la defense contre cette dissertation. 3v. 16°. London and Berlin, 1771–70.

Peabody, George. Proceedings at the Reception and Dinner in honor of, Danvers, October, 1856. Boston, 1856.

Peale, Titian R. See under UNITED STATES, p. 63, *ante*.

Pearson, Emily C. Gutenburg and the Art of Printing. 12°. Boston, 1871.

Pearson, Thomas Scott. Catalogue of the Graduates of Middlebury College. Windsor, 1853.

Peirce, Bradford K. A Half Century with Juvenile Delinquents ; or the New York House of Refuge and its Times. New York, 1869.

Penhallow, Samuel. History of the Wars of New England with the Eastern Indians, or a Narrative of their continued Perfidy and Cruelty. 4°. Cincinnati, 1859.

Pennsylvania, Historical Society of. Memoirs. Vol. 1. Reprint. Philadelphia, 1864 ; Vol. 3, Part 2, Philadelphia, 1836 ; Vol. 4, Part 1, Philadelphia, 1840 ; Vol. 7, Philadelphia, 1860 ; Vol. 9, [being vol. 1 Penn and Logan Correspondence], Philadelphia, 1870.

Pennsylvania Hospital for the Insane. Reports 1846 to 1850. Philadelphia, 1851.

Pepys, Samuel. Diary and Correspondence in the Reigns of Charles II. and James II. With life and notes, by Lord Braybrooke. 4v. Philadelphia, 1866.

Perce, Elbert. Battle Roll : An Encyclopædia containing Descriptions of the most famous Land Battles and Sieges in all ages.

Percival, James Gates. Life. See Ward, J. H.

Periodical Accounts relating to the Missions of the Church of the United Brethren, established among the Heathen. Vols. 5 ; 6 (imperfect) ; 14 ; 15 (imperfect). London, 1814—39.

Pernety, Antoine J. Dissertation sur l'Amerique et les Americains, contre les Recherches Philosophiques de M. de P. 16°. Berlin, 1770. (V. 3 of De Pauw, Recherches Philosophiques sur les Americains.)

Perry, Amos. Carthage and Tunis, past and present. Providence, 1869.

Pettigrew, Thomas Joseph. Chronicles of the Tombs; a Collection of Epitaphs, preceded by an Essay on Monumental Inscriptions. 12°. London, 1857.

Peyton, John Lewis. American Crisis; or Pages from the Note-Book of a State Agent during the Civil War. 2v. 12°. London, 1867.

——— Over the Alleghanies and Across the Prairies. 2d edition. 12°. London, 1870.

Phelps, Almira Lincoln. Our Country. A National Book consisting of Original Articles by American Writers. Edited by Mrs. Phelps for the Benefit of the Christian and Sanitary Commissions. 12°. Baltimore, 1864.

Phelps, Noah A. History of Simsbury, Granby and Canton, from 1642 to 1645. Hartford, 1845.

Phelps, Richard H. History of the Newgate of Connecticut. Small 4°. Albany, 1860.

Philadelphia. Annual Reports of Comptrollers of the Public Schools, 1845 to 1849 and 1855 to 1857. [Bound in 4v.] Philadelphia, 1845–57.

Phillips, Henry, Jr. Historical Sketches of the Paper Currency of the American Colonies. First series. Small 4°. Roxbury, 1865.

——— The Same. Second series. Small 4°. Roxbury, 1866.

Phillips, Wendell. Speeches, Lectures and Letters. 12°. Boston, 1864.

Pickering, Charles. See under UNITED STATES, p. 64, *ante*.

Pickering, Octavius. Life of Timothy Pickering. Vol. 1. Boston, 1867.

Pickett, Albert James. History of Alabama; and incidentally of Georgia and Mississippi. 2d edition. 2v. 12°. Charleston, S. C., 1851.

Pitkin, Timothy. Political and Civil History of the United States of America, from 1763 to 1797. 2v. New Haven, 1828.

Plan for shortening time of passage between New York and London, with proceedings of the Railway Convention at Portland. Portland, 1850.

Plato. Tou theiou Platonos apanta ta sozomena. Divini Platonis opera omnia quæ extant. Marsilio Ficino interprete. Folio. Francofurit, 1602.

——— See Grote.

Plumer, William, Jr. Life of William Plumer, by his son. Edited by A. P. Peabody. Boston, 1856.

Plutarch's Lives. The translation called Dryden's. Corrected and revised by A. H. Clough. 5v. Boston, 1859.

Plutarch's Morals. Translated from the Greek. Revised by William W. Goodwin; with introduction by R. W. Emerson. 5v. Boston, 1870.

Poe, Edgar Allan. Works. With a memoir by Rufus W. Griswold, and notices of his life and genius, by N. P. Willis and J. R. Lowell. 4v. 12°. New York, 1868.

CONTENTS.

Arthur Gordon Pym, etc., v. 4.
Eureka; an essay on the material and spiritual universe, v. 2.
Literati, v. 3.
Memoir of Poe, by R. W. Griswold, v. 1.
Poems, v. 2.
Tales, v. 1–2.

Poets and Poetry of Vermont. Edited by A. M. Hemenway. 2d edition.

Politianus, Angelus. Opera. 4°. Basileæ, 1553.

Pollard, Edward A. First Year of the War. Reprinted from the Richmond corrected edition. New York, 1863.

——— Lost Cause; a new Southern history of the War of the Confederates. New York, 1867.

——— Lost Cause Regained. 12°. New York, 1868.

Pond, Enoch. Lives of Increase Mather and Sir William Phipps. Boston, 1870. [Vol. 5, Lives of Chief Fathers of N. E.]

Poole, William Frederick. Index to Periodical Literature. New York, 1853.

Poor, John A. Memoir of Reuel Williams. [Cambridge,] 1864.

Pope, Alexander. Essay on Man. [Phonetic printing.] 32°. Cincinnati, 1851.

——— Poetical Works. With a Life by Alex. Dyce. 3v. 16°. Boston, 1859.

——— See Homer.

Popham Celebration. See Ballard, Edward.

Port Folio, The. Vol. 2. Philadelphia, 1802.

——— The Same. New Series. Vols. 2; 6 to 10. 6v. Philadelphia, 1806–13.

Portland. Annual Reports, 1867 and 1868. 2v. Portland, 1867–68.

Portlock, J. E. Report of the Geology of Londonderry, and of parts of Tyrone and Fermanagh. Dublin, 1843.

Portlock, Nathaniel. Voyage Round the World; but more particularly to the Northwest Coast of America; performed in 1785–1788. 4°. London, 1789.

Potts, Thomas. Gazetteer of England and Wales; containing the statistics, agriculture and mineralogy of the Counties; with history, &c., of the Cities, Towns and Boroughs, and a complete index villaris. 2v. London, 1810.

Pouchet, Felix Archimede. The Universe; or the infinitely great and the infinitely little. Small 4°. New York, 1870.

Pouchot. Memoir upon the Late War in North America, between the French and English, 1755—60. Translated and edited by F. B. Hough. 2v. 4°. [Albany], 1866.

Prentiss, Sergeant Smith. Memoir of. Edited by his brother. 2v. 12°. New York, 1858.

Prescott, William Hickling. Biographical and Critical Miscellanies. Boston, 1858.

——— History of the Conquest of Mexico. With a preliminary View of the Ancient Mexican Civilization, and the Life of the Conqueror, Hernando Cortes. 3v. New York, 1855,

——— History of the Conquest of Peru. With a preliminary View of the Civilization of the Incas. 2v. Philadelphia, 1860.

——— History of the Reign of Ferdinand and Isabella, the Catholic, of Spain. 9th edition. 3v. New York, 1854. (Vol. 1 *wanting.*)

——— History of the Reign of Philip the Second, King of Spain. 3v. 1859.

Present State of Peru. See Joseph Skinner.

Presidents' Messages, Inaugural, Annual and Special, from 1789 to 1846. Compiled by Edwin Williams. 2v. New York, 1847.

Price, Richard. See Miscellanies.

Priestley, Joseph. See Miscellanies.

Prime, William C. Coins, Medals and Seals, Ancient and Modern. Illustrated and Described. New York, 1861.

Prince Society. Publications of. Containing:

Hutchinson Papers, 2 vols.;
Wood's New England Prospect;
John Dunton's Letters from New England;
The Andros Tracts, 2 vols. 6v. 4°. Albany and Boston.

Prior, James. Life of Edmund Burke. 12°. London, 1854.

Prior, Matthew. Poetical Works. With a Life by John Mitford. 2v. 16°. Boston, 1860.

Prison Discipline Society, Boston. Reports, 1826 to 1854. 3v. Boston, 1855.

Prize Essays on a Congress of Nations for the Promotion of Universal Peace; with a sixth essay. By J. A. Bolles, T. C. Upham, William Ladd and others. Boston, 1840.

Protestant Episcopal Church in Vermont. See Documentary History; also Indices to Pamphlets for Reports of late Conventions of the Diocese.

Provancher, L. Flore Canadienne. 2v. Quebec, 1862.

Punchard, George. History of Congregationalism from about A. D. 250 to the present time; a Continuation of "A view of Congregationalism." 2d edition. Vols. 1—3. 12°. New York, 1865—67.

—— View of Congregationalism, its Principles and Doctrines, 3d edition. 12°. Boston, 1856.

Pulteney, Richard. Sketch of the Progress of Botany in England. 2v. London, 1790.

Q.

Quincy, Josiah. History of Harvard University. 2v. Boston, 1860.

—— Memoir of the Life of John Quincy Adams. Boston, 1860.

—— Municipal History of the Town and City of Boston from 1630 to 1830. Boston, 1852.

Quint, Alonzo H. Potomac and the Rapidan. Army Notes, 1861—63. 12°. Boston, 1864.

—— Record of the Second Massachusetts Infantry, 1861—65. Boston, 1867.

R.

Raleigh. Walter. Abridgment of [his] History of the World. Published by Philip Raleigh. 12°. London, 1700.

Ramsay, David. History of South Carolina from 1670 to 1808. 2v. Charleston, 1809.

—— Life of George Washington. London, 1807.

Ramsey, J. G. M. Annals of Tennessee, to the end of the 18th century. Philadelphia, 1853.

Randall, Henry S. Life of Thomas Jefferson. 3v. New York, 1858.

Randall, S. S. Digest of the Common School System of the State of New York. 16°. Albany, 1844.

Randolph, Sarah N. Domestic Life of Thomas Jefferson, compiled from Family Letters and Reminiscences. By his Great-Granddaughter. New York, 1871.

Ranney, Darwin H. Evangelical Church; or, True Grounds for the Union of the Saints. 12°. Woodstock, 1840.

Rantoul, Robert, Jr. Memoirs, Speeches and Writings. Edited by Luther Hamilton. Boston, 1854.

Rapin de Thoyras, Paul. History of England. Translated by N. Tindal. 2v. Folio. London, 1732-3. [Continued by Nicholas Tindal, *q. v.*]

—— The same. 3v. Folio. London, 1786-4. [Continued by Nicholas Tindal, *q. v.*]

Raymond, Henry J. Life and Public Services of Abraham Lincoln : together with his State Papers, including Speeches, Addresses, Messages, Letters and Proclamations. With Personal Reminiscences of President Lincoln by F. B. Carpenter. New York, 1865.

Raynal, Guillaume Thomas Francois. Philosophical and Political History of the Settlement and Trade of the Europeans in the East and West Indies. Translated by J. O. Justamond. 8v. London, 1788.

Reavis, L. U. See Saint Louis.

Rebellion Record. A Diary of American Events. With Documents, Narratives, Illustrative Incidents. Poetry, etc. Edited by Frank Moore. 11v. New York, 1864—68.

——— The same. Supplement. 1st volume. New York, 1869.

Records of Salem Witchcraft. See Woodward, W. E.

Reed and Cadwalader Pamphlets. A Reprint of the. With an appendix. 1863.

Reed, William B. Life and Correspondence of Joseph Reed. 2v. Philadelphia, 1857.

Reichel, W. J. Memorial of the Dedication of Monuments erected by the Moravian Historical Society in New York and Connecticut. Philadelphia and New York, 1860.

Relation of Maryland. Reprinted [from edition of 1635], with note and appendix by Francis L. Hawks. 4°. New York, 1865. [Sabin's Reprints, No. 2].

Relations des Jesuites ; contenant ce qui s'est passe de plus remarquable dans les Missions des Peres de la Campagnie de Jesus dans la Nouvelle France. 3v. Quebec, 1858.

Report on History and Progress of the American Coast Survey to 1858. By Committee of American Association for Advancement of Science. [Cambridge, 1858].

Reporter: [Brattleboro. By William Fessenden.] Vols. 1 and 2, (February 9, 1803 to February 9, 1805).

Rerum Brittanicarum Medii Ævi Scriptores. See Chronicles.

Rerum Hungaricarum Scriptores Varii, [J. de Thurocz, P. Ranzani, P. Callimachus, etc.] 4°. Francofurti, 1600.

Rhode Island Historical Society. Collections. 6v. Providence, 1827—67.

Richards, William C. Great in Goodness ; a Memoir of George N. Briggs, Governor of Massachusetts from 1844 to 1851. 12°. Boston, 1867.

Richardson, Charles, *LL. D.* New Dictionary of the English Language. 2v. 4°. London, 1858.

Riddle, Joseph Esmond, and Thomas Kerchever Arnold. Copious and Critical English-Latin Lexicon, founded on the German-Latin Dictionary of Charles Ernest Georges. Edited by C. Anthon. New York, 1849.

Riedesel. Friederike Charlotte Luise von. Letters and Journals relating to the War of the American Revolution, and the Capture of the German Troops at Saratoga. From the German, by W. L. Stone. Albany, 1867.

Riedesel, Friedrich Adolph von. Memoirs and Letters and Journals during his residence in America. From the German, by W. L. Stone. 2v. Albany, 1868.

Ripley, George. See Appleton.

Rives, William Cabell. History of the Life and Times of James Madison. 3v. Boston, 1866–68.

Robertson, Frederick W. Life and Letters. Edited by Stopford A. Brooke. 2v. Boston, 1866.

——— Sermons preached at Trinity Chapel, Brighton. 5th series. Boston, 1864.

Robertson, William. History of America. 2d edition. 2v. 4°. London, 1778.

——— The Same. 9th edition. 4v. London. 1800.

——— History of the Discovery and Settlement of America. New York, 1855.

Rochefoucauld-Liancourt. See La Rochefoucauld-Liancourt.

Roe, Alva Dunning. Home Scenes and Heart Tints ; a memorial of Mrs. Marion H. Roe. 12°. New York, 1865.

Roger, Charles, (of Quebec.) Rise of Canada from Barbarism to Wealth and Civilization. Vol. 1. Quebec, 1856.

Rogers, Henry Darwin. See under PENNSYLVANIA, p. 48, *ante*.

Rollin, Charles. Ancient History of the Egyptians, Carthaginians, Assyrians, Babylonians, Medes and Persians, Grecians and Macedonians ; including a History of the Arts and Sciences of the Ancients. 2v. New York, 1855.

Rondthaler, Edward. Life of John Heckewelder. Edited by B. H. Coates. 12°. Philadelphia, 1847.

Ross, Alexander. History of the World ; the second part, in six books ; being a continuation of the famous history of Sir Walter Raleigh, Knight ; beginning where he left ; from 160 B. C., to 1640 after Christ ; together with a chronologie of those times. 4°. London, 1652.

Rousseau, Jean Jacques. Confessions. Translated from the French. 12°. London, 1861.

Ruffin, E. See Addresses on Agriculture.

Rumford, Count. See Thompson, Benjamin.

Rural Magazine, or Vermont Repository. Devoted to literary, moral, historical and political improvement. Vols. 1 and 2. Rutland, 1795–96.

Rush, Benjamin. Essays, Literary, Moral and Philosophical. Philadelphia, 1798.

Ruskin, John. Elements of Drawing ; in three letters to beginners ; with illustrations. 12°. New York, 1859.

——— Elements of Perspective. 12°. New York, 1860.

——— Lectures on Architecture and Painting. 12°. New York, 1859.

——— Modern Painters. 4v. New York, 1860–58.

——— Political Economy of Art. New York, 1858.

——— Stones of Venice. Vol. 1. New York, 1860.

——— The Two Paths ; being lectures on art, and its application to decoration and manufacture. 12°. New York, 1859.

Russell, William Howard. My Diary North and South. 12°. Boston, 1863.

Rutland. See Williams, Charles K.

Ruttenber, E. M. History of the Indian Tribes of Hudson's River. Albany, 1872.

S.

Sabin, Joseph. [Bibliotheca Americana.] A Dictionary of Books relating to America, from its discovery to the present time. Vols. 1—4. New York, 1868–71.

Sabin's Reprints. Small Quarto Series Nos. 1 to 10. 4°. New York, 1865. See A Further Accompt ; Byfield ; Certain Inducements ; Daybreaking ; Further Queries ; New England's First Fruits ; Relation of Maryland ; Shepard, Thomas ; Whitfield, Henry.

——— Octavo Series No. 7. New York, 1869. See Mason, John.

Sabine, Lorenzo. Biographical Sketches of Loyalists of the American Revolution. With an Historical Essay. 2v. Boston, 1864.

Sackville, *Lord* George. See Miscellanies.

Safford, William H. See Blennerhassett Papers.

St. Louis. Annual Reports of the Board of Directors of the Public Schools, 1865–6 ; 1867–8 to 1870–71. 5v.

——— Catalogue of the Public School Library. Prepared by John Jay Bailey. 4°. St. Louis, 1870.

St. Louis Law Library Association. Descriptive Catalogue of Books. St. Louis, 1870.

Saint Louis, the Future Great City of the World. By L. U. Reavis. 2d edition. St. Louis, 1870.

Salem. City Documents for 1869–70. Salem, 1870.

Salmon, Thomas. Modern History ; or present state of all Nations. Illustrated with cuts and maps, by H. Moll. 5v in 6. Small 4°. London, 1755.

Samford, William F. Letter to Gov. Wise, with Wise's reply. See Wise, H. A.

Samuels, Edward A. Ornithology and Oology of New England; containing full descriptions of the birds of N. E. and adjacent country, with complete history of their habits, etc. Boston, 1867.

Sanborn, A. J. See Green Mountain Poets.

Sanders, Daniel Clarke. History of the Indian Wars with the first settlers of the United States, particularly in New England. Written in Vermont. 24°. Montpelier, 1812.

San Francisco. Municipal Reports, 1868–69; 1869–70. 2v.

——— Report of Superintendent of Public Schools, Oct. 15, 1867.

Sanger, William W. History of Prostitution; its Extent, Causes and Effects throughout the World. New York, 1858.

Sangster, Charles. Hesperus and other Poems and Lyrics. 12°. Montreal, 1860.

Sargent, Winthrop. Life and Career of Major John Andre, Adjutant General of the British Army in America. 12°. Boston, 1861.

Sarmiento, Domingo Faustino. Life in the Argentine Republic in the Days of the Tyrants; or, Civilization and Barbarism. From the Spanish, and with a Biographical Sketch of the Author by Mrs. Horace Mann. 12°. New York, 1868.

Sauzay, A. Wonders of Glass-Making in all Ages. 16°. New York, 1870.

Savage, James. Genealogical Dictionary of the First Settlers of New England; showing Three Generations of those who came before May, 1692. 4v. Boston, 1860—62.

Scaeva. See Stuart, Isaac W.

Schoolcraft, Henry Rowe. Historical and Statistical Information respecting the History, Condition and Prospects of the Indian Tribes of the United States. Collected and prepared under direction of the Bureau of Indian Affairs. Illustrated. Parts 1—5. 5v. 4°. Philadelphia, 1851—55.

Schouler, William. History of Massachusetts in the Civil War. Boston, 1868.

Scott, Henry L. Military Dictionary. New York, 1861.

Scott, *Sir* Walter. Poetical Works. With Memoir of Author. 9v. 16°. Boston, 1857.

——— Waverley Novels. [Adam and Charles Black's Centenary edition.] 25v. 12°. Edinburgh, 1871.

CONTENTS.

Vol.	Novel.	First Published.	Time of Tale.	
1.	Waverley,	1814.	George II.,	1745.
2.	Guy Mannering,	1815.	George III.,	1760.
3.	The Antiquary,	1816.	George III.,	1798.
4.	Rob Roy,	1817.	George I.,	1715.
5.	Old Mortality,	1816.	Charles II.,	1679.
6.	A Legend of Montrose,	1819.	Charles I.,	1644.
	The Black Dwarf,	1816.	Anne,	1708.

Vol.	Novel.	First Published.	Time of Tale.	
7.	The Heart of Mid-Lothian,	1818.	George II.,	1736.
8.	The Bride of Lammermoor,	1819.	William III.,	1700.
9.	Ivanhoe,	1819.	Richard I.,	1194.
10.	The Monastery,	1820.	Elizabeth,	1559.
11.	The Abbot,	1820.	Elizabeth,	1570.
12.	Kenilworth,	1821.	Elizabeth,	1575.
13.	The Pirate,	1821.	William III.,	1700.
14.	The Fortunes of Nigel,	1822.	James I.,	1620.
15.	Peveril of the Peak,	1823.	Charles II.,	1660.
16.	Quentin Durward,	1823.	Edward IV.,	1470.
17.	St. Ronan's Well,	1823.	George III..	1800.
18.	Redgauntlet,	1824.	George III.,	1770.
19.	The Betrothed,	1825.	Henry II.,	1187.
	Chronicles of the Canongate.			
	The Highland Widow.	1827.	George II..	1755.
20.	The Talisman,	1825.	Richard I.,	1193.
	Chronicles of the Canongate.			
	The Two Drovers,	1827.	George III.,	1765.
	My Aunt Margaret's Mirror,	1828.	William III,	1700.
	The Tapestried Chamber,	1828.	George III.,	1780.
	The Laird's Jock,	1828.	Elizabeth,	1600.
21.	Woodstock,	1826.	Cromwell,	1654.
22.	The Fair Maid of Perth,	1828.	Henry IV.,	1402.
23.	Anne of Geiersetein,	1829.	Edward IV.,	1474.
24.	Count Robert of Paris,	1831.	William Rufus,	1090.
25.	The Surgeon's Daughter,	1827.	George II.,	1755.
	Castle Dangerous,	1831.	Edward I.,	1306.

——— See Hunnewell, J. F.

Scrope, George Poulett. Volcanos. Character of their Phenomena; their Share in the Structure of the Surface of the Globe and their Relation to its Internal Forces: with descriptive catalogue of volcanos. 2d edition. London, 1862.

Seybert, Adam. Statistical Annals of the United States, 1789—1818; embracing views of the population, commerce, fisheries, public lands, revenues, mint, &c. 4°. Philadelphia, 1818.

Shakspeare, William. Dramatic Works. With notes by Samuel Waller Singer, and Life and Essays by William Watkins Lloyd. 10v. 12°. London, 1856.

——— Poems. With Memoir by Alex. Dyce. 16°. Boston, 1856.

——— Works. Edited by Richard Grant White. Vol. 1. 12°. Boston, 1865.

——— See Clarke, *Mrs.* Cowden; and Holmes, Nathaniel.

Shaw, Alexander. Narrative of the Discoveries of Sir Charles Bell in the Nervous System. London, 1839.

Sheffield, John, *Lord.* Observations on the Manufactures, Trade and Present State of Ireland. London, 1785.

——— See Gibbon.

Shelley, Percy Bysshe. Poetical Works. Edited by Mrs. Shelley. With a Memoir. 3v. 16°. Boston, 1857.

Shepard, Thomas. Clear Sunshine of the Gospel breaking forth upon the Indians in New England. Reprinted [from edition of 1648.] 4°. New York, 1865. [Sabin's Reprints No. 10.]

Sherlock, Thomas. See Miscellanies.

Shirley, Walter Waddington. See Chronicles.

Sidney, *Sir* Philip. Miscellaneous Works. With a life of the Author, and notes, by William Gray. Boston, 1860.

Simms, Jeptha R. Trappers of New York. Albany, 1871.

Skelton, John. Poetical Works. Principally according to Alex. Dyce's edition. 3v. 16°. Boston, 1856.

Skinner, Joseph. Present State of Peru; from original and authentic documents. 4°. London, 1805.

Slafter, Edmund F. Memoir of John Slafter. Boston, 1869.

Slade, William, Jr. See Vermont State Papers, p. 72, *ante*.

Smiles, Samuel. Life of George Stephenson and of his son Robert Stephenson; comprising also a History of the Invention and Introduction of the Railway Locomotive. New York, 1868.

Smith, Adam. Inquiry into the Nature and Causes of the Wealth of Nations. With Life of the Author, notes, etc. by J. R. M'Culloch. Edinburgh, 1863.

Smith, Edward P. Incidents of the U. S. Christian Commission. Philadelphia, 1869.

Smith, Goldwin. Three English Statesmen, [Pym, Cromwell, Pitt]; a Course of Lectures on the Political History of England. 12°. New York, 1867.

Smith, *Captain* John. True Relation of Virginia. With notes by Charles Deane. 4°. Boston, 1866. [Virginia Series, No. 1.]

——— See Veazie.

Smith, William, *LL. D.* Dictionary of the Bible; comprising its Antiquities, Biography, Geography and Natural History. 3v. Boston, 1863.

——— History of Greece, from the earliest times to the Roman Conquest. With Supplementary chapters on the History of Literature and Art. Revised, with an appendix, by George W. Greene. 12°. New York, 1863.

——— Dictionary of Greek and Roman Antiquities. Boston, 1865.

——— Dictionary of Greek and Roman Biography and Mythology. 3v. Boston, 1859.

——— Dictionary of Greek and Roman Geography. 2v. Boston, 1865.

Smith, *Hon.* William, (formerly of New York, and late Chief Justice of Canada.) History of the late Province of New York, from its Discovery to 1762. 2v. New York, 1830,

Smith, William Prescott. Book of the Great Railway Celebrations of 1857. New York, 1858.

Smithsonian Institution. See p. 66, *ante*.

Smollett, T., *D. D.* [Tobias George ?] See Nicholas Tindal.

Snow, William Parker. Southern Generals, their Lives and Campaigns. New York, 1866.

Snowden, James Ross. Description of Ancient and Modern Coins in the Cabinet Collection at the Mint of the United States. Philadelphia, 1860.

Solis, Antonio de. History of the Conquest of Mexico by the Spaniards. Translated by T. Townsend. Revised by N. Hooke. 3d edition. 2v. London, 1753.

Some Reflections on the Disputes between New York, New Hampshire and Col. John Henry Lydius of Albany. 12°. New Haven, 1764.

Soule, Frank, John H. Gihon and James Nisbet. Annals of San Francisco. New York, 1855.

South Carolina Historical Society. Collections. Vol. 1. Charleston, 1857.

South, Robert. Sermons preached upon several occasions. Edited by William Greenough Thayer Shedd. Vols. 1 and 2. New York, 1866—67.

Southey, Robert. Poetical Works. With a Memoir of the Author. 10v. 16°. Boston, 1860.

Southey, Thomas. Chronological History of the West Indies. 3v. London, 1827.

Sparks, Jared, (*Editor*). Correspondence of the American Revolution; letters of eminent men to George Washington. 4v. Boston, 1853.

——— Library of American Biography. First Series, 10v. 16°. New York, 1854. Second Series, 15v. 16°. Boston, 1852.

CONTENTS.

Allen, Ethan. By J. Sparks, v. 1, first series.
Arnold, Benedict. By J. Sparks, v. 3, first series.
Bacon, Nathaniel. By W. Ware, v. 3, second series.
Boone, Daniel. By J. M. Peck, v. 13, second series.
Brainerd, David. By W. B. O. Peabody, v. 8, first series.
Brown, Charles B. By W. H. Prescott, v. 1, first series.
Cabot, Sebastian. By C. Hayward, Jr., v. 9, first series.
Calvert, Leonard. By G. W. Burnap, v. 9, second series.
Davidson, Lucretia M. By C. M. Sedgwick, v. 7, first series.
Davie, William R. By F. M. Hubbard, v. 15, second series.
Decatur, Stephen. By A. S. Mackenzie, v. 11 second series.
Dwight, Timothy. By W. B. Sprague, v. 4, second series.
Eaton, William. By C. C. Felton, v. 9, first series.
Edwards, Jonathan. By S. Miller, v. 8, first series.
Eliot, John. By C. Francis, v. 5, first series.
Ellery, William. By E. T. Channing, v. 6, first series.
Fitch, John. By C. Whittlesey, v. 6, second series.
Fulton, Robert. By J. Renwick, v. 10, first series.
Gorton, Samuel. By J. M. Mackie, v. 5, second series.
Greene, Nathanael. By G. W. Greene, v. 10, second series.
Henry, Patrick. By A. H. Everett, v. 1, second series.
Hudson, Henry. By H. R. Cleveland, v. 10, first series.
Hutchinson, Anne. By G. E. Ellis, v. 6, second series.
Kirkland, Samuel. By S. K. Lothrop, v. 15, second series.

La Salle, Robert Cavelier de. By J. Sparks, v. 1, second series.
Ledyard, John. By J. Sparks, v. 14, second series.
Lee, Charles. By J. Sparks, v. 8, second series.
Leisler, Jacob. By C. F. Hoffman, v. 3, second series.
Lincoln, Benjamin. By F. Bowen, v. 13, second series.
Marquette, Father. By J. Sparks, v. 10, first series.
Mason, John. By G. E. Ellis, v. 3, second series.
Mather, Cotton. By W. B. O. Peabody, v. 6, first series.
Montgomery, Richard. By J. Armstrong, v. 1, first series.
Oglethorpe, James. By W. B. O. Peabody, v. 2, second series.
Otis, James. By F. Bowen, v. 2, second series.
Palfrey, William. By J. G. Palfrey, v. 7, second series.
Penn, William. By G. E. Ellis, v. 12, second series.
Phips, Sir William. By F. Bowen, v. 7, first series.
Pike, Zebulon M. By H. Whiting, v, 5, second series.
Pinkney, William. By H. Wheaton, v. 6, first series.
Posey, Thomas. By J. Hall, v. 9, second series.
Preble, Edward. By L. Sabine, v. 12, second series.
Pulaski, Count Casimir. By J. Sparks, v. 4, second series.
Putnam, Israel. By O. W. B. Peabody, v. 7, first series.
Rale, Sebastian. By C. Francis, v. 7, second series.
Reed, Joseph. By H. Reed, v. 8, second series.
Ribault, John. By J. Sparks, v. 7, second series.
Rittenhouse, David. By J. Renwick, v. 7, first series.
Rumford, Benjamin, (Count). By J. Renwick, v. 5, second series.
Smith, Capt. John. By G. S. Hillard, v. 2, first series.
Stark, John. By E. Everett, v. 1, first series.
Steuben, Baron. By F. Bowen, v. 9, first series.
Stiles, Ezra. By J. L. Kingsley, v. 6, second series.
Sullivan, John. By O. W. B. Peabody, v. 3, second series.
Vane, Sir Henry. By C. W. Upham, v. 4, first series.
Ward, Samuel. By W. Gammell, v. 9, second series.
Warren, Joseph. By A. H. Everett, v. 10, first series.
Wayne, Anthony. By J. Armstrong, v. 4, first series,
Williams, Roger. By W. Gammell, v. 4, second series.
Wilson, Alexander. By W. B. O. Peabody, v. 2, first series.

——— Life of Gouverneur Morris. With Selections from his Correspondence and Miscellaneous Papers. 3v. Boston, 1832.

——— Remarks on a "Reprint of the Original Letters from Washington to Joseph Reed, during the American Revolution, referred to in the pamphlets of Lord Mahon and Mr. Sparks." Boston, 1853.

——— Reply to the Strictures of Lord Mahon and others, on the mode of editing the Writings of Washington. Cambridge, 1852.

——— Catalogue of [his] Library. Cambridge, 1871.

——— See Diplomatic Correspondence, p. 60, *ante*.

Spencer, Herbert. Social Statics; or, the Conditions essential to Human Happiness specified, and the first of them developed. New York, 1865.

Spenser, Edmund. Poetical Works. Edited by Francis J. Child. 5v. 16°. Boston, 1860.

Spiers, A. French and English Pronouncing Dictionary. Revised by G. P. Quackenbos. New York, 1861.

Spofford, Harriett Prescott. New England Legends. Boston, 1871.

Spooner's Vermont Journal. [Windsor. First called *Vermont Journal and Universal Advertiser*, which see.] Vol. 24, last 25 Nos., Vols. 25, 26, 27, first 25 Nos., (Jan. 1, 1807 to Dec. 31, 1810); and Vol. 32, last 47 Nos., and Vol. 33, first 25 Nos., (Aug. 8, 1814, to Dec. 18, 1815).

Sprague, William Buell. Annals of the American Pulpit; or, Commemorative Notices of Distinguished American Clergymen of Various Denominations, from the Settlement of the country to 1855. Vols. 1—8. New York, 1859—65.

Staples, William R. Rhode Island in the Continental Congress. Edited by Reuben Aldridge Guild. Providence, 1870.

Statesman's Manual. See Presidents' Messages.

Staunton, Howard. Great Schools of England; an Account of the Foundation, Endowment and Discipline of the Chief Seminaries of Learning in England; including Eton, Winchester, Rugby, etc. London, 1865.

Stearns, Samuel. American Oracle; comprehending an Account of Recent Discoveries in the Arts and Sciences. London, 1791.

Stedman, C., (*who served under Howe, Clinton and Cornwallis.*) History of the Origin, Progress and Termination of the American War. 2v. Dublin, 1794.

Stedman, John Gabriel. Narrative of a Five Years' Expedition against the Revolted Negroes of Surinam, from 1772 to 1777. 2v. 4°. London, 1796.

Steele, Ashbel. Chief of the Pilgrims; or, Life and Time of William Brewster. Philadelphia, 1857.

Steele, Zadock. Indian Captive; or a Narrative of the Captivity and Sufferings of Zadock Steele. To which is prefixed an Account of the Burning of Royalton. 16°. Montpelier, 1818.

Steinmetz, Andrew. Romance of Duelling in all Times and Countries. 2v. London, 1868.

Stephens, Alexander H. Constitutional View of the late War between the States; its Causes, Conduct and Results. 2v. Philadelphia, [1868—70].

Stephens, John Langdon. Incidents of Travel in Central America, Chiapas, and Yucatan. 12th edition. 2v. New York, 1855.

Stevens, Henry, *G. M. B., of* 4 *Trafalgar Square, London.* Bibliotheca Geographica & Historica; or a Catalogue of a nine days' sale [Nov. 19-29, 1872,] of books, maps, charts, manuscripts, autograph letters *et cetera*, illustrative of historical geography, &c. With introduction and notes, together with an essay upon the Stevens system of photobibliography. Part I. London, 1872.

——— Bibliotheca Historica; or Catalogue of five thousand books relating chiefly to America, to be sold by auction in Boston, April, 1870. With introduction and notes. Boston, 1870.

——— Historical and Geographical Notes of the Earliest Discoveries in America; 1453—1530: with the Tehuantepec Railway

Company's Map of the World and photo-lithographic fac-similes of many of the earliest maps and charts of America. New Haven, 1869.

——— Mr. George Peabody's Parting Dinner to the Americans connected with the Great Exhibition; given at the London Coffee House, Ludgate Hill. London, 1851.

Stevens, William Bacon. History of Georgia, from its Discovery by Europeans to the Adoption of the Present Constitution in 1796. 2v. New York and Philadelphia, 1847—59.

Stewart, Dugald. Collected Works. Edited by Sir William Hamilton. 10v. and supplement. Edinburgh, 1854—60.

CONTENTS.

Dissertation, exhibiting the progress of Metaphysical, Ethical, and Political Philosophy, v. 1.
Elements of the Philosophy of the Mind, v. 2—4.
Memoir of Stewart, by J. Veitch, v. 10.
Philosophical Essays, v. 5.
Philosophy of the Active and Moral Powers of Man, v. 6—7.
Political Economy, Lectures on, v. 8—9.
Reid, Thomas. Life and Writings of, v. 10.
Robertson, William. Life and Writings of, v. 10.
Smith, Adam. Life and Writings of, v. 10.
Translations of passages in Foreign Languages contained in Stewart's Works and Index, v. 11.

Stiles, Henry Reed. Bundling; its Origin, Progress and Decline in America. 12°. Albany, 1869.

——— Letters from the Prisons and Prison-Ships of the Revolution. 4°. New York, 1865.

Stille, Charles J. History of the U. S. Sanitary Commission. New York, 1869.

Stith, William. History of the First Discovery and Settlement of Virginia. New York, 1865.

Stone, Edwin W. Rhode Island in the Rebellion. 12°. Providence, 1865.

Stone, William Leete. Life and Times of Sa-go-ye-wat-ha, or Red Jacket. With a Memoir of the Author by his son. Albany, 1866.

——— Life and Times of Sir William Johnson, Bart. (Completed by his son.) Albany, 1865.

——— Letters on Masonry and Anti-Masonry, addressed to John Quincy Adams. New York, 1832.

——— Life of Joseph Brant—Thayendanegea. Including the Border Wars of the American Revolution, and Sketches of the Indian Campaigns of Generais Harmar, St. Clair, and Wayne. 2v. Albany, 1865.

——— Poetry and History of Wyoming; containing Campbell's Gertrude, with a Biographical Sketch of the Author, by W. Irving; and the History of Wyoming to the beginning of the present century. 3d edition. 12°. Albany, 1864.

Story, Joseph. Miscellaneous Writings, literary, critical, juridical and poetical. Boston, 1835.

Story, William W. Life and Letters of Joseph Story. 2v. Boston, 1851.

Stowe, Calvin Ellis. Origin and History of the Books of the Bible, both Canonical and Apocryphal; to show what the Bible is not, what it is, and how to use it. Hartford, 1868.

Stuart, Isaac W. Hartford in the Olden Time; its first thirty years. By Scaeva. Edited by W. M. B. Hartley. Hartford, 1853.

—— Life of Jonathan Trumbull, Senior, Governor of Connecticut. Boston, 1859.

Sumner, Charles. Works. 4v. Boston, 1870—71.

Sumner, William H. History of East Boston. Boston, 1858.

Surrey, Henry Howard, *Earl of.* Poetical Works. With a Memoir. 16°. Boston, 1854.

Swift, Jonathan. Poetical Works. With a Life by John Mitford. 3v. 16°. Boston, 1859.

—— Works. With Notes and Additions, and a Memoir of the Author by Thomas Roscoe. 6v. New York, 1859. (*Vol. 1 wanting.*)

CONTENTS.

Gulliver's Travels, etc., v. 2.
Journal to Stella, etc., v. 3.
Miscellaneous, vols. 4, 5 and 6.

Swift, Samuel. History of the Town of Middlebury, to which is prefixed an account of Addison County, Vermont. Middlebury, 1859.

Swinton, William. Rambles among Words; their Poetry, history and wisdom. Revised edition. 12°. New York, 1864.

—— Twelve Decisive Battles of the War; a History of the Eastern and Western Campaigns in relation to the Actions that decided their Issue. New York, 1867.

Symmes, Thomas. See Kidder, F.

T.

Taine, Hippolyte Adolphe. History of English Literature. Translated by H. Van Laun. 2d edition. 2v. Edinburgh, 1872.

Taylor, Bayard. Works. 13v. 12°. New York, 1865—69.

CONTENTS.

Africa.
By Ways of Europe.
California and Mexico.
Europe; or, Views Afloat.
Greece and Russia.
Hannah Thurston.
Home and Abroad, 1st series.
Home and Abroad, 2d series.
India, China and Japan.
John Godfrey's Fortunes.
Lands of the Saracen.
Northern Travel.
Story of Kennett.

—— Poems of the Orient. 5th edition. 12°. Boston, 1856.

Tehuantepec Railway. Its location, features and advantages under the La Sere grant of 1869; [to which is added a second part being] historical and geographical notes by Henry Stevens. New York, 1869.

Tenney, Jonathan. Memorial of the Class graduated at Dartmouth College July 27, 1843. Albany, 1869.

Thacher, James. Military Journal during the American Revolutionary War. Boston, 1827.

Thaer, Albert D. Principles of Practical Agriculture. Translated (from the German) by W. Shaw and C. W. Johnson. New York, 1856.

Thatcher, Benjamin Bussey. Indian Biography; historical account of those individuals who have been distinguished among the North American natives. 2v. 18°. New York, 1832.

Thiers, Louis Adolphe. History of the French Revolution. Translated, with notes, by Frederick Shoberl. 3d American edition. 4v. in 2. Philadelphia, 1845.

Thomas, John J. Farm Implements and Principles of their Construction and Use. New York, 1855.

Thomas, Joseph. See Lippincott.

Thompson, Benjamin, [Count Rumford.] Complete Works. Vol. 1. Boston. 1870.

Thompson, Daniel P. Gaut Gurley; or the Trappers of Umbagog. 12°. Philadelphia, [1860].

——— Green Mountain Boys. 12°. Boston, 1870.

——— History of the Town of Montpelier, from 1781 to 1860, with Biographical Sketches. Montpelier, 1860.

——— Locke Amsden; or, the Schoolmaster. 12°. Boston, 1869.

——— May Martin, and other Tales. 12°. Boston, 1869.

——— Rangers; or, the Tory's Daughter. 12°. Boston, 1869.

Thompson, Zadock. Gazetteer of the State of Vermont, containing a brief View of the State, Description of all the Counties, Towns, &c. 12°. Montpelier, 1824.

——— Geography and Geology of Vermont. 16°. Burlington, 1848.

——— History of the State of Vermont, for the Use of Families and Schools. 16°. Burlington, 1858.

——— History of the State of Vermont, from its Earliest Settlement to 1832. 16°. Burlington, 1833.

——— History of Vermont, Natural, Civil and Statistical, in Three Parts, with a new Map of the State and Two Hundred Engravings. Burlington, 1842.

——— The same, with an appendix. Burlington, 1853.

Thomson, James. Poetical Works. 2v. 16°. Boston, 1857.

Thornton, John Wingate. The Pulpit of the American Revolution; or, the Political Sermons of the Period of 1776, with notes. 12°. Boston, 1860.

Thorpe, B. See Yule Tide Stories.

Tickell, Thomas. Poetical Works. With a Life by Dr. Johnson. [Bound with Parnell's Poetical Works.] 16°. Boston, 1854.

Ticknor, George. History of Spanish Literature. 4th edition. 3v. Boston, 1872.

——— Life of William Hickling Prescott. Boston, 1864.

Tindal, Nicholas. History of England from the Revolution to the Accession of George II., with the Reign of George II. by T. Smollett, D. D. 2v. Folio. [No date.] London.

——— Continuation of M. Rapin de Thoyras's History of England from the Revolution to the Accession of George II. [With Smollett's George II., as above.] 2v. Folio. London, 1787.

——— See Rapin.

Tocqueville, Charles Alexis Henri Maurice Clerel de. Democracy in America; the Republic of the U. S. of A. reviewed and examined. Translated by Henry Reeves, with original preface and notes by John C. Spencer. 2 vols. in 1. New York, 1856.

Tooke, John Horne. Epea pteroenta; or the Diversions of Purley; with numerous additions from the copy prepared by the author for publication; also his letter to John Dunning. Revised and corrected, with additional notes, by Richard Taylor. London, 1857.

Torrey, John. See Natural History, p. 46, *ante*.

Tour of H. R. H., the Prince of Wales, through British America and the United States. By a British Canadian. Montreal, 1860.

Tracy, Joseph. Great Awakening; a history of the revival of religion in the time of Edwards and Whitfield. Boston, 1842.

Tribune Almanac for the years 1838 to 1868 inclusive; comprehending the Politician's Register and the Whig Almanac. 2v. 12°. New York, 1868.

Trowbridge, John. See Annual of Scientific Discovery, of which he was principal editor in 1870.

Troy Young Men's Association. Catalogue of the Library. Troy, 1859.

Trumbull, Benjamin. Complete History of Connecticut, from 1630 to 1764. 2v. New Haven, 1818.

Trumbull, John. Autobiography, Reminiscences and Letters, from 1756 to 1841. New York, 1841.

——— Poetical Works. 2v. in 1. Hartford, 1820.

Trumbull, J. Hammond. Public Records of the Colony of Connecticut, prior to the Union with New Haven Colony, May, 1665. Hartford, 1850.

——— The Same, from 1665 to 1678. With the journal of the council of war, 1675 to 1678. Hartford, 1852.

——— The Same; from 1678 to 1689. With notes and appendix illustrating the administration of Sir Edmund Andros. Hartford, 1859.

[For continuation of above records see C. J. Hoadly.]

Tuckerman, Henry Theodore. America and her Commentators. With a critical sketch of travel in the United States. New York, 1864.

——— Book of the Artists. American Artist Life. Comprising sketches of American Artists and an account of the rise and progress of Art in America. New York, 1867.

——— Essays, Biographical and Critical ; or studies of character. Boston, 1857.

Tudor, William. Life of James Otis, of Massachusetts. Boston, 1823.

Turkish Spy. See Marana.

Twining, Thomas. Science for the People ; a memorandum for propagating knowledge among the working classes. London, 1870.

Tyerman, L. Life and Times of John Wesley, Founder of the Methodists. 3v. New York, 1872.

U.

Ulloa, Antonio de. Voyage. See Juan y Santacilea.

United States Sanitary Commission. Memoirs. See Gould, B. A. ; Flint, Austin ; Lidell, John A. ; Stille, Charles J.

Universal History, from the earliest account of time. Compiled from original authors. Ancient Part. 21v. London, 1747–54.

——— The Same. Modern Part, by the authors of the Antient Part. 44v. London, 1759–66.

University of Vermont. Catalogue of the Library. Burlington, 1854.

——— Historical Discourse by Rev. John Wheeler, Address by J. R. Spalding, and Poem by Rev. O. G. Wheeler, delivered at the Semi-Centennial Anniversary. Burlington, 1854.

Upham, Charles Wentworth. Salem Witchcraft ; with an account of Salem village. and history of opinions on witchcraft and kindred subjects. 2v. Boston, 1867.

Ure, Andrew. Dictionary of Arts, Manufactures and Mines. 2v. New York, 1858.

V.

Valentine, David T. History of the City of New York. New York, 1853.

——— Manual of the Corporation of the City of New York, 1861. 12°. New York, 1861.

Van Buren, Martin. Inquiry into the Origin and Course of Political Parties in the United States. Edited by his sons. New York, 1867.

Van Santvoord, George. Sketches of the Lives and Judicial Services of the Chief Justices of the Supreme Conrt of the United States. New York, 1854.

Vanuxem, Lardner. See Natural History under NEW YORK, p. 46, *ante*.

Vaughan, Henry. Sacred Poems and Private Ejaculations. With Memoir by H. F. Lyte. 16°. Boston, 1854.

Veazie, William. Reprints. 4v. 4°. Boston, 1865.

CONTENTS.

An Account of two voyages to New England, made 1638, 1663. By John Josselyn, Gent.

Chronological Observations of America, to 1673.

New England's Rarities discovered in birds, beasts, fishes, serpents and plants of that country. By John Josselyn, Gent, with notes by Edward Tuckerman.

Advertisements for the unexperienced Planters of New England, or anywhere; or the Pathway to erect a plantation. By Captain John Smith.

A Description of New England, or observations and diseoveries in 1641. By Captain John Smith.

Venegas, Miguel. History of California. Translated from the original Spanish. 2v. London, 1759.

Vermont Almanac, Pocket Memorandum and Statistical Register. Astronomical Calculations by Hosea Doton. 1844; 1845; 1846; 1849; 1854. 5v. 16°. Woodstock.

Vermont Capital. Journal of Special Session of 1857. See under VERMONT, p. 68, *ante*.

Vermont Directory and Commercial Almanac, 1855 to 1868. (1862 *wanting*.) 13v. 16°. Burlington, Rutland and Claremont.

Vermont Historical Gazetteer. See Hemenway, A. M.

Vermont Historical Society. Collections. Vols. 1—2. 2v. Montpelier, 1871—72.

——— Pamphlet Publications of. [Bound in 1 vol.]

CONTENTS.

James Davie Butler's Address, Oct. 16, 1846.
James Davie Butler and George Frederick Houghton's Addresses, Oct. 20, 1848.
P. H. White and A. D. Hager's Addresses, 1858.
D. P. Thompson's Address, Oct. 23, 1850.
Constitution, By-Laws, &c., 1860.
Proceedings, Oct. 16, 1860; Jan. 23, 1861; Oct. 15, 1861; Jan., 1862; Oct., 1862.
J. W. De Peyster's and W. C. Watson's Addresses, 1863.
E. J. Phelps' Sketch of Chas. Linsley.
Addresses by G. F. Edmunds and P. H. White, 1866.
Address by J. Barrett, 1868.
Proceedings 1869 and 1870.

Vermont Intelligencer. Vol. 3. New Series. (Feb. 26, 1832 to Feb. 16, 1833).

——— See Bellows Falls Intelligencer, p. 123, *ante*.

Vermont Journal and Universal Advertiser. [By Hough and Spooner, Windsor. Afterwards called *Spooner's Vermont Journal*, which see.] Vol. 1, Nos. 1 to 37, (Aug. 7, 1783 to April 14, 1784.)

Vermont Mercury. [Woodstock.] Vols. 1 and 2. (April 6, 1837 to March 29, 1839).

Vermont Register and Almanac, 1812 to 1817. [6 pamphlet v. bound in 1.] 16°. Middlebury and Burlington.

NOTE.—See Vermont Directory, and Walton's Vermont Register.

Vermont Republican. [Windsor. In Vols. 11 and 12 called *Vermont Republican* and *American Yeoman.*] Vols. 6 and 7; (Dec. 27, 1813 to Dec. 17, 1815); and Vols. 11 and 12, (Dec. 21, 1818 to Nov. 27, 1820).

Vermont State Papers. Compiled by William Slade, Jr. See under VERMONT, p. 72, *ante*.

Vermont Stock Journal. Vols. 1 and 2, 1857 and 1858. 2v. Middlebury, 1857—58.

Viardot, Louis. Wonders of Italian Art. 12°. New York, 1870.

Victoria Regina. The Early Years of his Royal Highness the Prince Consort. Compiled under the direction of her Majesty, the Queen, by Lieut. General the Hon. C. Grey. 12°. New York, 1867.

Viele, Egbert L. Report [on Central Park.] 1857.

Vienna. Kaiserliche Akadamie der Wissenschaften in Wien. Mathem.-Naturw.Classe. Denkschriften. Vols 19—30. 4°. Wien, 1859—70.

—— —— —— Sitzungsberichte. Vols. 43 to 63. Wien, 1861—71.

—— —— —— Register zu den Baenden 43 bis 60 der Sitzungsberichte. 2v. Wien, 1865—70.

—— See Kreil, Karl.

Vinton, John Adams. Giles Memorial. Genealogical Memoirs of Families bearing the names of Giles, Gould, etc., with history of Pemaquid, &c. Boston, 1864.

—— Vinton Memorial; a genealogy of descendants of John Vinton, of Lynn, 1648, and sketches of other ancient families. Boston, 1858.

Virginia Series. Containing Smith's True Relation. 4°. Boston, 1866.

Voltaire, Francois Marie Arouet de. History of Charles XII, with Life of Voltaire by Lord Brougham, and critical notices by Macaulay and Carlyle. Edited by O. W. Wight. 12°. New York, 1864.

Voyages Round the World. See Historical Account, &c.

W.

Waite, Otis F. R. Claremont war History, 1861 to 1865. 12°. Concord, 1868.

—— Vermont in the Rebellion. With historical and biographical sketches, etc. 12°. Claremont, 1869.

Walker, Amasa. Science of Wealth. A manual of Political Economy. Embracing the laws of trade, currency and finance. Boston, 1867.

Walsh, M. McN. The Lawyer in the School Room, comprising the laws of all the States on important educational subjects. 12°. New York, 1867.

Walter, Richard, Voyage Round the World, in the years 1740–44, by George Anson. 9th edition. 4°. London, 1756.

Walton, Isaac. Complete Angler, or Contemplative Man's Recreation. And Instructions how to Angle for a Trout, etc., by Charles Cotton. 12°. New York, 1859.

Walton's Vermont Register and Farmer's Almanac, 1818 to 1872. [55 pamphlet v., of which those to 1870 are bound in 11 vols.] 16°. Montpelier and Claremont.

Ward, Julius H. Life and Letters of James Gates Percival. Boston, 1866.

Warden, David Baillie. Statistical, Political and Historical Account of the United States of North America. 3v. Edinburgh, 1819.

Warren, *Mrs.* Mercy. History of the Rise, Progress and Termination of the American Revolution. 3v. Boston, 1805.

Washburn, Charles A. History of Paraguay. 2v. Boston, 1871.

Washington. 22d Annnal Report of the Board of Trustees of the Public Schools of the City. Washington, 1867.

Washington, George. Farewell Address to the People of the United States of America. Folio. New York, 1850.

—— Writings; being his correspondence, addresses, messages, and other papers, official and private. With a life of the author, notes and illustrations, by Jared Sparks. 12v. Boston, 1858.

CONTENTS.

Life of Washington, by J. Sparks, v. 1.
Letters before the American Revolution, 1754–75, v. 2.
Correspondence relating to the American Revolution, 1775–83, v. 3—8.
Private Correspondence, 1783–89, v. 9.
Correspondence, [Official and Private,] 1789–99, v. 10–11.
Speeches, Addresses, Messages to Congress, Proclamations, &c., v. 12.

—— See Hough, Irving, Marshall, Ramsay, Sparks and others.

Waterland, Daniel. See Miscellanies.

Watson, Robert. History of the Reign of Philip the Second, King of Spain. 3v. London, 1812.

Watson, Winslow C. Men and Times of the Revolution, or Memoirs of Elkanah Watson. New York, 1856.

—— Military and Civil History of the County of Essex, New York; embracing an account of the Northern Wilderness, and military annals of Crown Point and Ticonderoga. Albany, 1869.

—— Pioneer History of the Champlain Valley; an account of the settlement of Willsborough by Wm. Gilliland, with his journal, etc. Albany, 1863.

Watts, Isaac. Horæ Lyricæ and Divine Songs. With a Memoir by Robert Southey. 16°. Boston, 1854.

Waverley Novels. See Scott, *Sir* Walter.

Wayland, Francis. Elements of Political Economy. 12°. Boston, 1860.

Webster, Daniel. Works. With a Biographical Memoir by Edward Everett. 6v. Boston, 1851. (Vols. 2 and 6 *wanting*).

CONTENTS.

Adams and Jefferson, 1826, v. 1.
Agriculture of England, 1840, v. 1.
Agricultural Society at Oxford, England, 1839, v. 1.
Albany Mass Meeting, 1844, v, 2.
Biographical Memoir, by E. Everett, v. 1.
Bunker Hill Monument, 1820, 1825, v. 1.
Capitol at Washington, Addition to the, 1851, v. 2.
Character of Washington, 1832, v. 1.
Congress, Speeches in, v. 3—4.
Diplomatic and Official Papers :
  "Amistad," Relations with Spain, 1841-42, v, 6.
  "Caroline," Case of 1842, v. 6.
  "Creole'" Case of, 1842, v. 6.
  Huelsemann, Correspondence with, 1850-51, v. 6.
  Impressment, 1842, v. 6.
  McLeod, Alexander, Case of, 1841-42, v. 6.
  Northeastern Boundary, 1842, v. 6.
  Right of Search, 1842, v. 6.
  Treaty of Washington, v. 6.
Election Speech in Faneuil Hall, 1848, v. 2.
Faneuil Hall, Public Dinner in, 1838, v. 1.
First Settlement of New England, 1820, v. 1,
Independence of the Judiciary, 1820, v. 3.
Legal Arguments and Speeches to the Jury :
  Bank of U. S. against W. D. Primrose, 1839, v. 6.
  Dartmouth College Case, 1818, v. 5.
  Gibbons and Ogden, Case of, 1824, v. 6.
  Girard's Will Case, 1844, v. 6.
  Kennistons, Defence of the, 1817, v. 5.
  Ogden and Saunders, Case of, 1827, v. 6.
  Prescott, Judge James, Defence of, 1821, v. 5.
  Rhode Island Government, 1848, v. 6.
  White, Joseph, Murder of, by Knapp, 1830, v. 6.
Mason, Jeremiah, Remarks on Death of, 1848, v. 2.
Miscellaneous Letters, v. 6.
National Republican Convention at Worcester, 1832, v. 1.
New England Society at New York, 1843, v. 2.
New Hampshire, Festival of the Sons of, at Boston, 1849, v. 2.
Niblo's Saloon, Speech in, 1837, v. 1.
Northeastern Boundary, before New York Historical Society, 1843, v. 2.
Philadelphia, Whig Convention at, 1844, v. 2.
Pilgrim Festival at New York, 1850, v. 2.
Reception at Boston, in Faneuil Hall, 1842, v. 2.
Richmond, Remarks to Ladies of, 1840, v. 2.
Richmond, Whig Convention at, October, 1840, v. 2.
Saratoga Mass Meeting, 1810, v. 2.
Southern Tour, 1847, v. 2.
Speeches in Congress :
  Apportionment of Representation, 1832, v, 3.
  Bank, National, 1837, v. 4.
  Bank of the United States, 1815 and 1832, v. 3.
  Bankruptcy, Uniform System of, 1840, v. 5.
  Calhoun, J. C., Remarks on Decease of, 1850, v. 5.
  Calhoun, Reply to, 1838, v. 4.
  California, Public Lands and Boundaries, 1850, v. 5.
  Compromise Bill, 1850, v. 5.

Constitution and the Union, 7th of March, 1850, v. 5.
Constitution not a Compact between Sovereign States, 1833, v. 3.
Currency, The, 1837, v. 4.
Currency, Legal, 1816, v. 3.
Distribution of Surplus Revenue, 1836, v. 4.
Expunging Resolution, 1837, v. 4.
Finances in 1840, State of, 1840, v. 5.
Foot's Resolution, Speeches on, 1830. v. 3.
Force Bill, Reply to Calhoun, 1833, v. 3.
French Spoliations prior to 1800, 1835, v. 4.
Fugitive Slave Bill, 1850, v. 5.
Greece, Revolution in, 1824, v. 3.
Hayne, Reply to, 1830, v. 3.
Judiciary, The, 1826, v. 4.
Louisville Canal, 1836, v. 4.
Madison Papers, Purchase of, 1837, v. 4.
Mexican War, Speeches on, 1847 and 1848, v. 5.
Oregon, Three Speeches, 1845 and 1846, v. 5.
Panama Mission, 1826, v. 3.
Panama Railroad, 1849, v. 5.
Preemption to Settlers on Public Lands, 1838, v. 4.
Presidential Protest, 1834, v. 4.
Protection, General Effects of, 1840, v. 4.
Public Lands, Graduation of Price of, 1839, v. 4.
Removal of Deposits, 1833-4, v. 3-4.
Slavery in the District of Columbia, 1836 and 1838, v. 4.
Specie Circular, 1836, v. 4.
Sub-Treasury, Speeches on, 1838, v. 4.
Sub-Treasury, The, 1846, v. 4.
Slavery, Exclusion of, from the Territories, 1848, v. 5.
Tariff, The, 1824, 1828, and 1846, v. 3-4.
Texas, Admission of, 1845, v. 5.
Texas, Boundaries of, 1850, v. 5.
Treasury-Note Bill, 1840, v. 4.
Treaty of Washington, Defence of, 1846, v. 5.
Van Buren, Nomination of, as Minister to England, 1832, v. 3.
Volunteer Force, Organization of, 1846, v. 5.
Story, Justice, Remarks on the Decease of, 1845, v. 2.
Wall Street, Speech in, 1840, v. 2.
Whig Principles and Purposes, 1840, v. 2.

——— Private Correspondence. Edited by Fletcher Webster. 2v. Boston, 1857.

——— See p. 65, *ante.*

Webster, Noah. American Dictionary of the English Language. Revised by C. A. Goodrich and N. Porter. Illustrated edition. 4°. Springfield, 1865.

——— A Grammatical Institute of the English Language. Part Second. 4th edition. 12°. Boston, 1796.

——— American Selection of Lessons in Reading and Speaking; being the Third Part of a Grammatical Institute. 13th edition. 12°. Boston, 1803.

Weekly Wanderer. [By Sereno Wright. Randolph, Vt.] Vols. 3, 4, 5, 6, 7 and 8. (Dec. 25, 1802 to Nov. 21, 1808).

Weiss, Charles. History of the French Protestant Refugees. From the French, by H. W. Herbert. 2v. 12°. New York, 1854.

Weed, Isaac. Travels through the States of North America, and the Provinces of Upper and Lower Canada, during the years 1795–97. 3d edition. 2v. London, 1800.

Wells, David A. See Annual of Scientific Discovery, of which he was editor from 1850 to 1867.

Wells, William V. Life and Public Services of John Adams. With extracts from his correspondence, etc. 3v. Boston, 1865.

Wheeler, William A. Explanatory and Pronouncing Dictionary of the noted Names of Fiction. 12°. Boston, 1866.

——— See Hole, Charles.

Wheler, George. Journey into Greece, in company of Dr. Spon, of Lyons. 4°. London, 1682.

Whipple, Edwin Percy. Character and Characteristic Men. 12°. Boston, 1868.

White, George. Historical Collections of Georgia. New York, 1854.

White, Henry. Indian Battles ; with incidents in the early history of New England. 12°. New York, (1859).

White, Henry Kirke. Poetical Works ; with a Memoir by Sir Harry Nicolas. 16°. Boston, 1859.

White, Pliny Holton. Bibliography of Vermont. [A newspaper article preserved in bound volume.]

Whitfield, Henry. Farther Discovery of the present state of the Indians in New England. Reprinted [from edition of 1651.] 4°. New York, 1865. [Sabin's Reprints No. 3.]

——— Strength out of Weakness ; the further progress of the Gospel among the Indians in New England. Reprinted [from one of the editions of 1652.] 4°. New York, 1865. [Sabin's Reprints No. 5.]

Whiting, William. Memoir of Rev. Samuel Whiting, D. D., and of his wife, Elizabeth St. John. Boston, 1872.

Whitmore, William H. Elements of Heraldry ; containing an explanation of principles, and a glossary of technical terms, with an essay on use of coat-armor in the U. S. Boston, 1866.

Wilberforce, William. Correspondence. Edited by his sons. 2v. 12°. Philadelphia, 1841.

Wilkes, Charles. See under UNITED STATES, pp. 63 and 64, *ante.*

Wilkinson, James. Memoirs of My Own Times. 3v. Philadelphia, 1816.

Willard, Joseph. Willard Memoir, or Life and Times of Major Simon Willard, with notices of his descendants, etc. Boston, 1858.

William of Malmesbury. Chronicle of the Kings of England, to the Reign of King Stephen. Edited by J. A. Giles. 12°. London, 1847.

Williams, Catherine R. Biography of Revolutionary Heroes; containing the Life of General William Barton, and also of Capt. Stephen Olney. 12°. Providence, R. I., 1839.

Williams, Charles K. Centennial Celebration of the settlement of Rutland, Vt., Oct. 2d, 3d, 4th and 5th, 1870. Rutland, 1870.

Williams, Eleazer. Life of Te-ho-ra-gwa-ne-gen, alias Thomas Williams. Albany, 1859.

Williams, *Rev.* John, *of Deerfield, Mass.* Redeemed Captive Returning to Zion; remarkable occurrences in the captivity and deliverance of Mr. John Williams; with notes, etc., by Stephen W. Williams. 12°. Northampton, 1853.

Williams, Samuel. Natural and Civil History of Vermont. Walpole, 1794.

Williamson, William B. History of the State of Maine; from its first discovery, A. D. 1602, to the separation, A. D. 1820. 2v. Hallowell, 1832.

Willis, William. See Maine Historical Society.

Willson, Marcius. American History; comprising sketches of Indian Tribes, description of American Antiquities, history of the United States, of British Provinces, of Mexico and of Texas. New York, 1858.

Wilson, Henry. History of the Anti-Slavery Measures of the 37th and 38th United States Congresses; 1861–64. 12°. Boston, 1864.

——— History of the Rise and Fall of the Slave Power in America. Vol. 1. Boston, 1872.

Wilson, James Grant. Life and Letters of Fitz-Greene Halleck. 12°. New York, 1869.

Wilson, William. Missionary Voyage to the Southern Pacific Ocean, performed in the years of 1796–98, in the ship Duff, commanded by Captain James Wilson; compiled from Journals of the Officers and Missionaries. 4°. London, 1799.

Winckelmann, John. History of Ancient Art. Translated from the German by G. Henry Lodge. Vols. 2 and 3. 4°. Boston, 1872.

Windsor Federal Gazette. [By Nahum Mower.] Vol. 3 and first 43 Nos. of Vol. 4. (March 1, 1803 to Dec. 25, 1804.)

Wingate, James. Maryland Register for 1860–61. A Legal, Political and Business Manual. Baltimore, 1860.

Winslow, Miron. A Sketch of Missions. 12°. Andover, 1819.

Winterbotham, William. Historical, Geographical, Commercial and Philosophical View of the American United States, and of the European Settlements in America and the West Indies. 4v. London, 1795.

Winthrop, John. History of New England from 1630 to 1649; with notes by James Savage. 2v. Boston, 1853.

Winthrop, Robert Charles. Addresses and Speeches on various occasions. Boston, 1852.

——— Addresses and Speeches on various occasions, from 1852 to 1867. Boston, 1867.

——— Life and Letters of John Winthrop. 2v. Boston, 1864–67.

Wisconsin Farmer and Northwestern Cultivator; a Monthly Journal; 1856; 1857. Vols. 8 and 9. Madison, 1856–57.

Wisconsin, State Historical Society of. Reports and Collections. 5v. Madison, 1855—69.

Wise, Henry A. Reply to Wm. A. Samford's Letter, [in which are reviewed Vermont "Joint Resolutions relating to Slavery and the Dred Scott Decision," passed in 1858.] [1859].

Wood, George B. and Bache, Franklin. Dispensatory of the United States of America. 13th edition. Philadelphia, 1870.

Wood, John George. Homes without Hands; being a description of the habitations of animals. New York, 1866.

Wood, William. See Prince Society.

Woodbury, Levi. Writings, Political, Judicial and Literary. 3v. Boston, 1852.

Woodfall, H. S. See Junius.

Woodruff, Hiram. Trotting Horse of America; how to train and drive him; with reminiscences of the trotting turf. 12°. New York, 1868.

Woodstock Observer. Vols. 1 and 2. [Jan. 11, 1820, to Jan. 1, 1822.)

Woodward, W. Elliot. Records of Salem Witchcraft, copied from the original documents. 2v. in 1. Small 4°. Roxbury, 1864. [Woodward's Historical Series, Nos. 1 and 2.]

Woodward's Historical Series. Nos. 1—8, containing Records of Salem Witchcraft, (1, 2); History of the Indian Wars, (3, 4); Witchcraft delusion in N. E., (5, 6, 7,) and Annals of Witchcraft, (8.) See Calef, R.; Drake, S. G.; Hubbard, Wm.; Mather, C.; and Woodward, W. E. 8v. in 6. Small 4°. Roxbury, 1864–69.

Woolman, John. Journal of; with an introduction by J. G. Whittier. 16°. Boston, 1871.

Woolsey, Theodore D. Essay on Divorce and Divorce Legislation, with special reference to the United States. 12°. New York, 1869.

Worcester, Joseph Emerson. Dictionary of the English Language. 4°. Boston, 1860.

Wordsworth, William. Poetical Works. 7v. 16°. Boston, 1859.

Wyatt, *Sir* Thomas. Poetical Works; with a Memoir. 16°. Boston, 1854.

Y.

Yates, Robert. Secret Proceedings and Debates of the Convention in 1787, from notes taken by R. Yates, and copied by J. Lansing, Jr.; with "the genuine information" laid before the Legislature of Maryland by Luther Martin. 12°. Richmond, 1839.

Youmans, Edward L. Culture Demanded by Modern Life; a Series of Addresses and Arguments by Eminent Scientific Men; with Introduction by E. L. Youmans. 12°. New York, 1867.

Young, Alexander. Chronicles of the First Planters of the Colony of Massachusetts Bay, from 1623 to 1636. Boston, 1846.

Young, Augustus. Unity of Purpose or Rational Analysis. Boston, 1846.

Young, Edward. Poetical Works. 2v. 16°. Boston, 1859. (Vol. 1 *wanting.*)

Ysabeau. See Maison Rustique.

Yule-Tide Stories. A Collection of Scandinavian and North German Tales and Traditions. Edited by B. Thorpe. 12°. London, 1853.

Z.

Zarate, D'Augustin de. Historie de la decouverte et de la conquete du Perou. Traduite de l'Espagnol. Vol. 2. 16°. Paris, 1716.

www.ingramcontent.com/pod-product-compliance
Lightning Source LLC
LaVergne TN
LVHW011206110826
845150LV00006B/1337

9781425517779